Rick Steves'

PORTUGUESE

PHRASE BOOK
& DICTIONARY

Avalon Travel
An imprint of Perseus Books
A Hachette Book Group company
1700 Fourth Street
Berkeley, CA 94710, USA

Printed in China by RR Donnelley.
Second edition. Fourth printing January 2018.

For the latest on Rick's lectures, guidebooks, tours, and public television
series, contact Rick Steves' Europe, 130 Fourth Avenue North, Edmonds,
WA 98020, tel. 425/771-8303, www.ricksteves.com, rick@ricksteves.com.

ISBN-13: 978-1-59880-189-7

Rick Steves' Europe Managing Editor: Risa Laib
Rick Steves' Europe Editors: Cameron Hewitt, Jill Hodges,
  Gretchen Strauch
Avalon Travel Editor: Jamie Andrade
Translation: Maria Antonia Campota Mafi,
  Luis F. Gonçalves Conde
Phonetics: Risa Laib, Cameron Hewitt
Production: Darren Alessi
Cover Design: Kimberly Glyder Design
Maps & Graphics: David C. Hoerlein, Zoey Platt
Photography: Rick Steves, Dominic Bonuccelli
Front Cover Photo: Coimbra © Robert Wright

CONTENTS

TABLE OF CONTENTS

Hi, I'm Rick Steves.

I'm the only monolingual speaker I know who's had the nerve to design a series of European phrase books. But that's one of the things that makes them better.

You see, after 30 summers of travel through Europe, I've learned first-hand: (1) what's essential for communication in another country, and (2) what's not. I've assembled the most important words and phrases in a logical, no-frills format, and I've worked with native Europeans and seasoned travelers to give you the simplest, clearest translations possible.

But this book is more than just a pocket translator. The words and phrases have been carefully selected to help you have a smarter, smoother trip in Portugal. The key to getting more out of every travel dollar is to get closer to the local people, and to rely less on entertainment, restaurants, and hotels that cater only to foreign tourists. This book will not only help you order a meal at a locals-only Lisbon restaurant—it will help you talk with the family who runs the place . . . about their kids, social issues, travel dreams, and favorite *música*. Long after your memories of museums have faded, you'll still treasure the personal encounters you had with your new Iberian friends.

A good phrase book should help you enjoy your Iberian experience—not just survive it—so I've added a healthy dose of humor. A few phrases are just for fun and aren't meant to be used at all. Most of the phrases are for real and should be used with "please" (*por favor*). I know you can tell the difference.

To get the most out of this book, take the time to internalize and put into practice my Portuguese pronunciation tips. Don't worry too much about memorizing grammatical rules, like the gender of a noun—the important thing is to communicate!

This book has a handy dictionary and a nifty menu decoder. You'll also find tongue twisters, international words, telephone tips, and a handy tear-out "cheat sheet." Tear it out and keep it in your pocket, so you can easily memorize key phrases during otherwise idle moments. As you prepare for your trip, you may want to read the most recent edition of my **Rick Steves Portugal** guidebook.

The Portuguese speak less English than their European neighbors. But while the language barrier may seem a little higher, the locals are happy to give an extra boost to any traveler who makes an effort to communicate.

My goal is to help you become a more confident, extroverted traveler. If this phrase book helps make that happen, or if you have suggestions for making it better, I'd love to hear from you. I personally read and value all feedback. My address is Rick Steves' Europe, 130 Fourth Avenue North, Edmonds, WA 98020, tel. 425/771-8303, rick@ricksteves.com.

Happy travels,

Rick Steves

GETTING STARTED

Portuguese

...is your passport to Europe's bargain basement. For its wonderful pricetag, you'll enjoy piles of fresh seafood, brilliant sunshine, and local character that often feels decades behind the rest of Europe. With its Old World charm comes a bigger language barrier than you'll find elsewhere in Europe. A phrase book is of greater value here than anywhere else in western Europe.

Here are a few tips on pronouncing Portuguese words:

C usually sounds like C in cat.
    But C followed by E or I sounds like S in sun.
Ç sounds like S in sun.
CH sounds like SH in shine.
G usually sounds like G in go.
    But G followed by E or I sounds like S in treasure.
H is silent.
J sounds like S in treasure.
LH sounds like LI in billion.
NH sounds like NI in onion.
R is trrrilled.
S can sound like S in sun (at the beginning of a word),
    Z in zoo (between vowels), or SH in shine.
SS sounds like S in sun.

GETTING STARTED

Portuguese vowels:

A can sound like A in father or A in sang.
E can sound like E in get, AY in play, or I in wish.
É sounds like E in get.
Ê sounds like AY in play.
I sounds like EE in seed.
O can sound like O in note, AW in raw, or OO in moon.
Ô and *OU* sound like O in note.
U sounds like OO in moon.

When you're speaking a Romance language, sex is unavoidable. A man is *simpático* (friendly), a woman is *simpática*. In this book, we show bisexual words like this: *simpático[a]*. If you're speaking of a female (which includes females speaking about themselves), use the *a* ending. It's always pronounced "ah." A word that ends in *r,* such as *cantor* (singer), will appear like this: *cantor[a]*. A *cantora* is a female singer. A word ending in *e*, such as *interessante* (interesting), applies to either sex.

Adjectives agree with the noun. A clean room is a *quarto limpo,* a clean towel is a *toalha limpa. Quartos limpos* have *toalhas limpas.* You'll be quizzed on this later.

If a word ends in a vowel, the Portuguese usually stress the second-to-last syllable. Words ending in a consonant are stressed on the last syllable. To override these rules, the Portuguese add an accent mark (such as ´, ~, or ^) to the syllable that should be stressed, like this: *rápido* (fast) is pronounced **rah**-pee-doo.

Just like French, its linguistic buddy, Portuguese has nasal sounds. A vowel followed by either *n* or *m* or topped with a ~ (such as *ã* or *õ*) is usually nasalized. In the phonetics, nasalized vowels are indicated by an underlined <u>n</u> or <u>w</u>. As you say the vowel, let its sound come through your nose as well as your mouth.

Here are the phonetics for nasal vowels:

ayn   nasalize the AY in day.
ohn   nasalize the O in bone.
oon   nasalize the O in moon.
ow   nasalize the OW in now.

Some words have only a slight nasal sound. To help you pronounce these words, I add an *ng* or *n* in the phonetics: *sim* (meaning "yes") is pronounced seeng, and *muito* (meaning "very") like **mween**-too.

Here's a quick guide to the rest of the phonetics used in this book:

a   like A in sang.
ah   like A in father.
ay   like AY in play.
ee   like EE in seed.
eh   like E in get.
ehr   sounds like "air."
g   like G in go.
i   like I in hit.
ī   like I in light.
o   like AW in raw.
oh   like O in note.
oo   like OO in moon.
or   like OR in core.
ow   like OW in now.
oy   like OY in toy.
s   like S in sun.
zh   like S in treasure.

Too often tourists insist on speaking Spanish to the Portuguese. Your attempts at Portuguese will endear you to the locals. And if you throw in "*por favor*" (please) whenever you can, you'll eat better, sleep easier, and make friends faster.

PORTUGUESE BASICS

In 1917, according to legend, the Virgin Mary visited Fatima using only these phrases.

Meeting and Greeting

Hello.	*Olá.*	oh-**lah**
Good morning.	*Bom dia.*	boh<u>n</u> **dee**-ah
Good afternoon.	*Boa tarde.*	boh-ah **tar**-deh
Good evening. /	*Boa noite.*	boh-ah **noy**-teh
Good night.		
Welcome!	*Bem-vindo[a]!**	behm-**veen**-doo
Mr.	*Senhor*	sin-**yor**
Mrs.	*Senhora*	sin-**yoh**-rah
Miss	*Menina*	meh-**nee**-nah
How are you?	*Como está?*	**koh**-moo ish-**tah**
Very well.	*Muito bem.*	**mween**-too bay<u>n</u>
Thank you.	*Obrigado.*	oh-bree-**gah**-doo
(said by a male)		
Thank you.	*Obrigada.*	oh-bree-**gah**-dah
(said by a female)		
And you?	*E você? / E tú?*	ee voh-**say** / ee too
(formal / informal)		

* Males use the "*o*" ending (*Bem-vindo*) when speaking; females use the "*a*" ending (*Bem-vinda*).

4

My name is ___.	Chamo-me ___.	**shah**-moo-meh
What's your name?	Como se chama?	**koh**-moo seh **shah**-mah
Pleased to meet you.	Prazer em conhecer.	prah-**zehr** ayn kohn-yeh-**sehr**
Where are you from?	De onde é que você é?	deh **ohn**-deh eh keh voh-**say** eh
I am / We are / Are you...?	Estou / Estamos / Estás...?	ish-**toh** / ish-**tah**-moosh / ish-**tash**
...on vacation	...de férias	deh **feh**-ree-ahsh
...on business	...em negócios	ayn neh-**gos**-ee-oosh
So long!	Até logo!	ah-**teh log**-oo
Goodbye.	Adeus.	ah-**deh**-oosh
Good luck!	Boa sorte!	**boh**-ah **sor**-teh
Have a good trip!	Boa-viagem!	boh-ah-vee-**ah**-zhayn

The Portuguese say *"Bom dia"* (Good morning) until noon, *"Boa
tarde"* (Good afternoon) until dark, and *"Boa noite"* (Good evening)
after dark. In Portugal, a woman who looks over 35 years old is
addressed as *senhora*, younger than 35 as *menina*. Good luck.

Essentials

Hello.	Olá.	oh-**lah**
Do you speak English?	Fala inglês?	**fah**-lah een-**glaysh**
Yes. / No.	Sim. / Não.	seeng / now
I don't speak Portuguese.	Não falo português.	now **fah**-loo poor-too-**gaysh**
I'm sorry. (said by a male)	Desculpe.	dish-**kool**-peh
I'm sorry. (said by a female)	Desculpa.	dish-**kool**-pah
Please.	Por favor.	poor fah-**vor**
Thank you.	Obrigado[a].	oh-bree-**gah**-doo
It's (not) a problem.	(Não) á problema.	(now) ah proo-**blay**-mah
Good / Great / Excellent.	Óptimo / Muito bom / Exelente.	**ot**-tee-moo / **mween**-too bohn / ehsh-eh-**layn**-teh

You are very kind.	É muito simpatico[a].	eh **mween**-too seeng-**pah**-tee-koo
Excuse me. (to pass)	Com licença.	kohn li-**sehn**-sah
Excuse me. (to get attention)	Desculpe[a].	dish-**kool**-peh
It doesn't matter.	Não faz mal.	now fahsh mahl
You're welcome.	De nada.	deh **nah**-dah
Sure.	Claro.	**klah**-roo
O.K.	Está bem.	ish-**tah** bayn
Let's go.	Vamos.	**vah**-moosh
Goodbye.	Adeus.	ah-**deh**-oosh

Where?

Where is...?	Onde é que é...?	**ohn**-deh eh keh eh
...the tourist information office	...a informação turistica	ah een-for-mah-**sow** too-**reesh**-tee-kah
...the train station	...a estação de comboio	ah ish-tah-**sow** deh kohn-**boy**-yoo
...the bus station	...a terminal das camionetas	ah tehr-mee-**nahl** dahsh kahm-yoo-**neh**-tahsh
...a cash machine	...uma caixa automática	**oo**-mah **kī**-shah ow-toh-**mah**-tee-kah
...the toilet	...a casa de banho	ah **kah**-zah deh **bahn**-yoo
men / women	homens / mulheres	**ah**-maynsh / mool-**yeh**-rish

You'll find some Portuguese words are similar to English if you're looking for a *hotel, restaurante, supermercado, banco,* or *farmacia.*

How Much?

How much is it?	Quanto custa?	**kwahn**-too **koosh**-tah
Write it?	Escreva?	ish-**kray**-vah
Is it free?	É grátis?	eh **grah**-teesh
Is it included?	Está incluido?	ish-**tah** een-kloo-**ee**-doo
Do you have...?	Tem...?	tayn
Where can I buy...?	Onde posso comprar...?	**ohn**-deh **pos**-soo kohn-**prar**

I would like...	*Gostaria...*	goosh-tah-**ree**-ah
We would like...	*Gostaríamos...*	goosh-tah-**ree**-ah-moosh
...this.	*...isto.*	**eesh**-too
...just a little.	*...só um bocadinho.*	soh oo<u>n</u> boo-kah-**deen**-yoo
...more.	*...mais.*	mīsh
...a ticket.	*...um bilhete.*	oo<u>n</u> beel-**yeh**-teh
...a room.	*...um quarto.*	oo<u>n</u> **kwar**-too
...the bill.	*...a conta.*	ah **koh<u>n</u>**-tah

PORTUGUESE BASICS

How Many?

one	*um*	oo<u>n</u>
two	*dois*	doysh
three	*três*	traysh
four	*quatro*	**kwah**-troo
five	*cinco*	**seeng**-koo
six	*seis*	saysh
seven	*sete*	**seh**-teh
eight	*oito*	**oy**-too
nine	*nove*	**nah**-veh
ten	*dez*	dehsh

You'll find more to count on in the "Numbers" section beginning on page 14.

When?

At what time?	*A que horas?*	ah kee **oh**-rahsh
open / closed	*aberto / fechado*	ah-**behr**-too / feh-**shah**-doo
Just a moment.	*Um momento.*	oo<u>n</u> moo-**mayn**-too
Now.	*Agora.*	ah-**goh**-rah
Soon.	*Breve.*	**bray**-veh
Later.	*Mais tarde.*	mīsh **tar**-deh
Today.	*Hoje.*	**oh**-zheh
Tomorrow.	*Amanhã.*	ah-ming-**yah**

Be creative! You can combine these phrases to say: "Two, please," or "No, thank you," or "Open tomorrow?" or "Please, where can I buy a ticket?" Please is a magic word in any language. If you want to buy something and you don't know the word for it, just point and say *por favor* (please). If you know the word for what you want, such as the bill, simply say, *"A conta, por favor"* (The bill, please). If you add *por favor* to most of the phrases in this book, you'll have a smoother trip.

Struggling with Portuguese

Do you speak English?	Fala inglês?	**fah**-lah een-**glaysh**
A teeny weeny bit?	Um pouquinho?	oon poh-**keen**-yoo
Please speak English.	Por favor fale inglês.	poor fah-**vor** **fah**-leh een-**glaysh**
You speak English well.	Fala bem inglês.	**fah**-lah bayn een-**glaysh**
I don't speak Portuguese.	Não falo português.	now **fah**-loo poor-too-**gaysh**
We don't speak Portuguese.	Não falamos português.	now fah-**lah**-moosh poor-too-**gaysh**
I speak a little Portuguese.	Falo um pouco em português.	**fah**-loo oon poh-koo ayn poor-too-**gaysh**
Sorry, I speak only English.	Desculpe[a], só falo inglês.	dish-**kool**-peh soh **fah**-loo een-**glaysh**
Sorry, we speak only English.	Desculpe, só falamos inglês.	dish-**kool**-peh soh fah-**lah**-moosh een-**glaysh**
Does somebody nearby speak English?	Alguem aqui fala inglês?	**ahl**-kayn ah-kee **fah**-lah een-**glaysh**
Who speaks English?	Quem fala inglês?	kayn **fah**-lah een-**glaysh**
What does this mean?	O que quer dizer isto?	oo keh kehr dee-**zehr** **eesh**-too
What is this in Portuguese / English?	Como se diz isto em português / inglês?	**koh**-moo seh deez **eesh**-too ayn poor-too-**gaysh** / een-**glaysh**

Repeat?	*Repita?*	ray-**pee**-tah
Please speak	*Por favor fale*	poor fah-**vor** fah-leh
slowly.	*devegar.*	deh-vah-**gar**
Slower.	*Mais devagar.*	mīsh deh-vah-**gar**
I understand.	*Compreendo.*	kohn-pree-**ayn**-doo
I don't understand.	*Não compreendo.*	now kohn-pree-**ayn**-doo
Do you understand?	*Compreende?*	kohn-pree-**ayn**-deh
Write it?	*Escreva?*	ish-**kray**-vah

Handy Questions

How much?	*Quanto custa?*	**kwahn**-too **koosh**-tah
How many?	*Quantos?*	**kwahn**-toosh
How long	*Quanto tempo*	**kwahn**-too **tayn**-poo
is the trip?	*é a viagem?*	eh ah vee-**ah**-zhayn
How many	*Quantos*	**kwahn**-toosh
minutes / hours?	*minutos / horas?*	mee-**noo**-toosh / **oh**-rahsh
How far?	*A que distância?*	ah keh deesh-**tahn**-see-ah
How?	*Como?*	**koh**-moo
Can you help me?	*Pode ajudar-me?*	**pod**-eh ah-zhoo-**dar**-meh
Can you help us?	*Pode ajudar-nos?*	**pod**-eh ah-zhoo-**dar**-noosh
Can I / Can we...?	*Posso / Podemos...?*	**pos**-soo / poo-**day**-moosh
...have one	*...ter um*	tehr oon
...go in for free	*...ir gratis*	eer **grah**-teesh
...borrow that	*...emprestar isto*	ayn-prehsh-**tar** **eesh**-too
for a moment /	*por um momento /*	poor oon moh-**mayn**-too /
an hour	*uma hora*	**oo**-mah **oh**-rah
...use the toilet	*...usar a casa*	oo-**zar** ah **kah**-sah
	de banho	deh **bahn**-yoo
What? (didn't hear)	*Diga?*	**dee**-gah
What is this / that?	*O que é isto /*	oo keh eh **eesh**-too /
	aquilo?	ah-**kee**-loo
What is better?	*O que é melhor?*	oo keh eh mil-**yor**
What's going on?	*Que se passa?*	keh seh **pah**-sah
When?	*Quando?*	**kwahn**-doo
What time is it?	*Que horas são?*	kee **oh**-rahsh sow
At what time?	*A que horas?*	ah kee **oh**-rahsh

PORTUGUESE BASICS

On time?	Pontual?	pohn-too-**ahl**
Late?	Atrasado?	ah-trah-**zah**-doo
How long will it take?	Quanto tempo leva?	**kwahn**-too **tayn**-poo leh-vah
What time does this open / close?	A que horas é que abre / fecha?	ah kee **oh**-rahsh eh keh **ah**-breh / **fay**-shah
Is this open daily?	Está aberto todos os dias?	ish-**tah** ah-**behr**-too **toh**-doosh oosh **dee**-ahsh
What day is this closed?	Que dia fecha?	keh **dee**-ah **feh**-shah
Do you have...?	Tem...?	tayn
Where is...?	Onde é...?	**ohn**-deh eh
Where are...?	Onde estão...?	**ohn**-deh ish-**tow**
Where can I find...?	A onde posso encontrar...?	ah **ohn**-deh **pos**-soo ayn-kohn-**trar**
Where can we find...?	A onde podemos encontrar...?	ah **ohn**-deh poo-**day**-moosh ayn-kohn-**trar**
Where can I buy...?	A onde posso comprar...?	ah **ohn**-deh **pos**-soo kohn-**prar**
Where can we buy...?	A onde podemos comprar...?	ah **ohn**-deh poo-**day**-moosh kohn-**prar**
Is it necessary?	É necessário?	eh neh-seh-**sah**-ree-oo
Is it possible...?	É possível...?	eh **pos**-see-vehl
...to enter	..entrar	ayn-**trar**
...to picnic here	...fazer picnic aqui	fah-**zehr** peek-neek ah-**kee**
...to sit here	...sentar aqui	sayn-**tar** ah-**kee**
...to look	...olhar	ohl-**yar**
...to take a photo	...tirar uma foto	tee-**rar** oo-mah **foh**-toh
...to see a room	...ver um quarto	vehr oon **qwar**-too
Who?	Quem?	kayn
Why?	Porquê?	poor-**kay**
Why not?	Porquê não?	poor-**kay** now
Yes or no?	Sim ou não?	seeng oh now

To prompt a simple answer, ask, "*Sim ou não?*" You can turn a word or sentence into a question by asking it in a questioning tone. "*Isso é bom*" (It's good) becomes "*Isso é bom?*" (Is it good?).

Yin and Yang

good / bad	bom / mau	bohn / mow
best / worst	melhor / pior	mil-**yor** / pee-**yor**
a little / lots	um pouco / muito	oon **poh**-koo / **mween**-too
more / less	mais / menos	mīsh / **may**-noosh
cheap / expensive	barato / caro	bah-**rah**-too / **kah**-roo
big / small	grande / pequeno	**grahn**-deh /pay-**kay**-noo
hot / cold	quente / frio	**kayn**-teh / **free**-oo
cool / warm	fresco / quente	**frehsh**-koo / **kayn**-teh
open / closed	aberto / fechado	ah-**behr**-too / feh-**shah**-doo
push / pull	empurre / puxe	**ayn**-poor / push
entrance / exit	entrada / saída	ayn-**trah**-dah / sah-**ee**-dah
arrive / depart	chegar / partir	shay-**gar** / par-**teer**
early / late	cedo / tarde	**say**-doo / **tar**-deh
soon / later	breve / mais tarde	**bray**-veh / mīsh **tar**-deh
fast / slow	rápido / lento	**rah**-pee-doo / **layn**-too
here / there	aqui / ali	ah-**kee** / ah-**lee**
near / far	perto / longe	**pehr**-too / **lohn**-zheh
indoors / outdoors	dentro / fora	**dayn**-troo / **for**-ah
mine / yours	meu / vosso	**meh**-oo / **vas**-soo
this / that	isto / aquilo	**eesh**-too / ah-**kee**-loo
everybody / nobody	toda gente / ninguem	**toh**-dah **zhayn**-teh / neeng-**gayn**
easy / difficult	fácil / difícil	**fah**-seel / dee-**fee**-seel
left / right	esquerda / direita	ish-**kehr**-dah / dee-**ray**-tah
up / down	cima / baixo	**see**-mah / **bī**-shoo
above / below	em cima / em baixo	ayn **see**-mah / ayn **bī**-shoo
young / old	jovem / velho	**zhav**-ayn / **vehl**-yoo
new / old	novo / velho	**noh**-voo / **vehl**-yoo
heavy / light	pesado / leve	peh-**zah**-doo / **leh**-veh
dark / light	escuro / claro	ish-**koo**-roo / **klah**-roo
happy / sad	feliz / triste	feh-**leesh** / **treesh**-teh
beautiful / ugly	lindo / feio	**leen**-doo / **fay**-oo
nice / mean	boa / má	**boh**-ah / mah

smart / stupid	*inteligente /*	in-teh-leh-**zhayn**-teh /
	estúpido	ish-**too**-pee-doo
vacant / occupied	*livre / ocupado*	**lee**-vreh / oh-koo-**pah**-doo
with / without	*com / sem*	koh<u>n</u> / say<u>n</u>

Big Little Words

I	*eu*	**eh**-oo
you (formal)	*você*	voh-**say**
you (informal)	*tu*	too
we	*nós*	nohsh
he	*ele*	**eh**-leh
she	*ela*	**eh**-lah
they	*eles*	**eh**-lish
and	*e*	ee
at	*á*	ah
because	*porque*	**poor**-keh
but	*mas*	mahsh
by (train, car, etc.)	*via*	**vee**-ah
for	*para*	**pah**-rah
from	*de*	deh
here	*aqui*	ah-**kee**
if	*se*	seh
in	*em*	ay<u>n</u>
it	*isto*	**eesh**-too
not	*não*	no<u>w</u>
now	*agora*	ah-**goh**-rah
only	*só*	soh
or	*ou*	oh
that	*aquilo*	ah-**kee**-loo
this	*isto*	**eesh**-too
to	*para*	**pah**-rah
very	*muito*	**mween**-too

Perfectly Portuguese Expressions

Fantastic!	*Fantástico!*	fahn-**tahsh**-tee-koo
Perfect.	*Perfeito.*	pehr-**fay**-too
Wow!	*Fiche!*	**fee**-sheh
Good!	*Porreiro! Óptimo!*	poo-**ray**-roo, **ot**-tee-moo
Congratulations!	*Parabéns!*	pah-rah-**baynsh**
Really?	*A sério?*	ah **seh**-ree-oo
That's life.	*É a vida.*	eh ah **vee**-dah
No problem.	*Não tem problema.*	no<u>w</u> tay<u>n</u> proo-**blay**-mah
O.K.	*Está bem.*	ish-**tah** bay<u>n</u>
Good luck!	*Boa-sorte!*	boh-ah-**sor**-teh
Let's go!	*Vamos!*	**vah**-moosh

COUNTING

NUMBERS

0	*zero*	**zeh**-roo
1	*um*	oo<u>n</u>
2	*dois*	doysh
3	*três*	traysh
4	*quatro*	**kwah**-troo
5	*cinco*	**seeng**-koo
6	*seis*	saysh
7	*sete*	**seh**-teh
8	*oito*	**oy**-too
9	*nove*	**nah**-veh
10	*dez*	dehsh
11	*onze*	**ohn**-zeh
12	*doze*	**doh**-zeh
13	*treze*	**tray**-zeh
14	*catorze*	kah-**tor**-zeh
15	*quinze*	**keen**-zeh
16	*dezasseis*	deh-**zah**-saysh
17	*dezassete*	deh-zah-**seh**-teh
18	*dezoito*	deh-**zoy**-too
19	*dezanove*	deh-zah-**nah**-veh
20	*vinte*	**veen**-teh
21	*vinte e um*	**veen**-teh ee oo<u>n</u>
22	*vinte e dois*	**veen**-teh ee doysh

14

23	*vinte e três*	**veen**-teh ee traysh
30	*trinta*	**treen**-tah
31	*trinta e um*	**treen**-tah ee oo<u>n</u>
40	*quarenta*	kwah-**rayn**-tah
41	*quarenta e um*	kwah-**rayn**-tah ee oo<u>n</u>
50	*cinquenta*	seeng-**kwayn**-tah
60	*sessenta*	seh-**sayn**-tah
70	*setenta*	seh-**tayn**-tah
80	*oitenta*	oy-**tayn**-tah
90	*noventa*	noh-**vayn**-tah
100	*cem*	say<u>n</u>
101	*cento e um*	**sayn**-too ee oo<u>n</u>
102	*cento e dois*	**sayn**-too ee doysh
200	*duzentos*	doo-**zayn**-toosh
1000	*mil*	meel
2016	*dois mil e dezasseis*	doysh meel ee deh-zah-**saysh**
2017	*dois mil e dezessete*	doysh meel ee deh-zeh-**seht**
2018	*dois mil e dezoito*	doysh meel ee deh-**zoy**-too
2019	*dois mil e dezenove*	doysh meel ee deh-zah-**nah**-veh
2020	*dois mil e vinte*	doysh meel ee **veen**-teh
2021	*dois mil e vinte e um*	doysh meel ee **veen**-teh ee oo<u>n</u>
2022	*dois mil e vinte e dois*	doysh meel ee **veen**-teh ee doysh
million	*milhão*	mil-**yow**
billion	*bilhão*	bil-**yow**
number one	*número um*	**noo**-meh-roo oo<u>n</u>
first	*primeiro*	pree-**may**-roo
second	*segundo*	seh-**goon**-doo
third	*terceiro*	tehr-**say**-roo
once / twice	*uma vêz / duas vezes*	**oo**-mah vayz / **doo**-ahsh **veh**-zehsh
a quarter	*um quarto*	oo<u>n</u> **kwar**-too

COUNTING

a third	um terço	oon **tehr**-soo
half	metade	meh-**tah**-deh
this much	esta	**ehsh**-tah
	quantidade	kwahn-tee-**dah**-deh
a dozen	uma dúzia	**oo**-mah **dooz**-yah
some	alguns	**ahl**-goonsh
enough	suficiente	soo-fee-see-**yayn**-teh
a handful	uma porção	**oo**-mah poor-**sow**
50%	cinquenta	seeng-**kwayn**-tah
	per cento	pehr **sayn**-too
100%	cem per cento	**sayn** pehr **sayn**-too

MONEY

Where is a	Onde está	**ohn**-deh ish-**tah**
cash machine?	uma caixa	**oo**-mah **kī**-shah
	automática?	ow-toh-**mah**-tee-kah
My ATM card	O meu cartão	oo **meh**-oo kar-**tow**
has been...	ATM foi...	ah tay em foy
...demagnetized.	...desmagnetizado.	dish-mag-neh-tee-**zah**-doo
...stolen.	...roubado.	roh-**bah**-doo
...eaten by	...prêso na maquina.	**preh**-zoo nah **mah**-kee-nah
the machine.		
Do you accept	Aceitam cartões	ah-say-**tayn** kar-**towsh**
credit cards?	de credito?	deh **kreh**-dee-too
Can you change	Pode trocar	**pod**-eh troo-**kar**
dollars?	dollares?	**dol**-ah-rehsh
What is your	Qual é a taxa	kwahl eh ah **tah**-shah
exchange rate	de câmbio	deh **kahm**-bee-oo
for dollars...?	para o dollar...?	**pah**-rah oo **dol**-lar
...in traveler's	...em cheque	ayn **sheh**-keh
checks	de viagem	deh vee-**ah**-zhayn
What is the	Qual é a	kwahl eh ah
commission?	comissão?	koo-mee-**sow**
Any extra fee?	À taxa extra?	ah **tah**-shah **ish**-trah
Can you break this?	Pode trocar?	**pod**-eh troo-**kar**
(large to small bills)		

Key Phrases: Money

euro (€)	euro	**yoo**-roh
money	dinheiro	deen-**yay**-roo
cash	dinheiro	deen-**yay**-roo
credit card	cartão de	kar-**tow** deh
	crédito	**kreh**-dee-too
bank	banco	**bang**-koo
cash machine	caixa	**kī**-shah
	automática,	ow-toh-**mah**-tee-kah,
	Multibanco	mool-tee-**bahng**-koo
Where is a	Onde está	**ohn**-deh ish-**tah**
cash machine?	uma caixa	**oo**-mah **kī**-shah
	automática?	ow-toh-**mah**-tee-kah
Do you accept	Aceitam cartões	ah-say-**tayn** kar-**towsh**
credit cards?	de credito?	deh **kreh**-dee-too

COUNTING

I would like...	Gostaria...	goosh-tah-**ree**-ah
...small bills.	...notas pequenas.	**not**-ahsh peh-**kay**-nahsh
...large bills.	...notas grandes.	**not**-ahsh **grahn**-dish
...coins.	...moedas.	moo-**eh**-dahsh
€50	cinquenta	seeng-**kwayn**-tah
	euros	**yoo**-roosh
Is this a mistake?	Isto é um erro?	**eesh**-too eh oon **eh**-roo
This is incorrect.	Isto está	**eesh**-too ish-**tah**
	incorreto.	een-koo-**rehk**-too
Did you print	Foi imprimido	foy eem-pree-**mee**-doo
these today?	hoje?	**oh**-zheh
I'm broke.	Estou teso[a].	ish-**toh** tay-zoo
I'm poor.	Sou pobre.	soh **pob**-reh
I'm rich.	Sou rico[a].	soh **ree**-koo
I'm Bill Gates.	Sou o Bill Gates.	soh oo "Bill Gates"
Where is the	Onde é o	**ohn**-deh eh oo
nearest casino?	casino mais	kah-**zee**-noh mīsh
	próximo?	**proh**-see-moo

Portugal uses the euro currency. Euros (€) are divided into 100 cents. Use your common cents—cents are like pennies, and the currency has coins like nickels, dimes, and half-dollars.

Money Words

euro (€)	euro	**yoo**-roh
cents	cent	sehnt
money	dinheiro	deen-**yay**-roo
cash	dinheiro	deen-**yay**-roo
cash machine	caixa	**kï**-shah
	automática,	ow-toh-**mah**-tee-kah,
	Multibanco	mool-tee-**bahng**-koo
bank	banco	**bang**-koo
credit card	cartão de crédito	kar-**tow** deh **kreh**-dee-too
change money	troca de dinheiro	**troo**-kah deh deen-**yay**-roo
exchange	troca	**troo**-kah
buy / sell	comprar / vender	koh<u>n</u>-**prar** / vay<u>n</u>-**dehr**
commission	comissão	koo-mee-**sow**
traveler's check	cheques de	**sheh**-kehsh deh
	viagem	vee-**ah**-zhay<u>n</u>
cash advance	levantamento	leh-vahn-tah-**mayn**-too
	em caixa	ay<u>n</u> **kï**-shah
	automática	ow-toh-**mah**-tee-kah
cashier	caixa	**kï**-shah
bills	notas	**not**-ahsh
coins	moedas	moo-**eh**-dahsh
receipt	recibo	reh-**see**-boo

Cash machines are multilingual, but if you like to experiment, *anular* means "cancel," *corrigir* is "correct," and *continuar* means "continue."

TIME

What time is it?	Que horas são?	kee **oh**-rahsh so<u>w</u>
It's...	São...	so<u>w</u>

...8:00 in the morning.	...oito horas da manhã.	oy-too oh-rahsh dah ming-yah
...16:00.	...dezasseis horas.	deh-zah-saysh oh-rahsh
...4:00 in the afternoon.	...quatro da tarde.	kwah-troo dah tar-deh
...10:30 (in the evening).	...dez horas e meia (da noite).	dehsh oh-rahsh ee may-ah (dah noy-teh)
...a quarter past nine.	...nove e um quarto.	nah-veh ee oon kwar-too
...a quarter to eleven.	...um quarto para as onze.	oon kwar-too pah-rah ahz ohn-zeh
...noon.	...meio-dia.	may-oo-dee-ah
...midnight.	...meia-noite.	may-ah-noy-teh
...early / late.	...cedo / tarde.	say-doo / tar-deh
...on time.	...pontual.	pohn-too-ahl
...sunrise.	...nascer do sol.	nahsh-sehr doo sohl
...sunset.	...por do sol.	poor doo sohl
It's my bedtime.	Está na hora de dormir.	ish-tah nah oh-rah deh dor-meer

COUNTING

Timely Expressions

I'll return / We'll return at 11:20.	Volto / Voltamos as onze e vinte.	vohl-too / vohl-tah-moosh ahz ohn-zeh ee veen-teh
I'll / We'll be there by 18:00.	Vou / Vamos estar lá por volta das dezoito horas.	voh / vah-moosh ish-tar lah poor vohl-tah dahsh deh-zoy-too oh-rahsh
When is checkout time?	Qual é a hora da saída?	kwahl eh ah oh-rah dah sah-ee-dah
What time does...?	A que horas...?	ah kee oh-rahsh
...this open / close	...é que abre / fecha	eh keh ah-breh / fay-shah
...this train / bus leave for ___	...este comboio / auto-carro parte para ___	ehsh-tah kohn-boy-oo / ow-too-kah-roo par-teh pah-rah
...the next train / bus leave for ___	...o próximo comboio / auto-carro parte para___	oo proh-see-moo kohn-boy-oo / ow-too-kah-roo par-teh pah-rah

COUNTING

Key Phrases: Time

minute	*minuto*	mee-**noo**-too
hour	*hora*	**oh**-rah
day	*dia*	**dee**-ah
week	*semana*	seh-**mah**-nah
What time is it?	*Que horas são?*	kee **oh**-rahsh sow
It's...	*São...*	sow
...8:00.	*...oito horas.*	**oy**-too **oh**-rahsh
...16:00.	*...dezasseis horas.*	deh-zah-**saysh oh**-rahsh
What time does this open / close?	*A que horas é que abre / fecha?*	ah kee **oh**-rahsh eh keh **ah**-breh / **fay**-shah

...the train / bus arrive in ___	*...o comboio / auto-carro chega em ___*	oo kohn-**boy**-oo / ow-too-**kah**-roo **shay**-geh ayn
I want / We want to take the 16:30 train.	*Quero / Queremos apanhar o comboio das dezasseis e trinta.*	**kay**-roo / keh-**ray**-moosh ah-payn-**yar** oo kohn-**boy**-oo dahsh deh-zah-**saysh** ee **treen**-tah
Is the train...?	*O comboio está... ?*	oo kohn-**boy**-oo ish-**tah**
Is the bus...?	*O auto-carro está...?*	oo ow-too-**kah**-roo ish-**tah**
...early / late	*...adiantado / atrasado*	ah-dee-ahn-**tah**-doo / ah-trah-**zah**-doo
...on time	*...na hora*	nah **oh**-rah

In Portugal, the 24-hour clock (or military time) is used mainly for train, bus, and ferry schedules. Informally, the Portuguese use the same 12-hour clock we do.

About Time

minute	*minuto*	mee-**noo**-too
hour	*hora*	**oh**-rah
in the morning	*da manhã*	dah ming-**yah**

in the afternoon	da tarde	dah **tar**-deh
in the evening	da noite	dah **noy**-teh
at night	à noite	ah **noy**-teh
at 6:00 sharp	as seis horas	ahsh saysh **oh**-rahsh
	em ponto	ayn **pohn**-too
from 8:00 to 10:00	das oito ás dez	dahz **oy**-too ahz dehsh
in half an hour	daqui a	dah-**kee** ah
	meia hora	**may**-ah **oh**-rah
in one hour	em uma hora	ayn **oo**-mah **oh**-rah
in three hours	em trez horas	ayn traysh **oh**-rahsh
anytime	a qualquer hora	ah kwahl-**kehr oh**-rah
immediately	imediata-	ee-meh-dee-ah-tah-
	mente	**mayn**-teh
every hour	todas as	**toh**-dahsh ahsh
	horas	**oh**-rahsh
every day	todos os	**toh**-doosh oosh
	dias	**dee**-ahsh
daily	diário	dee-**ah**-ree-oh
last	último	**ool**-tee-moo
this	este	**ehsh**-teh
next	próximo	**proh**-see-moo
May 15	quinze de Maio	**keen**-zeh deh **mah**-yoo
high season	época alta	**eh**-poh-kah **ahl**-tah
low season	época baixa	**eh**-poh-kah **bī**-shah
in the future	no futuro	noo foo-**too**-roo
in the past	no passado	noo pah-**sah**-doo

The Day

day	dia	**dee**-ah
today	hoje	**oh**-zheh
yesterday	ontem	**ohn**-tayn
tomorrow	amanhã	ah-ming-**yah**
tomorrow	amanhã de	ah-ming-**yah** deh
morning	manhã	ming-**yah**
day after	depois de	day-**pwaysh** deh
tomorrow	amanhã	ah-ming-**yah**

COUNTING

The Week

week	*semana*	seh-**mah**-nah
last week	*na semana passada*	nah seh-**mah**-nah pah-**sah**-dah
this week	*esta semana*	**ehsh**-tah seh-**mah**-nah
next week	*para a próxima semana*	**pah**-rah ah **proh**-see-mah seh-**mah**-nah
Monday	*segunda-feira*	seh-goon-dah-**fay**-rah
Tuesday	*terça-feira*	tehr-sah-**fay**-rah
Wednesday	*quarta-feira*	kwar-tah-**fay**-rah
Thursday	*quinta-feira*	keen-tah-**fay**-rah
Friday	*sexta-feira*	saysh-tah-**fay**-rah
Saturday	*sábado*	**sah**-bah-doo
Sunday	*domingo*	doo-**meeng**-goo

The Month

month	*mês*	maysh
January	*Janeiro*	zhah-**nay**-roo
February	*Fevereiro*	feh-veh-**ray**-roo
March	*Março*	**mar**-soo
April	*Abril*	**ah**-breel
May	*Maio*	**mah**-yoo
June	*Junho*	**zhoon**-yoo
July	*Julho*	**zhool**-yoo
August	*Agosto*	ah-**gohsh**-too
September	*Setembro*	seh-**tayn**-broo
October	*Outubro*	oh-**too**-broo
November	*Novembro*	noo-**vayn**-broo
December	*Dezembro*	deh-**zayn**-broo

The Year

year	*ano*	**ah**-noo
spring	*primavera*	pree-mah-**veh**-rah
summer	*verão*	veh-**row**
fall	*outono*	oh-**toh**-noo
winter	*inverno*	een-**vehr**-noo

COUNTING

Holidays and Happy Days

holiday	feriado	feh-ree-**ah**-doo
national holiday	feriado	feh-ree-**ah**-doo
	nacional	nah-see-oo-**nahl**
religious holiday	feriado	feh-ree-**ah**-doo
	religioso	ray-lee-zhee-**oh**-zoo
Is today / tomorrow	Hoje / Amanhã	**oh**-zheh / ah-ming-**yah**
a holiday?	é feriado?	eh feh-ree-**ah**-doo
Is a holiday	Há um feriado	ah oon feh-ree-**ah**-doo
coming up	em bréve?	ayn **breh**-veh /
soon? When?	Quando?	**kwahn**-doo
What is the	Qual é o	kwahl eh oo
holiday?	feriado?	feh-ree-**ah**-doo
Merry Christmas!	Feliz Natal!	feh-**leesh** nah-**tahl**
Happy New Year!	Feliz Ano Novo!	feh-**leesh** ah-noo **noh**-voo
Easter	Páscoa	**pahsh**-kwah
Happy wedding	Feliz	feh-**leesh**
anniversary!	aniversário	ah-nee-vehr-**sah**-ree-oo
	de casamento!	deh kah-zah-**mayn**-too
Happy birthday!	Feliz	feh-**leesh**
	aniversário!	ah-nee-vehr-**sah**-ree-oo

The Portuguese sing "Happy Birthday" to the same tune we do, but they sing the tune twice, using these words: *Parabéns a você, nesta data querida, muitas felicidades, muitos anos de vida. Hoje é dia de festa, cantam as nossas almas, para* (fill in name), *uma salva de palmas!* Whew!

Portugal celebrates its Independence Day on December 1. Other major holidays include Liberty Day (April 25), Good Friday and Easter, Camões Day (June 10, in honor of the Portuguese poet Luis de Camões), Assumption of Mary (August 15), and Republic Day (October 5).

TRAVELING

FLIGHTS

All Portuguese airports post bilingual signs in Portuguese and English. Also, nearly all airport service personnel and travel agents speak English these days. Still, these words and phrases could conceivably come in handy.

Making a Reservation

I'd like to... my reservation / ticket.	*Quero... minha reserva / bilhete.*	**kay**-roo... **meen**-yah ray-**zehr**-vah / beel-**yeh**-teh
We'd like to... our reservation / ticket.	*Queremos... nossa reserva / bilhetes.*	keh-**ray**-moosh... **noh**-sah ray-**zehr**-vah / beel-**yeh**-tish
...confirm	*...confirmar*	kohn-feer-**mar**
...change	*...mudar*	moo-**dar**
...cancel	*...cancelar*	kahn-seh-**lar**
aisle seat	*assento sobre o corredor*	ah-**sayn**-too **soh**-breh oo koo-ray-**dor**
window seat	*assento à janela*	ah-**sayn**-too ah zhah-**neh**-lah

At the Airport

Which terminal?	*Qual terminal?*	kwahl tehr-mee-**nahl**
...national flights	*vôos internacionais*	vohz **een**-tehr-nah-see-oh-nīsh

24

domestic flights	vôos internos, vôos domesticos	vohz een-**tehr**-noosh, vohzh doh-**maysh**-tee-koosh
arrival	chegada	shay-**gah**-dah
departure	partida	par-**tee**-dah
baggage check or claim	bagagem	bah-**gah**-zhay<u>n</u>
check in	check in	"check in"
Nothing to declare.	Nada a declarar.	**nah**-dah ah deh-klah-**rar**
I have only carry-on luggage.	Só tenho bagagem de mão.	soh **tayn**-yoo bah-**gah**-zhayn deh mo<u>w</u>
flight number	numero do vôo	**noo**-meh-roh doo voh
departure gate	porta de partida	**por**-tah deh par-**tee**-dah
duty free	imposto não pago, tax free	eem-**pohsh**-too no<u>w</u> **pah**-goo, "tax free"
luggage cart	carrinho de malas	kah-**reen**-yoh deh **mah**-lahsh
jet lag	jet lag	"jet lag"

TRAVELING

Getting to/from the Airport

Approximately how much is a taxi ride to...?	Mais ou menos quanto custa a viagem por taxi para...?	mīsh oh **may**-noosh **kwahn**-too **koosh**-tah ah vee-**ah**-zhay<u>n</u> poor **tahk**-see **pah**-rah
...downtown	...o centro	oo **sayn**-troo
...the train station	...a estação de comboio	ah ish-tah-**sow** deh koh<u>n</u>-**boy**-yoo
...the airport	...o aeroporto	oo ah-roh-**por**-too
Does a bus (or train) run...?	O auto-carro (o comboio) vai...?	oo ow-too-**kah**-roo (oo koh<u>n</u>-**boy**-yoo) vī
...from the airport to downtown	...do aeroporto até o centro	doo ah-roh-**por**-too ah-**tay** oo **sayn**-troo
...to the airport from downtown	...para o aeroporto do centro	**pah**-rah oo ah-roh-**por**-too doo **sayn**-troo
How much is it?	Quanto custa?	**kwahn**-too **koosh**-tah
Where does it leave from...?	De onde parte...?	deh **ohn**-deh **par**-teh

Where does it arrive...?	De onde chega...?	deh **ohn**-deh **shay**-gah
...at the airport	...no aeroporto	noo ah-roh-**por**-too
...downtown	...no centro	noo **sayn**-troo
How often does it run?	Com que frequência passa?	kohn keh freh-**kwayn**-see-ah **pah**-sah

TRAINS

The Train Station

Where is the...?	Onde é a...?	**ohn**-deh eh ah
...train station	...estação de comboio	ish-tah-**sow** deh kohn-**boy**-yoo
Portuguese State Railways	Caminhos de Ferro	kah-**meen**-yoosh deh **fehr**-roo
train information	informação sobre comboios	een-for-mah-**sow** **soh**-breh kohn-**boy**-yoosh
train	comboio	kohn-**boy**-yoo
high-speed train	comboio expresso	kohn-**boy**-yoo ish-**pray**-soo
fast / faster	rápido / mais rápido	**rah**-pee-doo / mīsh **rah**-pee-doo
arrival	chegada	shay-**gah**-dah
departure	partida	par-**tee**-dah
delay	atraso	ah-**trah**-zoo
toilet	casa de banho	**kah**-zah deh **bahn**-yoo
waiting room	sala de espera	**sah**-lah deh ish-**peh**-rah
lockers	depósito de bagagem	day-**poh**-see-too deh bah-**gah**-zhayn
baggage check room	despacho de bagagem	dish-**pah**-shoo deh bah-**gah**-zhayn
lost and found office	perdidos e achados	pehr-**dee**-doosh ee ah-**shah**-doosh
tourist information	informação turística	een-for-mah-**sow** too-**reesh**-tee-kah

to the trains	para os comboios	**pah**-rah oosh kohn-**boy**-yoosh
to the platforms	acesso ão cais	ah-**seh**-soo ow kīsh
platform	cais	kīsh
track	linha	**leen**-yah
train car	carruagem	kar-**wah**-zhayn
dining car	carruagem restaurante	kar-**wah**-zhayn rish-toh-**rahn**-teh
sleeper car	carruagem cama	kar-**wah**-zhayn **kah**-mah
conductor	condutor	kohn-doo-**toor**

Trains in Portugal come in several types. Along with the various local and milk-run trains (**Regional, Suburbano**), there are:

• the slow **Interregional** (**IR**) trains,
• the medium-speed **Intercidades** (**IC**) trains, and
• the fast **Alfa Pendular** (**AP**) train between Lisbon and Porto.

Faster trains are more expensive, but all are cheaper per mile than their northern European counterparts. Off the main Lisbon-Coimbra-Porto train lines, buses are usually a better bet. In cases where buses and trains serve the same destination, the bus is often more efficient, offering more frequent connections and sometimes a more central station.

Getting a Ticket

Where can I buy a ticket?	Onde posso comprar um bilhete?	**ohn**-deh **pos**-soo kohn-**prar** oon beel-**yeh**-teh
A ticket to ___.	Um bilhete para ___.	oon beel-**yeh**-teh **pah**-rah
Where can we buy tickets?	Onde podemos comprar bilhetes?	**ohn**-deh poo-**day**-moosh kohn-**prar** beel-**yeh**-tish
Two tickets to ___.	Dois bilhetes para ___.	doysh beel-**yeh**-tish **pah**-rah
Is this the line for...?	Esta é a fila para...?	**ehsh**-tah eh ah **fee**-lah **pah**-rah

TRAVELING

TRAVELING

Key Phrases: Trains

train station	*estação de comboio*	ish-tah-**sow** deh kohn-**boy**-yoo
train	*comboio*	kohn-**boy**-yoo
ticket	*bilhete*	beel-**yeh**-teh
transfer (verb)	*mudar*	moo-**dar**
supplement	*suplemento*	soo-pleh-**mayn**-too
arrival	*chegada*	shay-**gah**-dah
departure	*partida*	par-**tee**-dah
platform	*cais*	kīsh
track	*linha do comboio*	**leen**-yah doo kohn-**boy**-yoo
train car	*carruagem*	kar-**wah**-zhayn
A ticket to ___.	*Um bilhete para ___.*	oon beel-**yeh**-teh **pah**-rah
Two tickets to ___.	*Dois bilhetes para ___.*	doysh beel-**yeh**-tish **pah**-rah
When is the next train?	*Quando é o próximo comboio?*	**kwahn**-doo eh oo **proh**-see-moo kohn-**boy**-oo
Where does the train leave from?	*De onde é que parte o comboio?*	deh **ohn**-deh eh keh **par**-teh oo kohn-**boy**-yoo
Which train to ___?	*Que comboio para ___?*	keh kohn-**boy**-yoo **pah**-rah

...tickets	*...bilhetes*	beel-**yeh**-tish
...reservations	*...reservas*	reh-**zehr**-vahsh
How much is a ticket to ___?	*Quanto custa o bilhete para ___?*	**kwahn**-too **koosh**-tah oo beel-**yeh**-teh **pah**-rah
Is this ticket valid for ___?	*Este bilhete é válido por___?*	**ehsh**-teh beel-**yeh**-teh eh **vah**-lee-doo poor
How long is this ticket valid?	*Por quanto tempo é válido o bilhete?*	poor **kwahn**-too **tayn**-poo eh **vah**-lee-doo oo beel-**yeh**-teh

When is the next train?	Quando é o próximo comboio?	**kwahn**-doo eh oo **proh**-see-moo kohn-**boy**-oo
Do you have a schedule for all trains departing for ___ today / tomorrow?	Você tem o horário dos comboios que partem para ___ hoje / amanhã?	voh-**say** tayn oo oh-**rah**-ree-oo doosh kohn-**boy**-oosh keh **par**-tayn **pah**-rah ___ **oh**-zheh / ah-ming-**yah**
I'd like to leave...	Gostaria de partir...	goosh-tah-**ree**-ah deh par-**teer**
We'd like to leave...	Gostaríamos de partir...	goosh-tah-**ree**-ah-moosh deh par-**teer**
I'd like to arrive...	Gostaria de chegar...	goosh-tah-**ree**-ah deh shay-**gar**
We'd like to arrive...	Gostaríamos de chegar...	goosh-tah-**ree**-ah-moosh deh shay-**gar**
...by ___.	...por ___.	poor
...in the morning.	...de manhã.	deh ming-**yah**
...in the afternoon.	...de tarde.	deh **tar**-deh
...in the evening.	...ao anoitecer.	ow ah-noy-teh-**sehr**
Is there a...?	Há um...?	ah oon
...earlier train	...comboio mais cedo	kohn-**boy**-oo mīsh **say**-doo
...later train	...comboio mais tarde	kohn-**boy**-oo mīsh **tar**-deh
...overnight train	...comboio durante a noite	kohn-**boy**-oo doo-**rayn**-teh ah **noy**-teh
...cheaper train	...comboio mais barato	kohn-**boy**-oo mīsh bah-**rah**-too
...local train	...comboio local	kohn-**boy**-oo loo-**kahl**
...express train	...comboio rápido (expresso)	kohn-**boy**-oo **rah**-pee-doo (ish-**pray**-soo)
Is there a cheaper option?	Há um opção mais barata?	ah oon ohp-**sow** mīsh bah-**rah**-tah
What track does it leave from?	De que linha parte?	deh keh **leen**-yah **par**-teh
What track?	Que linha sai?	keh **leen**-yah sī

| On time? | Pontual? | pohn-too-**ahl** |
| Late? | Atrasado? | ah-trah-**zah**-doo |

Reservations, Supplements, and Discounts

Is a reservation required?	É preciso reservar?	eh preh-**see**-zoo reh-zehr-**var**
I'd like to reserve a...	Gostaria de reservar um...	goosh-tah-**ree**-ah deh reh-zehr-**var** oon
...seat.	...assento.	ah-**sayn**-too
...berth (couchette).	...lugar sentado.	loo-**gar** sayn-**tah**-doo
...sleeper.	...camarote.	kah-mah-**roh**-teh
...the entire train.	...o comboio todo.	oo kohn-**boy**-oo **toh**-doo
We'd like to reserve...	Gostaríamos de reservar...	goosh-tah-**ree**-ah-moosh deh reh-zehr-**var**
...two seats.	...dois lugares.	doysh loo-**garsh**
...two berths (couchettes).	...dois lugares sentados.	doysh loo-**garsh** sayn-**tah**-doosh
...two beds in a sleeper car.	...dois camarotes.	doysh kah-mah-**roh**-tish
Is there a supplement?	Há um suplemento?	ah oon soo-pleh-**mayn**-too
Does my railpass cover the supplement?	O meu passe cobre os extras?	oo **meh**-oo **pah**-seh **koh**-breh ooz **ish**-trahsh
Is there a discount for...?	Tem desconto para...?	tayn dish-**kohn**-too **pah**-rah
...youth	...jovens	**zhah**-vaynsh
...seniors	...pessoas de terceira idade	peh-**soh**-ahsh deh tehr-**say**-rah ee-**dah**-deh
...families	...famílias	fah-**meel**-yahsh

Ticket Talk

| ticket window | bilhetes, bilhetaria | beel-**yay**-tish, beel-yeh-tah-**ree**-ah |
| reservations window | reservas | reh-**zehr**-vahsh |

national /	nacional /	nah-see-oh-**nahl** /
international	internacional	**een**-tehr-nah-see-oh-nahl
ticket	bilhete	beel-**yeh**-teh
one way	uma ida	**oo**-mah **ee**-dah
roundtrip	ida e volta	**ee**-dah ee **vohl**-tah
first class	primeira classe	pree-**may**-rah **klah**-seh
second class	segunda classe	seh-**goon**-dah **klah**-seh
non-smoking	não fumar	now foo-**mar**
validate	validade	vah-lee-**dah**-deh
schedule	horário	oh-**rah**-ree-oo
departure	partida	par-**tee**-dah
direct	directo	dee-**reh**-too
transfer (verb)	mudar	moo-**dar**
connection	conexão	koo-nehk-**sow**
with supplement	com suplemento	kohn soo-pleh-**mayn**-too
reservation	reserva	ray-**zehr**-vah
seat...	assento...	ah-**sayn**-too
...by the window	...à janela	ah zhah-**neh**-lah
...on the aisle	...sobre o corredor	**soh**-breh oo koo-ray-**dor**
berth	beliche	beh-**lee**-sheh
...upper	...em cima	ayn **see**-mah
...middle	...no meio	noo **may**-oh
...lower	...em baixo	ayn **bī**-shoo
refund	reembolso	reh-ayn-**bohl**-soo
reduced fare	tarifa	tah-**ree**-fah
	reduzida	reh-doo-**zee**-dah

TRAVELING

Changing Trains

Is it direct?	É directo?	eh dee-**reh**-too
Must I transfer?	É preciso mudar?	eh preh-**see**-zoo moo-**dar**
Must we transfer?	Precisamos	preh-see-**zah**-moosh
	de mudar?	deh moo-**dar**
When? Where?	Quando? Onde?	**kwahn**-doo / **ohn**-deh
Do I / Do we	Faço / Fazemos	**fah**-soo / fah-**zeh**-moosh
change	mudança	moo-**dahn**-sah
here for ___?	aqui para ___?	ah-**kee pah**-rah

Where do I / do we change for ___?	Onde faço / fazemos mudança para ___?	**ohn**-deh **fah**-soo / fah-**zeh**-moosh moo-**dahn**-sah pah-**rah**
At what time...?	A que horas...?	ah kee **oh**-rahsh
From what track does my / our connecting train leave?	De qual linha a minha / nossa conexão parte?	deh kwahl **leen**-yah ah **meen**-yah / **noh**-sah koo-nehk-**sow par**-teh
How many minutes in ___ to change trains?	Quantos minutos em ___ para mudar de comboios?	**kwahn**-toosh mee-**noo**-toosh ay<u>n</u> ___ pah-rah moo-**dar** deh koh<u>n</u>-**boy**-oosh

On the Platform

Where is...?	Onde é...?	**ohn**-deh eh
Is this...?	Isto é ...?	**eesh**-toh eh
...the train to ___	...o comboio para ___	oo koh<u>n</u>-**boy**-yoo pah-**rah**
Which train to ___?	Que comboio para ___?	keh koh<u>n</u>-**boy**-yoo pah-**rah**
Which train car for ___?	Que carruagem para ___?	keh kar-**wah**-zhay<u>n</u> pah-**rah**
Where is first class?	Onde é a primeira classe?	**ohn**-deh eh ah pree-**may**-rah **klah**-seh
...front / middle / back	...frente / meio / trás	**fray<u>n</u>**-teh / **may**-oh / trahsh
Where can I validate my ticket?	Onde posso validar o meu bilhete?	**ohn**-deh **pos**-soo vah-lee-**dar** oo **meh**-oo beel-**yeh**-teh

On the Train

Is this (seat) free?	Está livre?	ish-**tah** lee-vreh
May I / May we...?	Posso / Podemos...?	**pos**-soo / poo-**day**-moosh
...sit here (I / we)	...sentar-me / sentar-nos aqui	say<u>n</u>-**tar**-meh / say<u>n</u>-**tar**-nooz ah-**kee**
...open the window	...abra a janela	**ah**-brah ah zhah-**neh**-lah
...eat your meal	...coma a sua comida	**koh**-mah ah **soo**-ah koh-**mee**-dah
Save my place?	Guarde o meu lugar?	**gwar**-deh oo **meh**-oo loo-**gar**

TRAVELING

Save our places?	Guarde os nossos lugares?	**gwar**-deh oosh **nos**-oosh loo-**garsh**
That's my seat.	Este é o meu lugar.	**ehsh**-teh eh oo **meh**-oo loo-**gar**
These are our seats.	Esses são os nossos lugares.	**ays**-sehsh so<u>w</u> oosh **nos**-oosh loo-**garsh**
Where are you going?	Onde é que vai?	**ohn**-deh eh keh vī
I'm going to ___.	Vou para ___.	**voh** pah-rah
We're going to ___.	Nós vamos para ___.	nohsh **vah**-moosh **pah**-rah
Tell me when to get off?	Diga-me quando devo sair?	**dee**-gah-meh **kwahn**-doo **deh**-voo sah-**eer**
Tell us when to get off?	Diga-nos quando devemos sair?	**dee**-gah-noosh **kwahn**-doo deh-**veh**-moosh sah-**eer**
Where is a (good-looking) conductor?	Onde está o condutor (bonitaô)?	**ohn**-deh ish-**tah** oo kohn-doo-**toor** (boo-nee-to<u>w</u>)
Does this train stop in ___?	Esse comboio para em ___?	**ays**-seh kohn-**boy**-oo **pah**-rah ay<u>n</u>
When will it arrive in ___?	Quando chega em ___?	**kwahn**-doo **shay**-gah ay<u>n</u>
When will it arrive?	Quando é que vai chegar?	**kwahn**-doo eh keh vī shay-**gar**

TRAVELING

Reading Train and Bus Schedules

até	until
atrasado	late
chegada	arrival
de	from
destino	destination
diário	daily
dias	days
dias de semana	weekdays
domingos e feriados	Sundays and holidays
excepto	except
hora	time

Major Transportation Lines in Portugal

TRAVELING

linha	track
para	to
partida	departure
sabádo	Saturday
só	only

também	also	
todo	every	
1-5, 6, 7	Monday–Friday, Saturday, Sunday	

European schedules use the 24-hour clock. It's like American time until noon. After that, subtract twelve and add P.M. So 13:00 is 1 P.M., 20:00 is 8 P.M., and 24:00 is midnight. One minute after midnight is 00:01.

Going Places

Portugal	*Portugal*	poor-too-**gahl**
Lisbon	*Lisboa*	leezh-**boh**-ah
Spain	*Espanha*	ish-**pahn**-yah
Morocco	*Marrocos*	mah-**rak**-oosh
Gibraltar	*Gibraltar*	zhee-brahl-**tar**
Austria	*Austria*	**owsh**-tree-ah
Belgium	*Belgica*	behl-**zhee**-kah
Czech Republic	*Republica Checa*	reh-**poob**-lee-kah **sheh**-kah
France	*França*	**frahn**-sah
Germany	*Alemanha*	ah-leh-**mahn**-yah
Great Britain	*Inglaterra*	eeng-glah-**tehr**-rah
Greece	*Grécia*	**gray**-see-ah
Ireland	*Irlanda*	eer-**lahn**-dah
Italy	*Italia*	ee-**tahl**-yah
Netherlands	*Holanda*	oh-**lahn**-dah
Scandinavia	*Escandinavia*	ish-kan-dee-**nahv**-yah
Switzerland	*Suiça*	**swee**-sah
Turkey	*Turkia*	**toor**-kee-ah
Europe	*Europa*	eh-oo-**roh**-pah
EU (European Union)	*UE (União Europeia)*	oo eh (oo-nee-**ow** eh-oo-roh-peh-**ee**-ah)
Russia	*Russia*	**roo**-see-ah
Africa	*Africa*	**ah**-free-kah
United States	*Estados Unidos*	ish-**tah**-doosh oo-**nee**-doosh
Canada	*Canadá*	kah-nah-**dah**
the world	*o mundo*	oo **moon**-doo

TRAVELING

BUSES AND SUBWAYS

At the Bus Station or Metro Stop

ticket	*bilhete*	beel-**yeh**-teh
city bus	*autocarro*	ow-too-**kah**-roo
long-distance bus	*camioneta*	kahm-yoo-**neh**-tah
bus stop	*paragem de autocarro*	pah-**rah**-zhay<u>n</u> deh ow-too-**kah**-roo
bus station	*terminal das camionetas*	tehr-mee-**nahl** dahsh kahm-yoo-**neh**-tahsh
subway	*metro*	**meh**-troo
subway station	*estação do metro*	ish-tah-**sow** doo **meh**-troo
subway map	*mapa do metro*	**mah**-pah doo **meh**-troo
subway entrance	*entrada do metro*	ay<u>n</u>-**trah**-dah doo **meh**-troo
subway stop	*paragem do metro*	pah-**rah**-zhay<u>n</u> doo **meh**-troo
subway exit	*saída do metro*	sah-**ee**-dah doo **meh**-troo
direct	*directo*	dee-**reh**-too
connection	*conexão*	koo-nehk-**sow**
pickpocket	*carteirista*	kar-tay-**rish**-tah

Taking Buses and Subways

How do I get to ___?	*Como vou para ___?*	**koh**-moo voh **pah**-rah
How do we get to ___?	*Como vamos para ___?*	**koh**-moo **vah**-moosh **pah**-rah
How much is a ticket?	*Quanto custa um bilhete?*	**kwahn**-too **koosh**-tah oon beel-**yeh**-teh
Where can I buy a ticket?	*A onde posso comprar um bilhete?*	ah **ohn**-deh **pos**-soo koh<u>n</u>-**prar** oo<u>n</u> beel-**yeh**-teh
Where can we buy tickets?	*Onde podemos comprar bilhetes?*	**ohn**-deh poo-**day**-moosh koh<u>n</u>-**prar** beel-**yeh**-tish
Is this ticket valid (for ___)?	*Este bilhete é válido (por ___)?*	**ehsh**-teh beel-**yeh**-teh eh **vah**-lee-doo (poor)

Key Phrases: Buses and Subways

bus	*auto-carro*	ow-too-**kah**-roo
subway	*metro*	**meh**-troo
ticket	*bilhete*	beel-**yeh**-teh
How do I get to ___?	*Como vou para ___?*	**koh**-moo voh **pah**-rah
How do we get to ___?	*Como vamos para ___?*	**koh**-moo **vah**-moosh **pah**-rah
Which stop for ___?	*Qual é a paragem para ___?*	kwahl eh ah pah-**rah**-zhayn **pah**-rah
Tell me when to get off?	*Diga-me quando devo sair?*	**dee**-gah-meh **kwahn**-doo **deh**-voo sah-**eer**
Tell us when to get off?	*Diga-nos quando devemos sair?*	**dee**-gah-noosh **kwahn**-doo deh-**veh**-moosh sah-**eer**

TRAVELING

Is there a one-day pass?	*Há bilhetes para um dia inteiro?*	ah beel-**yeh**-tish **pah**-rah oon **dee**-ah een-**tay**-roo
Which bus to ___?	*Que autocarro para ___?*	keh ow-too-**kah**-roo **pah**-rah
Does it stop at ___?	*Para em ___?*	**pah**-rah ayn
Which metro stop for ___?	*Qual é a paragem para ___?*	kwahl eh ah pah-**rah**-zhayn **pah**-rah
One ticket, please.	*Um bilhete, por favor.*	oon beel-**yeh**-teh poor fah-**vor**
Two tickets.	*Dois bilhetes.*	doysg beel-**yeh**-tish
Must I transfer?	*É preciso mudar?*	eh preh-**see**-zoo moo-**dar**
Must we transfer?	*Precisamos de mudar?*	preh-see-**zah**-moosh deh moo-**dar**
When does the... leave?	*Quando é que... parte?*	**kwahn**-doo eh keh... **par**-teh
...first	*...o primeiro*	oh pree-**may**-roo
...next	*...o próximo*	oh **proh**-see-moo

...last	...o último	oh **ool**-tee-moo
...bus / subway	...autocarro / metro	ow-too-**kah**-roo / **meh**-troo
What's the frequency per hour / day?	Quantas vêzes por hora / dia?	**kwahn**-tahsh **vay**-zish poor **oh**-rah / **dee**-ah
Where does it leave from?	De onde parte?	deh **ohn**-deh **par**-teh
What time does it leave?	A que horas parte?	ah kee **oh**-rahsh **par**-teh
I'm going to___.	Vou para ___.	voh **pah**-rah
We are going to___.	Nós vamos para ___.	nohsh **vah**-moosh **pah**-rah
Tell me when to get off?	Diga-me quando devo sair?	**dee**-gah-meh **kwahn**-doo **deh**-voo sah-**eer**
Tell us when to get off?	Diga-nos quando devemos sair?	**dee**-gah-noosh **kwahn**-doo deh-**veh**-moosh sah-**eer**

TRAVELING

TAXIS

Getting a Taxi

Taxi!	Táxi!	**tahk**-see
Can you call a taxi?	Pode chamar um táxi?	**pod**-eh shah-**mar** oon **tahk**-see
Where is a taxi stand?	Onde é uma paragem de táxis?	**ohn**-deh eh **oo**-mah pah-**rah**-zhayn deh **tahk**-seesh
Where can I get a taxi?	Onde posso apanhar um táxi?	**ohn**-deh **pos**-soo ah-pahn-**yar** oon **tahk**-see
Where can we get a taxi?	Onde podemos apanhar um táxi?	**ohn**-deh poo-**day**-moosh ah-pahn-**yar** oon **tahk**-see
Are you free?	Está livre?	ish-**tah** lee-vreh
Occupied.	Ocupado.	oo-koo-**pah**-doo
To ___, please.	Para ___, por favor.	**pah**-rah ___ poor fah-**vor**
To this address.	Para este endereço.	**pah**-rah **ehsh**-teh ayn-deh-**ray**-soo

---

Key Phrases: Taxis

Taxi!	*Táxi!*	**tahk**-see
Are you free?	*Está livre?*	ish-**tah lee**-vreh
To ___, please.	*Para ___, por favor.*	**pah**-rah ___ poor fah-**vor**
meter	*medidor*	may-dee-**dor**
Stop here.	*Pare aqui.*	**pah**-reh ah-**kee**
Keep the change.	*Fique com o troco.*	**fee**-keh koh<u>n</u> oo **troh**-koo

---

Take me to ___.	*Leve-me para ___.*	**leh**-veh-meh **pah**-rah
Take us to ___.	*Leve-nos para ___.*	**leh**-veh-noosh **pah**-rah
Approximately how much will it cost to go to...?	*Mais ou menos quanto custa a viagem para...?*	mīsh oh **may**-noosh **kwahn**-too **koosh**-tah ah vee-**ah**-zhay<u>n</u> **pah**-rah
...the airport	*...o aeroporto*	oo ah-roh-**por**-too
...the train station	*...a estação do comboio*	ah ish-tah-**sow** doo koh<u>n</u>-**boy**-oo
...this address	*...este endereço*	**ehsh**-teh ay<u>n</u>-deh-**ray**-soo
Any extra supplement?	*Alguma tarifa extra?*	ahl-**goo**-mah tah-**ree**-fah **ish**-trah
Too much.	*É muito caro.*	eh **mween**-too **kah**-roo
Can you take ___ people?	*Pode levar ___ pessoas?*	**pod**-eh leh-**var** ___ peh-**soh**-ahsh
Any extra fee?	*À taxa extra?*	ah **tah**-shah **ish**-trah
How much per hour?	*Quanto é por hora?*	**kwahn**-too eh poor **oh**-rah
How much for a one-hour city tour?	*Quanto custa por visitar a cidade durante uma hora?*	**kwahn**-too **koosh**-tah poor vee-zee-**tar** ah see-**dah**-deh doo-**rahn**-teh **oo**-mah **oh**-rah

TRAVELING

If you have trouble flagging down a taxi, ask for directions to a *paragem de táxis* (taxi stand). The simplest way to tell a cabbie where you want to go is by stating your destination followed by "please" (*Belém, por favor.*) Tipping isn't expected, but it's polite to round up. So if the fare is €19, round up to €20.

In the Taxi

The meter, please.	O medidor, por favor.	oo may-dee-**dor** poor fah-**vor**
Where is the meter?	Onde está o medidor?	**ohn**-deh ish-**tah** oo may-dee-**dor**
I'm / We're in a hurry.	Estou / Estamos com presa.	ish-**toh** / ish-**tah**-moosh koh<u>n</u> **preh**-zah
Slow down.	Mais devagar.	mīsh deh-vah-**gar**
If you don't slow down, I'll throw up.	Se não for mais devagar, vou vomitar.	seh no<u>w</u> for mīsh day-vah-**gar** voh voo-mee-**tar**
Right / Left / Straight.	Direita / Esquerda / Em frente.	dee-**ray**-tah / ish-**kehr**-dah / ay<u>n</u> **frayn**-teh
I'd like / We'd like to stop here briefly.	Gostaria / Gostaríamos de parar aqui por uns minutos.	goosh-tah-**ree**-ah / goosh-tah-**ree**-ah-moosh deh pah-**rar** ah-**kee** poor oon<u>sh</u> mee-**noo**-toosh
Please stop here for ___ minutes.	Por favor, pare aqui por ___ minutos.	poor fah-**vor** **pah**-reh ah-**kee** poor ___ mee-**noo**-toosh
Can you wait?	Pode esperar?	**pod**-eh ish-peh-**rar**
Crazy traffic, isn't it?	Este trânsito é doido, não é?	**ehsh**-teh **trayn**-see-too eh **doy**-doo, no<u>w</u> eh
You drive like ...	O senhor conduz como...	oo sin-**yor** koh<u>n</u>-**doosh koh**-moo
...a madman!	...um louco!	oo<u>n</u> **low**-koo
...Michael Schumacher.	...Michael Schumacher.	Miguel "Schumacher"
You drive very well.	O senhor conduz muito bem.	oo sin-**yor** koh<u>n</u>-**doosh mween**-too bay<u>n</u>
Where did you learn to drive?	Onde é que aprendeu a conduzir?	**ohn**-deh eh keh ah-**prayn**-doo ah koh<u>n</u>-doo-**zeer**
Stop here.	Pare aqui.	**pah**-reh ah-**kee**
Here is fine.	Aqui está bom.	ah-**kee** ish-**tah** boh<u>n</u>
At this corner.	Nesta esquina.	**nehsh**-tah ehsh-**kee**-nah

The next corner.	*Na próxima esquina.*	nah **proh**-see-mah ehsh-**kee**-nah
My change, please.	*O meu troco, por favor.*	oo **meh**-oo **troh**-koo poor fah-**vor**
Keep the change.	*Fique com o troco.*	**fee**-keh kohn oo **troh**-koo
This ride is / was more fun than Disneyland.	*Esta viagem é / foi mais agradavel do que na Disneyland.*	**ehsh**-tah vee-**ah**-zhayn eh / foy mîsh ah-grah-**dah**-vehl doo keh nah "Disneyland"

DRIVING

Rental Wheels

car rental agency	*companhia de carros de aluguel*	kohn-pahn-**yee**-ah deh **kah**-roosh deh ah-loo-**gehl**
I'd like to rent...	*Gostaria de alugar...*	goosh-tah-**ree**-ah deh ah-loo-**gar**
We'd like to rent...	*Gostaríamos de alugar...*	goosh-tah-**ree**-ah-moosh deh ah-loo-**gar**
...a car.	*...um carro.*	oon **kah**-roo
...a station wagon.	*...uma carrinha.*	**oo**-mah kah-**reen**-yah
...a van.	*...uma furgoneta.*	**oo**-mah foor-goo-**nay**-tah
...a motorcycle.	*...uma mota.*	**oo**-mah **moh**-tah
...a motor scooter.	*...uma motocicleta.*	**oo**-mah moh-toh-see-**kleh**-tah
How much...?	*Quanto custa...?*	**kwahn**-too **koosh**-tah
...per hour	*...á hora*	ah **oh**-rah
...per half day	*...por meio-dia*	poor may-oh-**dee**-ah
...per day	*...ao dia*	ow **dee**-ah
...per week	*...á semana*	ah seh-**mah**-nah
Unlimited kilometers?	*Quilômetragem ilimitada?*	kee-**loh**-meh-trah-zhayn ee-lee-mee-**tah**-dah
When must I bring it back?	*Quando é para devolver?*	**kwahn**-doo eh **pah**-rah deh-vohl-**vehr**
Is there...?	*Há...?*	ah
...a helmet	*...um capacete*	oon kah-pah-**say**-teh

TRAVELING

Key Phrases: Driving

car	carro	**kah**-roo
gas station	estação de gasolina	ish-tah-**sow** deh gah-zoo-**lee**-nah
parking lot	estaciona-mento	ish-tah-see-oo-nah-**mayn**-too
accident	acidente	ah-see-**dayn**-teh
left / right	esquerda / direita	ish-**kehr**-dah / dee-ray-tah
straight ahead	em frente	ayn **frayn**-teh
downtown	centro	**sayn**-troo
How do I get to __?	Como vou para__?	**koh**-moo voh **pah**-rah
Where can I park?	Onde é que posso estacionar?	**ohn**-deh eh keh **pos**-soo ish-tah-see-oo-**nar**

...a discount	...um desconto	oon dish-**kohn**-too
...a deposit	...um depósito	oon deh-**poh**-zee-too
...insurance	...seguro	say-**goo**-roo

At the Gas Station

gas station	stação de gasolina	ish-tah-**sow** deh gah-zoo-**lee**-nah
The nearest gas station?	A próxima estação de gasolina?	ah **proh**-see-mah ish-tah-**sow** deh gah-zoo-**lee**-nah
Self-service?	Self-service?	"self-service"
Fill the tank.	Abastecer o carro.	ah-bahsh-teh-**sehr** oo **kah**-roo
Wash the windows.	Lave os vidros do carro.	**lah**-veh oosh **veed**-roosh doo **kah**-roo
I need...	Preciso...	preh-**see**-zoo
We need...	Precisamos...	preh-see-**zah**-moosh
...gas.	...gasolina.	gah-zoo-**lee**-nah
...unleaded.	...sem chumbo.	sayn **shoon**-boo

...regular.	...normal.	nor-**mahl**
...super.	...super.	soo-**pehr**
...diesel.	...diesel.	dee-**zehl**
Check...	Verifique...	vehr-ee-**feek**
...the oil.	...o óleo.	oo **ahl**-yoh
...the air in the tires.	...o ar nos pneus.	oo ar noosh **pehn**-yoosh
...the battery.	...a bateria.	ah bah-teh-**ree**-ah
...the sparkplugs.	...as velas.	ahsh veh-**lahsh**
...the headlights.	...os faróis da frente.	oosh fah-**roysh** dah **frayn**-teh
...the tail lights.	...as luzes traseiras.	ahsh **loo**-shish trah-**zay**-rahsh
...the directional signal.	...o pisca-pisca.	oo **pish**-kah-**pish**-kah
...the brakes.	...os travões.	oosh trah-**vowsh**
...the transmission fluid.	...o óleo de transmissão.	oo **ahl**-yoh deh trah<u>n</u>s-mee-**show**
...the windshield wipers.	...o para-brisas.	oo pah-rah-**bree**-zahsh
...the fuses.	...o fussil.	oo **foo**-zeel
...the fan belt.	...a correia de ventoinha.	ah koh-**ray**-ah deh vehn-toh-**een**-yah
...the radiator.	...o radiador.	oo rah-dee-ah-**dor**
...my pulse.	...a minha pulsação.	ah **meen**-yah pool-sah-**sow**
...my husband / my wife.	...meu marido / minha mulher.	**meh**-oo mah-**ree**-doo / **meen**-yah mool-**yehr**

Gas prices are listed per liter; there are about four liters in a gallon.

Car Trouble

accident	acidente	ah-see-**dayn**-teh
breakdown	parado	pah-**rah**-doo
dead battery	sem bateria	say<u>n</u> bah-teh-**ree**-ah
funny noise	barulho estranho	bah-**rool**-yoo ish-**trahn**-yoo
electrical problem	problema elétrico	proo-**blay**-mah eh-**leh**-tree-koo

flat tire	*pneu furado*	**pehn**-yoo foo-**rah**-doo
shop with parts	*loja de peças*	**loh**-zhah deh **peh**-sahsh
My car won't start.	*O meu carro não arranca.*	oo **meh**-oo **kah**-roo now ah-**rang**-kah
My car is broken.	*Meu carro está avariado.*	**meh**-oo **kah**-roo ish-**tah** ah-vah-ree-**ah**-doo
This doesn't work.	*Isto não funciona.*	**eesh**-too now foon-see-**oh**-nah
It's overheating.	*Está muito quente.*	ish-**tah** mween-too **kayn**-teh
It's a lemon ("rattletrap")	*É um calhambeque.*	eh oon kahl-yahm-**beh**-keh
I need...	*Preciso...*	preh-**see**-zoo
We need...	*Precisamos...*	preh-see-**zah**-moosh
...a tow truck.	*...um reboque.*	oon reh-**bah**-keh
...a mechanic.	*...um mecânico.*	oon meh-**kah**-nee-koo
...a stiff drink.	*...whiskey.*	"whiskey"

For help with repair, look up "Repair" on page 158 in the Services chapter.

Parking

parking lot	*(parque de) esta-cionamento*	(**par**-keh deh) ish-tah-see-oo-nah-**mayn**-too
parking garage	*garagem*	gah-**rah**-zhayn
Where can I park?	*Onde é que posso estacionar?*	**ohn**-deh eh keh **pos**-soo ish-tah-see-oo-**nar**
Is parking nearby?	*O estaciona-mento é perto de aqui?*	oo ish-tah-see-oo-nah-**mayn**-too eh **pehr**-too deh ah-**kee**
Can I park here?	*Posso estacionar aqui?*	**pos**-soo ish-tah-see-oo-**nar** ah-**kee**
Is this a safe place to park?	*É seguro estacionar aqui?*	eh say-**goo**-roo ish-tah-see-oo-**nar** ah-**kee**
How long can I park here?	*Quanto tempo posso estacionar aqui?*	**kwahn**-too **tayn**-poo **pos**-soo ish-tah-see-oo-**nar** ah-**kee**

| Must I pay to park here? | É preciso pagar para estacionar aqui? | eh preh-**see**-zoo pah-**gar pah**-rah ish-tah-see-oo-**nar** ah-**kee** |
| How much per hour / day? | Quanto é por hora / dia? | **kwahn**-too eh poor **oh**-rah / **dee**-ah |

There are no parking meters in Portugal; instead, you'll find machines (**bilhete de estacionamento**) from which you purchase timed tickets to place inside your car.

FINDING YOUR WAY

I'm going to ___.	Vou para ___.	voh **pah**-rah
We're going to ___.	Nós vamos para ___.	nohsh **vah**-moosh **pah**-rah
How do I get to ___?	Como vou para ___?	**koh**-moo voh **pah**-rah
How do we get to ___?	Como chegamos a ___?	**koh**-moo shay-**gah**-moosh ah
Do you have a...?	Tem um...?	tayn oon
...city map	...mapa da cidade	**mah**-pah dah see-**dah**-deh
...road map	...mapa da estrada	**mah**-pah dah ish-**trah**-dah
How many minutes / hours...?	Quantos minutos / horas...?	**kwahn**-toosh mee-**noo**-toosh / **oh**-rahsh
...on foot	...a pé	ah peh
...on bicycle	...de bicicleta	deh bee-see-**kleh**-tah
...by car	...de carro	deh **kah**-roo
How many kilometers to ___?	Quantos quilômetros para ___?	**kwahn**-toosh kee-**loo**-meh-troosh **pah**-rah
What's the... route to Lisbon?	Qual é a... estrada para Lisboa?	kwahl eh ah... ish-**trah**-dah **pah**-rah leezh-**boh**-ah
...most scenic	...mais bonito	mīsh boh-**nee**-too
...fastest	...mais rápida	mīsh **rah**-pee-dah
...most interesting	...mais interessante	mīsh een-teh-reh-**sahn**-teh
Point it out?	Aponte?	ah-**pohn**-teh
I'm lost.	Estou perdido[a].	ish-**toh** pehr-**dee**-doo

Where am I?	Onde é que estou?	**ohn**-deh eh keh ish-**toh**
Where is...?	Onde é que é...?	**ohn**-deh eh keh eh
The nearest...?	O próximo...?	oo **proh**-see-moo
Where is this address?	Onde é este endereço?	**ohn**-deh eh **ehsh**-teh ay<u>n</u>-deh-**ray**-soo

Route-Finding Words

city map	mapa da cidade	**mah**-pah dah see-**dah**-deh
road map	mapa da estrada	**mah**-pah dah ish-**trah**-dah
downtown	centro	**say<u>n</u>**-troo
straight ahead	em frente	ay<u>n</u> **fray<u>n</u>**-teh
left	esquerda	ish-**kehr**-dah
right	direita	dee-**ray**-tah
first	primeira	pree-**may**-rah
next	próximo	**proh**-see-moo
intersection	cruzamento	kroo-zah-**may<u>n</u>**-too
corner	esquina	ehsh-**kee**-nah
block	bloco	**bloh**-koo
roundabout	rotunda	roh-**too<u>n</u>**-dah
stoplight	sinal de luz	see-**nahl** deh loosh
square	praça	**prah**-sah
street	rua	**roo**-ah
bridge	ponte	**poh<u>n</u>**-teh
tunnel	túnel	**too**-nehl
highway, freeway	autoestrada	ow-too-ish-**trah**-dah
north	norte	**nor**-teh
south	sul	sool
east	este	**ehsh**-teh
west	oeste	**wehsh**-teh

The Police

In any country, the flashing lights of a patrol car are a sure sign that someone's in trouble. If it's you, try this handy phrase: "*Desculpe, mas sou turista.*" (Sorry, I'm a tourist.) Or, for the adventurous: "*Se não gostar da minha condução, fique lá fora.*" (If you don't like how I drive, stay off the sidewalk.)

Standard Road Signs

 AND LEARN THESE ROAD SIGNS

Speed Limit
(km/hr)

Yield

No Passing

End of
No Passing
Zone

One Way

Intersection

Main
Road

Freeway

Danger

No Entry

No Entry
for Cars

All Vehicles
Prohibited

Parking

No Parking

Customs

Peace

TRAVELING

I'm late for my tour.	Estou atrazado para o meu passeio turístico.	ish-**toh** ah-trah-**zah**-doo **pah**-rah oo **meh**-oo pah-**say**-oh too-**ree**-stee-koo
Can I buy your hat?	Posso comprar o seu chapeu?	**pos**-soo kohn-**prar** oo **seh**-oo chah-**pow**
What seems to be the problem?	Qual é o problema?	kwahl eh oo proo-**blay**-mah
Sorry, I'm a tourist.	Desculpe[a], mas sou turista.	dish-**kool**-peh mahsh **soh** too-ree-shtah

Reading Road Signs

abrandar	yield
baixa	center of town
construção na estrada	workers ahead
cuidado	caution
desvio	detour
devagar	slow
entrada	entrance
estacionamento proibido	no parking
obras	construction
outras as direçoes	other directions (out of town)
pare	stop
peões	pedestrians
próxima saída	next exit
saída	exit
sentido único	one-way street
todas as direçoes	all directions (out of town)

Other Signs You May See

aberto das ___ ás ___	open from ___ to ___
água não potável	undrinkable water
casa de banho	toilet
cuidado	be careful
cuidado com o cão	mean dog
empurre / puxe	push / pull (but pronounced "push"!)

fechado para férias	closed for vacation
fechado para restauração	closed for restoration
homens / mulheres	men / women
Informação de Turismo	Tourist Information Office
ocupado	occupied
para alugar / venda	for rent / sale
perigo	danger
proibido	forbidden
proíbida a entrada	no entry
proibido fumar	no smoking
não há vagas	no vacancy
saída de emergência	emergency exit
WC	toilet

SLEEPING

Places to Stay

hotel	*hotel*	oh-**tehl**
family-run hotel	*pensão,*	payn-**sow**,
	residência	reh-zee-**dayn**-see-ah
fancy historic hotel	*pousada*	poh-**zah**-dah
room in private home	*quarto*	**kwar**-too
youth hostel	*pousada de*	poh-**zah**-dah deh
	juventude	zhoo-vayn-**too**-deh
vacancy sign	*quartos*	**kwar**-toosh
	("rooms")	
no vacancy	*não há vagas*	no<u>w</u> ah **vah**-gahsh

Reserving a Room

I like to reserve rooms a few days in advance as I travel. But if my itinerary is set, I reserve before I leave home. To reserve from home by email or fax, use the handy form in the appendix (online at www.ricksteves.com/reservation).

Hello.	*Olá.*	oh-**lah**
Do you speak English?	*Fala inglês?*	**fah**-lah een-**glaysh**
Do you have a room for...?	*Tem um quarto para...?*	tay<u>n</u> oo<u>n</u> **kwar**-too **pah**-rah
...one person	*...uma pessoa*	**oo**-mah peh-**soh**-ah

50

Key Phrases: Sleeping

I want to make / confirm a reservation.	*Eu quero fazer / confirmar uma reserva.*	eh-oo **kay**-roo fah-**zehr** / kohn-feer-**mar** oo-mah reh-**zehr**-vah
I'd like a room (for two people), please.	*Queria um quarto (para duas pessoas), por favor.*	keh-**ree**-ah oon **kwar**-too (**pah**-rah **doo**-ahsh peh-**soh**-ahsh) poor fah-**vor**
...with / without / and	*...com / sem / e*	kohn / sayn / ee
...toilet	*...casa de banho*	**kah**-zah deh **bahn**-yoo
...shower	*...chuveiro*	shoo-**vay**-roo
Can I see the room?	*Posso ver o quarto?*	**pos**-soo vehr oo **kwar**-too
How much is it?	*Quanto custa?*	**kwahn**-too **koosh**-tah
Credit card O.K.?	*Cartão de crédito O.K.?*	kar-**tow** deh **kreh**-dee-too "O.K."

SLEEPING

...two people	*...duas pessoas*	**doo**-ahsh peh-**soh**-ahsh
...today / tomorrow	*...hoje / amanhã*	**oh**-zheh / ah-ming-**yah**
...the day after tomorrow	*...depois de amanhã*	day-**pwaysh** deh ah-ming-**yah**
...two nights	*...duas noites*	**doo**-ahsh **noy**-tehsh
...this Friday	*...esta sexta-feira*	**ehsh**-tah saysh-tah-**fay**-rah
...June 21	*...vinte e um de Junho*	**veen**-teh ee oo<u>n</u> deh **zhoon**-yoo
Yes or no?	*Sim ou não?*	seeng oh no<u>w</u>
I'd like...	*Gostaria...*	goosh-tah-**ree**-ah
...a private bathroom.	*...uma casa de banho privada.*	oo-mah **kah**-zah deh **bahn**-yoo pree-**vah**-dah
...your cheapest room.	*...o quarto mais barato.*	oo **kwar**-too mīsh bah-**rah**-too
...___ bed(s) for ___ person(s) in ___ room(s).	*...___ cama(s) para ___ pessoa(s) no ___ quarto(s).*	___ **kah**-mah(sh) **pah**-rah ___ peh-**soh**-ah(sh) noo ___ **kwar**-too(sh)

How much is it?	Quanto custa?	**kwahn**-too **koosh**-tah
Anything cheaper?	Nada mais barato?	**nah**-dah mīsh bah-**rah**-too
I'll take it.	Eu fico com ceste quarto.	**eh**-oo **fee**-koo koh<u>n</u> **ehsh**-teh **kwar**-too
My name is ___.	Chamo-me ___.	**shah**-moo-meh
I'll stay / We'll stay...	Fico / Ficamos...	**fee**-koo / fee-**kah**-moosh
...for ___ night(s).	...por ___ noite(s).	poor ___ **noy**-teh(sh)
I'll come / We'll come...	Venho / Vimos...	**vehn**-yoo / **vee**-moosh
...in the morning.	...de manhã.	deh ming-**yah**
...in the afternoon.	...de tarde.	deh **tar**-deh
...in the evening.	...ao anoitecer.	ow ah-noy-teh-**sehr**
...in one hour.	...dentro de uma hora.	**dayn**-troo deh **oo**-mah **oh**-rah
...before 4:00 in the afternoon.	...antes das quatro da tarde.	**ahn**-tish dahsh **kwah**-troo dah **tar**-deh
...Friday before 6 P.M.	...sexta-feira antes das seis horas da tarde.	saysh-tah-**fay**-rah **ahn**-tish dahsh saysh **oh**-rahsh dah **tar**-deh
Thank you.	Obrigado[a].	oh-bree-**gah**-doo

O Alfabeto

If phoning, you can use the code alphabet below to spell out your name if necessary. Unless you're giving the hotelier your name as it appears on your credit card, consider using a shorter version of your name to make things easier.

A	ah	Amélia	ah-**mehl**-yah
B	bay	Barco (boat)	**bar**-koo
C	say	Casa (house)	**kah**-zah
D	day	Dado (dice)	**dah**-doo
E	eh	Elefante	ehl-eh-**fahn**-teh
F	ehf	Faca (knife)	**fah**-kah
G	**gee**-ah	Girafa	**zhee**-rah-fah
H	**eh**-gah	Hora (hour)	**oh**-rah

I	ee	Inês	ī-**nehz**
J	**zhot**-teh	José	zhoh-**zeh**
K	**kah**-pah	Kapa	**kah**-pah
L	ehl	Lurdes	**loor**-dehsh
M	ehm	Maria	mah-**ree**-ah
N	ehn	Nadia	**nah**-dee-ah
O	oh	Orlando	or-**lahn**-doo
P	pay	Paulo	**pow**-loo
Q	kay	Quem (who)	kay<u>n</u>
R	ehr	Rui	**roo**-ee
S	ehs	Sonia	**sohn**-yah
T	tay	Tania	**tahn**-yah
U	oo	Uganda	oo-**gahn**-dah
V	vay	Victor	**veek**-tor
W	**doob**-leh-vay	William	"William"
X	sheesh	Xadres (chess)	**zhah**-drehsh
Y	**eep**-soh-loo	York	"York"
Z	zay	Zebra	**zeh**-brah

Using a Credit Card

If you need to secure your reservation with a credit card, here's the lingo.

Is a deposit required?	É preciso deixar depósito?	eh preh-**see**-zoo day-**shar** day-**poh**-zee-too
Credit card O.K.?	Cartão de crédito O.K.?	kar-**tow** deh **kreh**-dee-too "O.K."
credit card	cartão de crédito	kar-**tow** deh **kreh**-dee-too
debit card	cartão de debito	kar-**tow** deh **deh**-bee-too
The name on the card is ___.	O nome no cartão é ___.	oo **noh**-meh noo kar-**tow** eh
The credit card number is...	O numero do cartão é...	oo **noo**-meh-roh doo kar-**tow** eh
0	zero	**zeh**-roo
1	um	oo<u>n</u>
2	dois	doysh

3	*três*	traysh
4	*quatro*	**kwah**-troo
5	*cinco*	**seeng**-koo
6	*seis*	saysh
7	*sete*	**seh**-teh
8	*oito*	**oy**-too
9	*nove*	**nah**-veh
Valid until...	*Válido até...*	**vah**-lee-doo ah-**teh**
January	*Janeiro*	zhah-**nay**-roo
February	*Fevereiro*	feh-veh-**ray**-roo
March	*Março*	**mar**-soo
April	*Abril*	ah-**breel**
May	*Maio*	**mah**-yoo
June	*Junho*	**zhoon**-yoo
July	*Julho*	**zhool**-yoo
August	*Agosto*	ah-**gohsh**-too
September	*Setembro*	seh-**tayn**-broo
October	*Outubro*	oh-**too**-broo
November	*Novembro*	noo-**vayn**-broo
December	*Dezembro*	deh-**zayn**-broo
2016	*dois mil e dezasseis*	doysh meel ee deh-zah-**saysh**
2017	*dois mil e dezessete*	doysh meel ee deh-zeh-**seht**
2018	*dois mil e dezoito*	doysh meel ee deh-**zoy**-too
2019	*dois mil e dezenove*	doysh meel ee deh-zah-**nah**-veh
2020	*dois mil e vinte*	doysh meel ee **veen**-teh
Can I reserve with a credit card and pay in cash?	*Posso reservar com o cartão de crédito e depois pagar em dinheiro?*	**pos**-soo reh-zehr-**var** koh<u>n</u> oo kar-**tow** deh **kreh**-dee-too ee day-**pwaysh** pah-**gar** ay<u>n</u> deen-**yay**-roo
I have another card.	*Tenho outro cartão.*	**tayn**-yoo **oh**-troo kar-**tow**

If your *cartão de crédito* (credit card) is not approved, say "*Tenho outro cartão*" (I have another card)—if you do.

What Your Hotelier Wants to Know

Here's a sample email I'd send to make a reservation:

From:	rick@ricksteves.com
Sent:	Today
To:	info@hotelcentral.com
Subject:	Reservation request for 19-22 July

Dear Hotel Central,

I would like to reserve a room for 2 people for 3 nights, arriving 19 July and departing 22 July. If possible, I would like a quiet room with a double bed and a bathroom inside the room.

Please let me know if you have a room available and the price.

Thank you!
Rick Steves

Getting Specific

I'd like a room...	Queria um quarto...	keh-**ree**-ah oo<u>n</u> **kwar**-too
We'd like a room...	Queriamos um quarto...	keh-**ree**-ah-moosh oo<u>n</u> **kwar**-too
...with / without / and	...com / sem / e	koh<u>n</u> / say<u>n</u> / ee
...toilet	...casa de banho	**kah**-zah deh **bahn**-yoo
...shower	...chuveiro	shoo-**vay**-roo
...bathtub	...banheira	bahn-**yay**-rah
...double bed	...cama grande	**kah**-mah **grahn**-deh
...twin beds	...camas gémeas	**kah**-mahsh **zheh**-may-ahsh
...balcony	...varanda	vah-**rahn**-dah
...view	...vista	**veesh**-tah
...on the ground floor	...no rés-do-chão	noo **raysh**-doo-sho<u>w</u>
...television	...televisão	teh-leh-vee-**zow**
...telephone	...telefone	teh-leh-**foh**-neh

SLEEPING

...air conditioning	...ar condicionado	ar koh<u>n</u>-dee-see-oh-**nah**-doo
...kitchenette	...kitchenete	"kitchenette"
Do you have...?	Tem...?	tay<u>n</u>
...an elevator	...um elevador	oo<u>n</u> eh-leh-vah-**dor**
...a swimming pool	...uma piscina	**oo**-mah pee-**shee**-nah
I arrive Monday, depart Wednesday.	Chego segunda-feira, e parto quarta-feira.	**shay**-goo seh-goon-dah-**fay**-rah ee **par**-too kwar-tah-**fay**-rah
We arrive Monday, depart Wednesday.	Chegamos segunda-feira, e partimos quarta-feira.	shay-**gah**-moosh seh-goon-dah-**fay**-rah ee par-**tee**-moosh kwar-tah-**fay**-rah
I am / We are desperate.	Estou / Estamos desesperado(s).	ish-**toh** / ish-**tah**-moosh deh-zish-pehr-**ah**-doo(sh)
I will / We will sleep anywhere.	Dormo / Dormimos em qualquer lugar.	**dor**-moo / dor-**mee**-mooz ay<u>n</u> kwahl-**kehr** loo-**gar**
I have a sleeping bag.	Tenho um saco de dormir.	**tay<u>n</u>**-yoo oo<u>n</u> **sah**-koo deh dor-**meer**
We have sleeping bags.	Temos sacos de dormir.	**tay**-moosh **sah**-koosh deh dor-**meer**
Will you call another hotel for me?	Pode contactar outro hotel por mim?	**pod**-eh koh<u>n</u>-tahk-**tar** **oh**-troo oh-**tehl** poor meeng

Families

Do you have a...?	Tem um...?	tay<u>n</u> oo<u>n</u>
...family room	...quarto para familia	**kwar**-too **pah**-rah fah-**meel**-yah
...family rate	...preço para familia	**preh**-soo **pah**-rah fah-**meel**-yah
...discount for children	...disconto para crianças	deesh-**kohn**-too **pah**-rah kree-**ahn**-sahsh
I have / We have...	Tenho / Temos...	**tay<u>n</u>**-yoo / **tay**-moosh
...one child, age ___ months / years.	...uma criança de ___ mêses / anos.	**oo**-mah kree-**ahn**-sah deh ___ **may**-zish / **ah**-noosh

SLEEPING

...two children,	...duas crianças,	**doo**-ahsh kree-**ahn**-sahsh
ages __ and __ years.	de __ e __ anos.	deh __ ee __ **ah**-noosh
I'd like...	Gostaria...	goosh-tah-**ree**-ah
We'd like...	Gostaríamos...	goosh-tah-**ree**-ah-moosh
...a crib.	...um berço.	oon **behr**-soo
...a small	...uma cama extra	**oo**-mah **kah**-mah **ish**-trah
extra bed.	para crianças.	**pah**-rah kree-**ahn**-sahsh
...bunk beds.	...beliches.	beh-**lee**-shehsh
babysitting service	serviços de	sehr-**vee**-soosh deh
	ajuda com as	ah-**zhoo**-dah koh_n_ ahsh
	crianças	kree-**ahn**-sahsh
Is a... nearby?	Há um... perto?	ah oo_n_... **pehr**-too
...park	...parque	**par**-keh
...playground	...parque de	**par**-keh deh
	diversões	dee-vehr-**sowsh**
...swimming pool	...piscina	pee-**shee**-nah

The Portuguese call kids *miúdos* (little ones) or *marotos* (naughty ones).

Mobility Issues

Stairs are...	Escadas são...	ish-**kah**-dahsh sow
...impossible...	...impossíveis...	eem-poh-**see**-vaysh
...difficult...	...difíceis...	dee-**fee**-saysh
...for me / us.	...para mim / nós.	**pah**-rah meeng / nohsh
...for my husband /	...para meu	**pah**-rah **meh**-oo
my wife.	marido /	mah-**ree**-doo /
	minha mulher.	**meen**-yah mool-**yehr**
Do you have...?	Tem...?	tay_n_
...an elevator	...um elevador	oo_n_ eh-leh-vah-**dor**
...a ground	...um quarto no	oo_n_ **kwar**-too noo
floor room	rés-do-chão	**raysh**-doo-show
...a wheelchair-	...uma cadeira de	**oo**-mah kah-**day**-rah deh
accessible room	rodas-acesso	**roh**-dahz-ahsh-**seh**-soo
	ao quarto	ow **kwar**-too

Confirming, Changing, and Canceling Reservations

You can use this template for your telephone call.

I have / We have a reservation.	Tenho / Temos uma reserva.	**tayn**-yoo / **tay**-moosh **oo**-mah reh-**zehr**-vah
My name is ___.	Chamo-me ___.	**shah**-moo-meh
I want to... my reservation.	Quero... minha reserva.	**keh**-roo... **meen**-yah reh-**zehr**-vah
...confirm	...confirmar	kohn-feer-**mar**
...cancel	...cancelar	kahn-seh-**lar**
...change	...trocar	troh-**kar**
The reservation is / was for...	A reserva é / era para...	ah reh-**zehr**-vah eh / **eh**-rah **pah**-rah
...one person	...uma pessoa	**oo**-mah peh-**soh**-ah
...two people	...duas pessoas	**doo**-ahsh peh-**soh**-ahsh
...today / tomorrow	...hoje / amanhã	**oh**-zheh / ah-ming-**yah**
...August 13	...treze de Agosto	**tray**-zeh deh ah-**gohsh**-too
...one night / two nights	...uma noite / duas noites	**oo**-mah **noy**-teh / **doo**-ahsh **noy**-tehsh
Did you find my / our reservation?	Encontrou minha / nossa reserva?	ehn-**kohn**-troh **meen**-yah / **noh**-sah reh-**zehr**-vah
What is your cancellation policy?	Qual é a regra para cancelar?	kwahl eh ah **reh**-grah **pah**-rah kahn-seh-**lar**
Will I be billed for the first night if I can't make it?	Tenho que pagar se não chegar?	**tayn**-yoo keh pah-**gar** seh now shay-**gar**
I'd like to arrive instead on ___.	Em vez, gostaria de chega r___.	ayn vaysh goosh-tah-**ree**-ah deh shay-**gar**
We'd like to arrive instead on ___.	Em vez, gostaríamos de chegar ___.	ayn vaysh goosh-tah-**ree**-ah-moosh deh shay-**gar**
Is everything O.K.?	Tudo bem?	**too**-doo bayn
Thank you. See you then.	Obrigado[a]. Até á próxima.	oh-bree-**gah**-doo ah-**teh** ah **proh**-see-mah
I'm sorry, I need to cancel.	Desculpe, eu tenho que cancelar.	dish-**kool**-peh **eh**-oo **tayn**-yoo keh kahn-seh-**lar**

Nailing Down the Price

How much is...?	Quanto custa...?	kwahn-too koosh-tah
...a room	...um quarto	oon kwar-too
for ___ people	para ___ pessoas	pah-rah ___ peh-soh-ahsh
...your cheapest room	...o quarto mais barato	oo kwar-too mīsh bah-rah-too
Is breakfast included?	Pequeno almoço está incluído?	peh-kay-noo ahl-moh-soo ish-tah een-kloo-ee-doo
Is breakfast required?	É preciso pagar o pequeno almoço?	eh preh-see-zoo pah-gar oo peh-kay-noo ahl-moh-soo
How much without breakfast?	Quanto custa sem o pequeno almoço?	kwahn-too koosh-tah sayn oo peh-kay-noo ahl-moh-soo
Is half-pension required?	É preciso pagar as refeiçoes?	eh preh-see-zoo pah-gar ahsh reh-fay-soh-ish
Complete price?	Preço total?	pray-soo toh-tahl
Is it cheaper for three-night stays?	Há discontos para três noites?	ah deesh-kohn-toosh pah-rah traysh noy-tehsh
I will / We will stay three nights.	Vou / Vamos ficar três noites.	voh / vah-moosh fee-kar traysh noy-tehsh
Is it cheaper if I pay in cash?	Há algum disconto se eu pagar em dinheiro?	ah ahl-goon deesh-kohn-too seh eh-oo pah-gar ayn deen-yay-roo
What is the cost per week?	Quanto é por uma semana?	kwahn-too eh poor oo-mah seh-mah-nah

Choosing a Room

Can I see the room?	Posso ver o quarto?	pos-soo vehr oo kwar-too
Can we see the room?	Podemos ver o quarto?	poh-day-moosh vehr oo kwar-too
Show me / Show us another room?	Mostre-me / Mostre-nos outro quarto?	mohsh-treh-meh / mohsh-treh-nooz oh-troo kwar-too
Do you have a room that's...?	Tem um quarto...?	tayn oon kwar-too

...larger / smaller	...maior / pequeno	mī-**yor** / peh-**kay**-noo
...better / cheaper	...melhor / barato	mil-**yor** / bah-**rah**-too
...brighter	...mais claro	mīsh **klah**-roo
...in the back	...nas traseiras	nahsh trah-**zay**-rahsh
...quieter	...mais calmo	mīsh **kahl**-moo
Sorry, it's not right for me.	Desculpe, mas não para mim.	dish-**kool**-peh mahsh now **pah**-rah meeng
Sorry, it's not right for us.	Desculpe, mas não para nós.	dish-**kool**-peh mahsh now **pah**-rah nohsh
I'll take it.	Este quarto 'ta bem.	ehsh-teh **kwar**-too ta bayn
The key, please.	A chave, por favor.	ah **shah**-veh poor fah-**vor**
Sleep well.	Dorme bem.	**dor**-meh bayn
Good night.	Boa-noite.	boh-ah-**noy**-teh

Breakfast

Is breakfast included?	Pequeno almoço está incluido?	peh-**kay**-noo ahl-**moh**-soo ish-**tah** een-kloo-**ee**-doo
How much is breakfast?	Quanto custa o pequeno almoço?	**kwahn**-too **koosh**-tah oo peh-**kay**-noo ahl-**moh**-soo
When does breakfast start?	Quando começa o pequeno almoço?	**kwahn**-doo koh-**meh**-sah oo peh-**kay**-noo ahl-**moh**-soo
When does breakfast end?	Quando termina o pequeno almoço?	**kwahn**-doo tehr-**mee**-nah oo peh-**kay**-noo ahl-**moh**-soo
Where is breakfast served?	Quando servem o pequeno almoço?	**kwahn**-doo **sehr**-vayn oo peh-**kay**-noo ahl-**moh**-soo

Hotel Help

I'd like...	Gostaria...	goosh-tah-**ree**-ah
We'd like...	Gostaríamos...	goosh-tah-**ree**-ah-moosh
...a / another...	...um / outro...	oon / **oh**-troo
...different room.	...quarto diferente.	**kwar**-too dee-feh-**rehn**-teh
...towel.	...toalha.	too-**ahl**-yah

SLEEPING

...clean towel(s).	...toalha(s) limpa(s) .	too-**ahl**-yah(sh) **leem**-pah(sh)
...pillow.	...almofada.	ahl-moh-**fah**-dah
...clean sheets.	...lençois limpos.	**layn**-soysh **leem**-poosh
...blanket.	...cobertor.	koo-behr-**tor**
...glass.	...copo.	**koh**-poo
...sink stopper.	...tampa para lava louça.	**tahn**-pah **pah**-rah **lah**-vah **loh**-sah
...soap.	...sabão.	sah-**bow**
...toilet paper.	...papel higiénico.	pah-**pehl** ee-zhee-**ehn**-ee-koo
...electrical adapter.	...tomada.	toh-**mah**-dah
...brighter light bulb.	...lâmpada mais forte.	**lahm**-pah-dah mīsh **for**-teh
...lamp.	...luz.	loosh
...chair.	...cadeira.	kah-**day**-rah
...table.	...mesa.	**meh**-zah
...Internet access.	...acesso a Internet.	ahsh-**seh**-soo ah **een**-tehr-neht
...silence.	...silêncio.	see-**layn**-see-oo
...to speak to the manager.	...falar com o gerente.	fah-**lar** kohn oo zhehr-**ehn**-teh
I've fallen and I can't get up.	Eu caí e não posso levantar.	**eh**-oo kah-**ee** eh now **pos**-soo leh-vahn-**tar**
How can I make the room cooler / warmer?	Como posso por o quarto mais fresco / mais quente?	**koh**-moo **pos**-soo poor oo **kwar**-too mīsh **frehsh**-koo / mīsh **kayn**-teh
Where can I wash / hang my laundry?	Onde posso lavar / pendurar a minha roupa?	**ohn**-deh **pos**-soo lah-**var** / payn-doo-**rar** ah **meen**-yah **roh**-pah
Is a... laundry nearby?	Há uma... lavanderia por perto?	ah **oo**-mah... lah-vahn-dah-**ree**-ah poor **pehr**-too
...self-service	...self-service	"self-service"
...full service	...serviço completo	sehr-**vee**-soo kohn-**pleh**-too

I'd like to stay another night.	Gostaria de ficar outra noite.	goosh-tah-**ree**-ah deh fee-**kar** oh-trah **noy**-teh
We'd like to stay another night.	Gostaríamos de ficar outra noite.	goosh-tah-**ree**-ah-moosh deh fee-**kar** **oh**-trah **noy**-teh
Where can I park?	Onde é que estaciono?	**ohn**-deh eh keh ish-tah-see-**oh**-noo
What time do you lock up?	A que horas fecha?	ah kee **oh**-rahsh **fay**-shah
Please wake me at 7:00.	Acorde-me ás sete da manhã, por favor.	ah-**kor**-deh-meh ahsh **seh**-teh dah ming-**yah** poor fah-**vor**
Where do you go for lunch / dinner / coffee?	Onde se pode ir almoçar / jantar / tomar um café?	**ohn**-deh seh **pod**-eh eer ahl-moh-**sar** / zhahn-**tar** / toh-**mar** oon kah-**feh**

Chill Out

SLEEPING

Many hotel rooms in the Mediterranean part of Europe come with air-conditioning—often controlled with a stick (like a TV remote). Various sticks have the same basic features:

• fan icon (click to toggle through the wind power from light to gale)
• louver icon (click to choose: steady air flow or waves)
• snowflakes and sunshine icons (heat or cold, generally just one or the other is possible: cool air in summer, heat in winter)
• two clock settings (to determine how many hours the air-conditioning will stay on before turning off, or stay off before turning on)
• temperature control (20° or 21° is a comfortable temperature in Celsius—see the thermometer on page 187)

Hotel Hassles

Come with me.	Venha comigo.	**vayn**-yah koo-**mee**-goo
I have / We have a problem in the room.	Tenho / Temos um problema no quarto.	**tayn**-yoo / **tay**-moosh oon proo-**blay**-mah noo **kwar**-too
It smells bad.	Cheira mal.	**shay**-rah mahl

bugs	*insectos*	een-**seh**-toosh
mice	*ratos*	**rah**-toosh
cockroaches	*baratas*	bah-**rah**-tahsh
prostitutes	*prostitutas*	proosh-tee-**too**-tahsh
I'm covered with bug bites.	*Estou todo picado.*	ish-**toh toh**-doo pee-**kah**-doo
The bed is too soft / hard.	*Esta cama é muito mole / dura.*	**ehsh**-tah kah-mah eh **mween**-too **mah**-leh / **doo**-rah
I can't sleep.	*Não consigo dormir.*	now kohn-**see**-goo dor-**meer**
The room is too...	*O quarto é muito...*	oo **kwar**-too eh **mween**-too
...hot / cold.	*...quente / frio.*	**kayn**-teh / **free**-oo
...noisy / dirty.	*...barulhento / sujo.*	bah-rool-**yehn**-too / **soo**-zhoo
I can't open / shut...	*Não posso abrir / fechar...*	now **pos**-soo ah-**breer** / feh-**shar**
...the door / the window.	*...a porta / a janela.*	ah **por**-tah / ah zhah-**neh**-lah
Air conditioner...	*Ar condicionado...*	ar kohn-dee-see-oh-**nah**-doo
Lamp...	*Candeeiro...*	kahn-dee-**yay**-roo
Lightbulb...	*Lâmpada...*	**lahm**-pah-dah
Electrical outlet...	*Tomada...*	toh-**mah**-dah
Key...	*Chave...*	**shah**-veh
Lock...	*Fechadura...*	feh-shah-**doo**-rah
Window...	*Janela...*	zhah-**neh**-lah
Faucet...	*Torneira...*	tor-**nay**-rah
Sink...	*Lava louça...*	**lah**-vah **loh**-sah
Toilet...	*Lavatórios...*	lah-vah-**tah**-ree-oosh
Shower...	*Chuveiro...*	shoo-**vay**-roo
...doesn't work.	*...não funciona.*	now foon-see-**oh**-nah
There is no hot water.	*Não há água quente.*	now ah **ah**-gwah **kayn**-teh
When is the water hot?	*Quando há água quente?*	**kwahn**-doo ah **ah**-gwah **kayn**-teh

SLEEPING

Checking Out

English	Portuguese	Pronunciation
When is check-out time?	A que horas é preciso pagar a conta e sair?	ah kee **oh**-rahsh eh preh-**see**-zoo pah-**gar** ah **kohn**-tah ee sah-**eer**
I'll leave...	Parto...	**par**-too
We'll leave...	Partimos...	par-**tee**-moosh
...today / tomorrow.	...hoje / amanhã.	**oh**-zheh / ah-ming-**yah**
...very early.	...muito cedo.	mween-too **say**-doo
Can I pay now?	Posso pagar agora?	**pos**-soo pah-**gar** ah-**gor**-ah
Can we pay now?	Podemos pagar agora?	poh-**day**-moosh pah-**gar** ah-**gor**-ah
The bill, please.	A conta, por favor.	ah **kohn**-tah poor fah-**vor**
Credit card O.K.?	Cartão de crédito O.K.?	kar-**tow** deh **kreh**-dee-too "O.K."
Everything was great.	Tudo foi óptimo.	**too**-doo foy **ot**-tee-moo
I slept like an angel.	Dormi como um anjo.	**dor**-mee **koh**-moo oon **ahn**-zhoo
Will you call my next hotel...?	Pode telefonar para o meu próximo hotel...?	**pod**-eh teh-leh-foh-**nar** **pah**-rah oo **meh**-oo **proh**-see-moo oh-**tehl**
...for tonight	...para hoje a noite	**pah**-rah **oh**-zheh ah **noy**-teh
...to make a reservation	...para fazer uma reserva	**pah**-rah fah-**zehr oo**-mah reh-**zehr**-vah
...to confirm a reservation	...para confirmar uma reserva.	**pah**-rah kohn-feer-**mar oo**-mah reh-**zehr**-vah
I will pay for the call.	Pago a chamada.	**pah**-goo ah shah-**mah**-dah
Can I / Can we...?	Posso / Podemos...?	**pos**-soo / poo-**day**-moosh
...leave baggage here until ___?	...deixar a bagagem aqui até ___?	day-**shar** ah bah-**gah**-zhayn ah-**kee** ah-**teh**

SLEEPING

Camping

camping	*campismo*	kahm-**peesh**-moo
campsite	*campismo*	kahm-**peesh**-moo
tent	*tenda*	**tayn**-dah
The nearest campground?	*O próximo parque de campismo?*	oo **proh**-see-moo **par**-keh deh kahm-**peesh**-moo
Can I...?	*Posso...?*	**pos**-soo
Can we...?	*Podemos...?*	poo-**day**-moosh
...camp here for one night	*...campar aqui por uma noite*	kahm-**par** ah-**kee** poor **oo**-mah **noy**-teh
Are showers included?	*Os chuveiros estam incluidos?*	oosh shoo-**vay**-roosh ish-**tayn** een-kloo-**ee**-doosh

EATING

RESTAURANTS

Types of Restaurants

Restaurant—Dining establishment with cuisine and service rated *de luxo* (luxury), *de primeira, de segunda,* or *de terceira classe* (first, second, or third class)

Adega típica—Small restaurant serving local dishes (often with *fado* singing)

Casa de fados—Restaurant with fado singing

Churrasqueira—Barbeque and grill family-style restaurant

Comida a quilo—Lunch buffet restaurant (pay by weight)

Marisqueira—Seafood restaurant, sometimes expensive

Estalagem—Inn serving regional specialties

Casa de pasto—Informal, inexpensive eatery

Cervejaria—Pub or beer garden

Tasca—Small tavern

Finding a Restaurant

Where's a good... restaurant nearby?	Onde há um bom restaurante... por perto?	**ohn**-deh ah oo<u>n</u> boh<u>n</u> rish-toh-**rahn**-teh... poor **pehr**-too
...cheap	...barato	bah-**rah**-too
...local-style	...estilo regional	ish-**tee**-loo ray-zhee-oh-**nahl**

...untouristy	...não turístico	now too-**reesh**-tee-koo
...vegetarian	...vegetariano	veh-zheh-tar-ree-**ah**-noo
...fast food	...comida rápida	koo-**mee**-dah **rah**-pee-dah
...self-service buffet	...bufete de auto-serviço	boo-**fay** deh ow-toh-sehr-**vee**-soo
...Chinese	...chinês	shee-**naysh**
fried chicken restaurant	churrasqueira	shoo-rahsh-**kway**-rah
beer garden	cervejaria	sehr-vay-zhah-**ree**-ah
with terrace	com esplanada	koh<u>n</u> ish-plah-**nah**-dah
with a salad bar	com bufete de saladas	koh<u>n</u> boo-**fay** deh sah-**lah**-dahsh
with candles	com velas	koh<u>n</u> **veh**-lahsh
romantic	romântico	roh-**mahn**-tee-koo
moderate price	preço razoável	**pray**-soo rah-**zwah**-vehl
a splurge	uma extravagância	**oo**-mah ish-trah-vah-**gahn**-see-ah
Is it better than McDonald's?	É melhor doque no McDonald's?	eh **mil**-yor **doh**-keh noo "McDonald's"

The Portuguese serve lunch from noon to 2 P.M. and dinner from 7:30 to 10:00 P.M. Save money by considering a *meia dose* (half portion) or a *prato do dia* (menu of the day).

Getting a Table

What time does this open / close?	A que horas é que abre / fecha?	ah kee **oh**-rahsh eh keh **ah**-breh / **fay**-shah
Are you open...?	Está aberto...?	ish-**tah** ah-**behr**-too
...today / tomorrow	...hoje / amanhã	**oh**-zheh / ah-ming-**yah**
...for lunch / dinner	...para o almoço / o jantar	**pah**-rah oo ahl-**moh**-soo / oo zhahn-**tar**
Are reservations recommended?	Recomenda fazer reserva?	reh-koh-**mehn**-dah fah-**zehr** reh-**zehr**-vah
I'd like...	Gostaria...	goosh-tah-**ree**-ah
We'd like...	Gostaríamos...	goosh-tah-**ree**-ah-moosh
...a table for one / two.	...uma mesa para uma / duas.	**oo**-mah **may**-zah **pah**-rah **oo**-mah / **doo**-ahsh

Key Phrases: Restaurants

English	Portuguese	Pronunciation
Where's a good restaurant nearby?	Onde há um bom restaurante por perto?	**ohn**-deh ah oon bohn rish-toh-**rahn**-teh poor **pehr**-too
I'd like...	Gostaria...	goosh-tah-**ree**-ah
We'd like...	Gostaríamos...	goosh-tah-**ree**-ah-moosh
...a table for one / two.	...uma mesa para uma / duas.	**oo**-mah **may**-zah **pah**-rah **oo**-mah / **doo**-ahsh
...to sit inside / outside	...de sentar dentro / fora	deh sayn-**tar** **dent**-roo / **foh**-rah
Is this table free?	Esta mesa está livre?	**ehsh**-tah **meh**-zah ish-**tah lee**-vreh
The menu (in English), please.	A ementa (em inglês), por favor.	ah eh-**mayn**-tah (ayn een-**glaysh**) poor fah-**vor**
Bill, please.	Conta, por favor.	**kohn**-tah poor fah-**vor**
Credit card O.K.?	Cartão de crédito O.K.?	kar-**tow** deh **kreh**-dee-too "O.K."
Keep the change.	Fique com o troco.	**fee**-keh kohn oo **troh**-koo

EATING

English	Portuguese	Pronunciation
...to reserve a table for two people...	...de reservar uma mesa para duas pessoas...	deh reh-zehr-**var oo**-mah **may**-zah **pah**-rah **doo**-ahsh peh-**soh**-ahsh
...for today / tomorrow...	...para hoje / amanhã...	**pah**-rah **oh**-zheh / ah-ming-**yah**
...at 8:00 P.M.	...às oito.	ahz **oy**-too
My name is ___.	Chamo-me ___.	**shah**-moo-meh
I have a reservation for ___ people.	Tenho uma reserva para ___ pessoas.	**teyn**-yoo **oo**-mah reh-**zehr**-vah **pah**-rah ___ peh-**soh**-ahsh
I'd like / We'd like to sit...	Gostaria / Gostaríamos de sentar...	goosh-tah-**ree**-ah / goosh-tah-**ree**-ah-moosh deh sayn-**tar**
...inside / outside.	...dentro / fora.	**dehn**-troo / **foh**-rah

...by the window.	...perto da janela.	**pehr**-too dah zhah-**neh**-lah
...with a view.	...com uma vista.	kohn **oo**-mah **veesh**-tah
...where it's quiet.	...onde é sossegado.	**ohn**-deh eh soh-seh-**gah**-doo
Is this table free?	Esta mesa está livre?	**ehsh**-tah **meh**-zah ish-**tah** lee-vreh
Can I sit here?	Posso sentar-me aqui?	**pos**-soo sayn-**tar**-meh ah-**kee**
Can we sit here?	Podemos sentar-nos aqui?	poo-**day**-moosh sayn-**tar**-nooz ah-**kee**

The Menu

menu	ementa	eh-**mayn**-tah
special of the day	prato do dia	**prah**-too doo **dee**-ah
specialty of the house	especialidade da casa	ish-peh-see-ah-lee-**dah**-deh dah **kah**-zah
menu of the day	ementa do dia	eh-**mayn**-tah doo **dee**-ah
tourist menu	ementa turistica	eh-**mayn**-tah too-**reesh**-tee-kah
combination plate	prato misto	**prah**-too **meesh**-too
breakfast	pequeno almoço	peh-**kay**-noo ahl-**moh**-soo
lunch	almoço	ahl-**moh**-soo
dinner	jantar	zhahn-**tar**
appetizers	entradas	ayn-**trah**-dahsh
sandwiches	sanduíches, sandes	sahnd-**weesh**-ish, **sahn**-dish
bread	pão	pow
salad	salada	sah-**lah**-dah
soup	sopa	**soh**-pah
first course	primeira refeição	pree-**may**-rah reh-fay-**sow**
main course	refeição principal	reh-fay-**sow** preen-see-**pahl**
side dishes	complementares	kohn-pleh-mayn-**tah**-rish
meat	carne	**kar**-neh
poultry	aves	**ah**-vish
fish	peixes	**pay**-sheesh

seafood, shellfish	marisco	mah-**reesh**-koo
children's plate	prato de	**prah**-too deh
	criança	kree-**ahn**-sah
vegetables	legumes	lay-**goo**-mish
cheese	queijo	**kay**-zhoo
dessert	sobremesa	soo-breh-**may**-zah
munchies (tapas)	petiscos	peh-**teesh**-koosh
drink menu	ementa de	eh-**mayn**-tah deh
	bebidas	beh-**bee**-dahsh
beverages	bebidas	beh-**bee**-dahsh
beer	cerveja	sehr-**vay**-zhah
wine	vinho	**veen**-yoo
cover charge	tixa aplicada	**tī**-shah ah-plee-**kah**-dah
service included	serviço	sehr-**vee**-soo
	incluído	een-kloo-**ee**-doo
service not	serviço não	sehr-**vee**-soo no<u>w</u>
included	incluído	een-kloo-**ee**-doo
hot / cold	quente / frio	**kayn**-teh / **free**-oo
with / and / or /	com / e / ou /	koh<u>n</u> / ee / oh /
without	sem	say<u>n</u>

Waiters in many Portuguese restaurants will put appetizers on your table as a temptation before you even order. Just wave the food away if you don't want it. You'll pay (usually a per-person charge) if you consume even one olive.

Ordering

waiter	empregado	ehm-preh-**gah**-doo
waitress	empregada	ehm-preh-**gah**-dah
I'm / We're ready	Quero / Queremos	**kay**-roo / keh-**ray**-moosh
to order.	pedir.	peh-**deer**
I'd like / We'd like...	Queria /	keh-**ree**-ah /
	Queríamos...	keh-**ree**-ah-moosh
...just a drink.	...só uma bebida.	soh **oo**-mah beh-**bee**-dah
...a snack.	...um petisco.	oo<u>n</u> peh-**teesh**-koo
...just a salad.	...só uma salada.	soh **oo**-mah sah-**lah**-dah

...a half portion.	...meia dose.	**may**-ah **doh**-zeh
...a tourist menu (fixed-price meal).	...uma ementa turistica.	**oo**-mah eh-**mayn**-tah too-**rees**-tee-kah
...to see the menu.	...de ver a ementa.	deh vehr ah eh-**mayn**-tah
...to order.	...encomendar.	ayn-koo-mayn-**dar**
...to eat.	...de comer.	deh koo-**mehr**
...to pay.	...de pagar.	deh pah-**gar**
...to throw up.	...de vomitar.	deh voh-mee-**tar**
Do you have...?	Tem...?	tayn
...an English menu	...uma ementa em inglês	**oo**-mah eh-**mayn**-tah ayn een-**glaysh**
...a lunch special	...prato do dia	**prah**-too doo **dee**-ah
What do you recommend?	O que é que recomenda?	oo keh eh keh ray-koo-**mayn**-dah
What's your favorite dish?	Qual é seu prato preferido?	kwahl eh **seh**-oo **prah**-too pray-feh-**ree**-doo
Is it...?	Isto é...?	**eesh**-too eh
...good	...bom	bohn
...expensive	...caro	**kah**-roo
...light	...leve	**leh**-veh
...filling	...enche	**ayn**-sheh
What is...?	O que é...?	oo keh eh
...that	...aquilo	ah-**kee**-loo
...local	...da região	dah rayzh-**yow**
...fresh	...fresco	**frehsh**-koo
...cheap and filling	...barato e enche	bah-**rah**-too ee **ayn**-sheh
...fast	...rápido	**rah**-pee-doo
Can we split this and have an extra plate?	Podemos dividir e ter outro prato?	poo-**day**-moosh dee-vee-**deer** ee tehr **oh**-troo **prah**-too
I've changed my mind.	Mudei de ideia.	**moo**-day deh ee-**day**-ah
Nothing with eyeballs.	Nada com olhos.	**nah**-dah kohn **ohl**-yoosh
Can I substitute (anything) for the ___?	Posso substituir (algo) por___?	**pos**-soo soob-shtee-too-**eer** (**ahl**-goo) poor

| Can I / Can we get it "to go"? | Posso / Podemos levar esta comida? | **pos**-soo / poo-**day**-moosh leh-**var** ehsh-tah koo-**mee**-dah |
| "To go"? | Para levar? | **pah**-rah leh-**var** |

This is the procedure at a restaurant: To summon a waiter, say, *"Por favor"* (Please). The waiter brings a menu and asks what you'd like to drink (*Quer tomar alguma coisa?*). When ready to take your order, the waiter says, *"Está pronto?"* After you've eaten, the waiter will ask if you're finished (*Terminou?*), if you'd like dessert (*Quer sobremesa?*), and if you want anything else (*Quer tomar mais alguma coisa?*). You ask for the bill: *"A conta, por favor."*

Tableware and Condiments

plate	prato	**prah**-too
extra plate	outro prato	**oh**-troo **prah**-too
napkin	guardanapo	gwar-dah-**nah**-poo
silverware	talheres	tahl-**yehr**-ish
knife	faca	**fah**-kah
fork	garfo	**gar**-foo
spoon	colher	**kool**-yehr
cup	chávena	**shah**-veh-nah
glass	copo	**koh**-poo
carafe	jarro	**zhah**-roo
water	água	**ah**-gwah
bread	pão	pow
butter	manteiga	mahn-**tay**-gah
margarine	margarina	mar-gah-**ree**-nah
salt / pepper	sal / pimenta	sahl / pee-**mayn**-tah
sugar	açúcar	ah-**soo**-kar
artificial sweetener	sacarina	sah-kah-**ree**-nah
honey	mel	mehl
mustard	mostarda	moosh-**tar**-dah
ketchup	ketchup	"ketchup"
mayonnaise	maionese	mah-yoh-**neh**-zeh
toothpick	palito	pah-**lee**-too

EATING

The Food Arrives

Is this included with the meal?	Isto está incluido com a refeição?	eesh-too ish-**tah** een-kloo-**ee**-doo koh<u>n</u> ah reh-fay-**sow**
I did not order this.	Não pedi isto.	no<u>w</u> peh-**dee** eesh-too
We did not order this.	Não pedimos isto.	no<u>w</u> peh-**dee**-mooz eesh-too
Can you heat this up?	Pode aquecer a comida?	**pod**-eh ah-kay-**sehr** ah koo-**mee**-dah
A little.	Um pouco.	oon **poh**-koo
More. / Another.	Mais. / Outro.	mīsh / **oh**-troo
One more, please.	Mais um, por favor.	mīz oon poor fah-**vor**
The same.	O mesmo.	oo **mehsh**-moo
Enough.	Chega.	**shay**-gah
Finished.	Terminei.	tehr-mee-**nay**
I'm full.	Estou satisfeito[a].	ish-**toh** sah-teesh-**fay**-too

After bringing your meal, your server might wish you a cheery *"Bom-apetite!"* (pronounced boh<u>n</u>-ah-peh-**tee**-teh).

Complaints

This is...	Isto é...	**eesh**-too eh
...dirty.	...sujo.	**soo**-zhoo
...greasy.	...gorduroso.	gor-doo-**roh**-zoo
...salty.	...salgado.	sahl-**gah**-doo
...undercooked.	...malcozinhado.	mahl-koo-zeen-**yah**-doo
...overcooked.	...queimado.	kay-**mah**-doo
...inedible.	...não comestível.	no<u>w</u> koo-mish-**tee**-vehl
...cold.	...frio.	**free**-oo
Do any of your customers return?	Os seus clientes voltam?	oosh **seh**-oosh klee-**ayn**-tish **vohl**-toh<u>n</u>
Yuck!	Porcaria!	poor-kah-**ree**-ah

Compliments to the Chef

Yummy!	Óptimo!	**ot**-tee-moo
Delicious!	Delicioso!	deh-lee-see-**oh**-zoo

EATING

Very tasty!	Muito gostoso!	**mween**-too goosh-**toh**-zoo
I love Portuguese / this food.	Adoro português / esta comida.	ah-**doh**-roo por-too-**gaysh** / **ehsh**-tah koo-**mee**-dah
Better than mom's cooking.	Melhor doque a comida da minha mãe.	mil-**yor doh**-keh ah koo-**mee**-dah dah **meen**-yah **mayn**-eh
My compliments to the chef!	Os meus parabéns ao chefe!	oosh **meh**-oosh pah-rah-**baynsh ah**-oo sheh-feh

Paying for Your Meal

The bill, please.	A conta, por favor.	ah **kohn**-tah poor fah-**vor**
Together.	Junta.	**zhoon**-tah
Separate checks.	Conta separada.	**kohn**-tah seh-pah-**rah**-dah
Credit card O.K.?	Cartão de crédito O.K.?	kar-**tow** deh **kreh**-dee-too "O.K."
This is not correct.	Isto não está certo.	**eesh**-too now ish-**tah sehr**-too
Can you explain this?	Pode-me explicar isto?	pod-eh-meh ish-plee-**kar eesh**-too
Can you explain / itemize the bill?	Pode explicar / descriminar esta conta?	pod-eh ish-plee-**kar** / dish-kree-mee-**nar ehsh**-tah **kohn**-tah
What if I wash the dishes?	E se eu lavar a loiça?	ee seh **eh**-oo lah-**var** ah **loy**-sah
Is tipping expected?	Esperam gorjeta?	ehsh-**pehr**-ayn gor-**zheh**-tah
What percent?	Qual é a porcentagem?	kwahl eh ah por-sayn-**tah**-zhayn
tip	gorjeta	gor-**zheh**-tah
Keep the change.	Fique com o troco.	**fee**-keh kohn oo **troh**-koo
This is for you.	Isto é para si.	**eesh**-too eh **pah**-rah see
Could I have a receipt, please?	Posso ter o recibo, por favor?	**pos**-soo tehr oo reh-**see**-boo poor fah-**vor**

EATING

In most restaurants, service is included—your menu typically will indicate this by noting *serviço incluído*. Still, if you like to tip and you're pleased with the service, leave up to 5 percent. If service is not included (*serviço não incluído*), tip up to 10 percent. If you're uncertain whether to tip, ask another customer if tipping is expected (*Esperam gorjeta?*).

SPECIAL CONCERNS

In a Hurry

I'm / We're in a hurry.	Estou / Estamos com pressa.	ish-**toh** / ish-**tah**-moosh kohn **preh**-sah
I need / We need...	Preciso / Precisamos...	preh-**see**-zoo / preh-see-**zah**-moosh
...to be served quickly.	...ser servidos rápidamente.	sehr sehr-**vee**-doosh **rah**-pee-dah-mayn-teh
Is that a problem?	Há algum problema?	ah ahl-**goon** proo-**blay**-mah
I must / We must...	Preciso / Precisamos...	preh-**see**-zoo / preh-see-**zah**-moosh
...leave in a half hour / in one hour.	...ir embora daqui em meia hora / numa hora.	eer ayn-**boh**-rah dah-**kee** ayn **may**-ah **oh**-rah / **noo**-mah **oh**-rah
When will the food be ready?	Quando é que a comida vai estar pronta?	**kwahn**-doo eh keh ah koo-**mee**-dah vī ish-**tar prohn**-tah

Dietary Restrictions

I'm allergic to...	Sou alérgico[a] a...	soh ah-**lehr**-zhee-koo ah
I cannot eat...	Não posso comer...	now **pos**-soo koh-**mehr**
He / She cannot eat...	Ele / Ela não pode comer...	**eh**-leh / **eh**-lah now **pod**-eh koh-**mehr**
...dairy products.	...lacticínios.	lahk-tee-**see**-nee-oosh
...wheat.	...trigo.	**tree**-goo
...meat / pork.	...carne / porco.	**kar**-neh / **por**-koo

...salt / sugar.	...sal / açúcar.	sahl / ah-**soo**-kar
...shellfish.	...mariscos.	mah-**reesh**-koosh
...spicy foods.	...comidas picantes.	koo-**mee**-dahsh pee-**kahn**-tish
...nuts.	...nozes.	**noh**-zish
I am diabetic.	Sou diabético[a].	soh dee-ah-**beh**-tee-koo
I'd / We'd like a...	Queria / Queríamos uma...	keh-**ree**-ah / keh-**ree**-ah-mooz **oo**-mah
...kosher meal.	...comida kosher.	koo-**mee**-dah koh-shehr
...low-fat meal.	...comida com pouca gordura.	koo-**mee**-dah koh<u>n</u> **poh**-kah gor-**doo**-rah
I eat only insects.	Só como insectos.	soh **koh**-moo een-**seh**-toosh
No salt.	Sem sal.	say<u>n</u> sahl
No sugar.	Sem açucar.	say<u>n</u> ah-**soo**-kar
No fat.	Sem gordura.	say<u>n</u> gor-**doo**-rah
Minimal fat.	Pouca gordura.	**poh**-kah gor-**doo**-rah
Low cholesterol.	Colesterol baixo.	koo-**lehsh**-teh-rohl **bī**-shoo
No caffeine.	Descaféinado.	dish-kah-feh-ee-**nah**-doo
No alcohol.	Sem alcool.	say<u>n</u> **ahl**-kahl
Organic.	Orgânico.	or-**gah**-nee-koo
I'm a...	Sou...	soh
...vegetarian.	...vegetariano[a].	veh-zheh-tar-ree-**ah**-noo
...strict vegetarian.	...rigorosamente vegetariano[a].	ree-goh-roh-zah-**mayn**-teh veh-zheh-tar-ree-**ah**-noo
...carnivore.	...carnivoro[a].	kar-nee-**voh**-roo
...big eater.	...comilão.	koo-mee-**low**
Is any meat or animal fat used in this?	Tem carne ou gordura animal nisso?	tay<u>n</u> **kar**-neh oh gor-**doo**-rah ah-nee-**mahl nee**-soo

Many Portuguese think "vegetarian" means "no red meat" or "not much meat." If you're a strict vegetarian, you'll have to make it very clear.

EATING

Children

Do you have...?	Tem...?	tayn
...a children's portion	...uma refeição para criança	**oo**-mah reh-fay-**sow** **pah**-rah kree-**ahn**-sah
...a half portion	...uma meia dose	**oo**-mah **may**-ah **doh**-zeh
...a high chair	...uma cadeira alta	**oo**-mah kah-**day**-rah **ahl**-tah
...a booster seat	...um suporte para a cadeira	oon soo-**por**-teh **pah**-rah ah kah-**day**-rah
plain noodles	esparguete simples	ish-par-**geh**-teh **seem**-plish
plain rice	arroz simples	ah-**rohzh seem**-plish
with butter	com manteiga	kohn mahn-**tay**-gah
no sauce	sem molho	sayn **mohl**-yoo
sauce or dressing on the side	molho separado	**mohl**-yoo seh-pah-**rah**-doo
pizza	pizza	**pee**-zah
...cheese only	...só queijo	soh **kay**-zhoo
...pepperoni and cheese	...pepperoni e queijo	peh-peh-**roh**-nee ee **kay**-zhoo
peanut butter and jelly sandwich	sanduíche de manteiga de amendoim e geléia	sahnd-**weesh**-eh deh mahn-**tay**-gah deh ah-mayn-**dweem** ee zheh-**lay**-ah
cheese sandwich...	sanduíche de queijo...	sahnd-**weesh**-eh deh **kay**-zhoo
...toasted	...com pão torrado	kohn pow too-**rah**-doo
hot dog	cachrorro quente	kahsh-**roh**-roh **kayn**-teh
hamburger	hamburger	"hamburger"
cheeseburger	cheeseburger	"cheeseburger"
French fries	batatas fritas	bah-**tah**-tahsh **free**-tahsh
ketchup	ketchup	"ketchup"
crackers	bolaichas	boo-**lī**-shahsh
Nothing spicy.	Nada picante.	**nah**-dah pee-**kahn**-teh
Not too hot.	Não muito quente.	now **mween**-too **kayn**-teh

Please keep the food separate on the plate.	Por favor, deixe a comida separada no prato.	poor fah-**vor day**-sheh ah koo-**mee**-dah seh-pah-**rah**-dah noo **prah**-too
He / She will share....	Ele / Ela vai dividir...	**eh**-leh / **eh**-lah vī dee-vee-**deer**
They (m / f) will share...	Eles / Elas vão dividir...	**eh**-lish / **eh**-lahsh vo<u>w</u> dee-vee-**deer**
...our meal.	...a nossa comida.	ah **noo**-sah koo-**mee**-dah
Please bring the food quickly.	Por favor, traga a comida rápidamente.	poor fah-**vor trah**-gah ah koo-**mee**-dah **rah**-pee-dah-**mayn**-teh
I want / We want an extra...	Quero / Queremos... extra.	**kay**-roo / keh-**ray**-moosh... **ish**-trah
...plate.	...um prato	oo<u>n</u> **prah**-too
...cup.	...uma chávena	**oo**-mah **shah**-veh-nah
...spoon / fork.	...uma colher / um garfo	**oo**-mah **kool**-yehr / oo<u>n</u> **gar**-foo
I want / We want two extra...	Quero / Queremos dois... extras.	**kay**-roo / keh-**ray**-moosh doysh... **ish**-trahsh
...plates.	...pratos	**prah**-toosh
...cups.	...chávenas	**shah**-veh-nahsh
...spoons / forks.	...colheres / garfos	**kool**-yeh-rish / **gar**-foosh
Small milk (in a plastic cup).	Pouco leite (num copo plástico).	**poh**-koo **lay**-teh (noom **koh**-poo **plah**-shtee-koo)
straw(s).	palhinha(s).	pahl-**yeen**-yah(sh)
More napkins, please.	Mais guardanapos, por favor.	mīsh gwar-dah-**nah**-poosh poor fah-**vor**
Sorry for the mess.	Desculpe[a] a sujeira.	dish-**kool**-peh ah soo-**zhay**-rah

WHAT'S COOKING?

Breakfast

breakfast	pequeno almoço	peh-**kay**-noo ahl-**moh**-soo

Key Phrases: What's Cooking?

food	*comida*	koo-**mee**-dah
breakfast	*pequeno*	peh-**kay**-noo
	almoço	ahl-**moh**-soo
lunch	*almoço*	ahl-**moh**-soo
dinner	*jantar*	zhahn-**tar**
bread	*pão*	po<u>w</u>
cheese	*queijo*	**kay**-zhoo
soup	*sopa*	**soh**-pah
salad	*salada*	sah-**lah**-dah
meat	*carne*	**kar**-neh
fish	*peixe*	**pay**-sheh
fruit	*fruta*	**froo**-tah
vegetables	*legumes*	lay-**goo**-mish
dessert	*sobremesa*	soo-breh-**may**-zah
Delicious!	*Delicioso!*	deh-lee-see-**oh**-zoo

bread	*pão*	po<u>w</u>
toast	*torrada*	too-**rah**-dah
roll	*papo seco, pães*	**pah**-poo **seh**-koo, pay<u>n</u>sh
butter	*manteiga*	mahn-**tay**-gah
jelly	*geléia*	zheh-**lay**-ah
milk	*leite*	**lay**-teh
coffee / tea	*café / chá*	kah-**feh** / shah
Is breakfast included?	*O pequeno almoço está incluido?*	oo peh-**kay**-noo ahl-**moh**-soo ish-**tah** een-kloo-**ee**-doo

What's Probably Not for Breakfast

omelet	*omeleta*	oh-meh-**leh**-tah
egg...	*ovo...*	**oh**-voo
...boiled /	*...cozido / não*	koo-**zee**-doo / no<u>w</u>
soft boiled /	*muito cozido /*	**mween**-too koo-**zee**-doo /
hard boiled	*muito cozido*	**mween**-too koo-**zee**-doo

eggs...	ovos...	**oh**-voosh
...fried	...estrelados	ish-treh-**lah**-doosh
...scrambled	...mexidos	mish-**ee**-doosh
ham	fiambre	fee-**ahm**-breh
cheese	queijo	**kay**-zhoo
yogurt	yogurte	yoo-**goor**-teh
cereal	cereal	seh-ree-**ahl**
pastry	pastelaria	pahsh-teh-lah-**ree**-ah
fruit juice	sumo de fruta	**soo**-moo deh **froo**-tah
orange juice	sumo de laranja	**soo**-moo deh lah-**rahn**-zhah
hot chocolate	leite com chocolate quente	**lay**-teh koh<u>n</u> shoo-koo-**lah**-teh **kayn**-teh

Appetizers and Snacks

acepipes, petiscos	ah-seh-**pee**-pish, peh-**teesh**-koosh	appetizers
amêijoas à Bulhão Pato	ah-**may**-zhoo-ahsh ah bool-**yow pah**-too	small clams in wine, garlic, and cilantro broth
camarão-carne ou peixe	kah-mah-**row**-kar-neh oh **pay**-sheh	fried pastry filled with meat or fish
camarões com piri piri	kah-mah-**rowsh** koh<u>n</u> **pee**-ree **pee**-ree	sautéed shrimp with garlic and hot pepper
chouriço assado	shoh-**ree**-soo ah-**sah**-doo	grilled smoked pork sausage flavored with garlic and paprika
crepe de galinha / legumes	**kreh**-peh deh gah-**leen**-yah / lay-**goo**-mish	fried, crispy crepe with chicken / vegetables
gambas fritas com alho	**gahm**-bahsh **free**-tahsh koh<u>n</u> **ahl**-yoo	sautéed garlic prawns
pasta de atum	**pahsh**-tah deh ah-**toon**	tuna paté
pasties / bolinhos de bacalhau	**pahsh**-tee-ish / boh-**leen**-yoosh deh bah-kahl-**yow**	cod fish cakes / balls

salgados	sahl-**gah**-doosh	savory pastries
santola	sahn-**toh**-lah	spider crab stuffed with
recheada	reh-shee-**ah**-dah	its own meat

Sandwiches

I'd like a sandwich.	*Gostaria uma sanduíche.*	goosh-tah-**ree**-ah **oo**-mah sahnd-**weesh**-eh
We'd like two sandwiches.	*Gostaríamos duas sanduíches.*	goosh-tah-**ree**-ah-moosh **doo**-ahsh sahnd-**weesh**-ish
bread	*pão*	po<u>w</u>
toasted	*torrada*	too-**rah**-dah
toasted ham and cheese	*tosta mista*	**toosh**-tah **meesh**-tah
cheese	*queijo*	**kay**-zhoo
tuna	*atum*	ah-**toon**
fish	*peixe*	**pay**-sheh
chicken	*frango*	**frang**-goo
turkey	*peru*	peh-**roo**
ham	*fiambre*	fee-**ahm**-breh
salami	*salame*	sah-**lah**-meh
egg salad	*salada de ovo*	sah-**lah**-dah deh **oh**-voo
lettuce	*alface*	ahl-**fah**-seh
tomatoes	*tomates*	too-**mah**-tish
onions	*cebolas*	seh-**boh**-lahsh
mustard	*mostarda*	moosh-**tar**-dah
ketchup	*ketchup*	"ketchup"
mayonnaise	*maionese*	mah-yoh-**nay**-zeh
peanut butter	*manteiga de amendoim*	mahn-**tay**-gah deh ah-may<u>n</u>-**dweem**
jelly	*geléia*	zheh-**lay**-ah
pork sandwich	*bifana no pão*	bee-**fah**-nah noo po<u>w</u>
meat and fried egg on a roll	*prego no pão*	**preh**-goo noo po<u>w</u>
Does this come cold or warm?	*É servido frio ou quente?*	eh sehr-**vee**-doo **free**-oo oh **kay<u>n</u>**-teh
Heated, please.	*Aquecido, por favor.*	ah-keh-**see**-doo poor fah-**vor**

The Portuguese like pork sandwiches (*bifana no pão*) and meat and fried egg on a roll (*prego no pão*).

Say Cheese

cheese	queijo	**kay**-zhoo
sheep's cheese	queijo da serra	**kay**-zhoo dah **seh**-rah
fresh goat's cheese	queijo fresco	**kay**-zhoo **frehsh**-koo
ricotta-style cheese	requeijão	reh-kay-**zhow**
cheese plate	porção de queijo	por-**sow** deh **kay**-zhoo
Can I try a taste?	Posso provar?	**pos**-soo proh-**var**

Soups

soup...	sopa...	**soh**-pah
...of the day	...do dia	doo **dee**-ah
...vegetable	...de legumes	deh lay-**goo**-mish
broth...	canja...	**kayn**-zhah
...chicken	...de galinha	deh gah-**leen**-yah
...beef	...de bife	deh **bee**-feh
...fish	...de peixe	deh **pay**-sheh
...with noodles	...com massa	kohn **mah**-sah
...with rice	...com arroz	kohn ah-**rohsh**

Soup Specialties

caldo verde	**kahl**-doo **vehr**-deh	potato and kale soup with smoked sausage
creme de camarão	**kreh**-meh deh kah-mah-**row**	pureed, spicy shrimp soup
sopa de alentejana	**soh**-pah deh ah-**lehn**-teh-zhah-nah	soup with egg, bread, herbs and garlic
sopa de mariscos	**soh**-pah deh mah-**reesh**-koosh	shellfish soup
sopa de peixe	**soh**-pah deh **pay**-sheh	fish soup
sopa de pedra	**soh**-pah deh **pehd**-rah	vegetable soup with red beans and sausage

EATING

| sopa de tomate com ovo | **soh**-pah deh too-**mah**-teh koh<u>n</u> **oh**-voo | tomato soup with poached egg |

Salads

salad...	salada...	sah-**lah**-dah
...green / mixed	...de alface / mista	deh ahl-**fah**-seh / **meesh**-tah
...with octopus	...de polvo	deh **pohl**-voo
...with green peppers and grilled sardines	...de pimento	deh pee-**may<u>n</u>**-too
...with tuna, potatoes, and egg	...de atum	deh ah-**too<u>n</u>**
...Russian (tuna with lots of mayo)	...Russa	**roo**-sah
...with ham and cheese	...com fiambre e queijo	koh<u>n</u> fee-**ahm**-breh ee **kay**-zhoo
...with egg	...com ovo	koh<u>n</u> **oh**-voo
lettuce	alface	ahl-**fah**-seh
tomato	tomate	too-**mah**-teh
onion	cebola	seh-**boh**-lah
cucumber	pepino	peh-**pee**-noo
oil / vinegar	óleo / vinagre	**ahl**-yoh / vee-**nah**-greh
dressing	molho	**mohl**-yoo
dressing on the side	molho separado	**mohl**-yoo seh-pah-**rah**-doo
What is in this salad?	O que tem na salada?	oo keh tay<u>n</u> nah sah-**lah**-dah

Seafood

seafood	marisco	mah-**reesh**-koo
assorted seafood	diversos mariscos	dee-**vehr**-soosh mah-**reesh**-koosh
fish	peixe	**pay**-sheh
fried white fish	filetes	feh-**leh**-tish
anchovies	anchovas	ahn-**shoh**-vahsh
barnacles	percebes	pehr-**sheh**-bish

bream (fish)	*pargo*	**par**-goo
clams	*amêijoas*	ah-**may**-zhoo-ahsh
cod	*bacalhau*	bah-kahl-**yow**
crab	*caranguejo*	kah-rahn-**gay**-zhoo
crayfish	*lagostins*	lah-**gohsh**-teengsh
cuttlefish	*chocos*	**shoh**-koosh
dungeness crab	*sapateira*	sah-pah-**tay**-rah
eel	*enguia*	ayn-**gwee**-ah
herring	*arenque*	ah-**rehn**-keh
lobster	*lagosta*	lah-**gohsh**-tah
mussels	*mexilhões*	meh-sheel-**yohnsh**
octopus	*polvo*	**pohl**-voo
oysters	*ostras*	**ohsh**-trahsh
prawns	*gambas*	**gahm**-bahsh
salmon	*salmão*	sahl-**mow**
sardines	*sardinhas*	sar-**deen**-yahsh
scad (like mackerel)	*carapaus*	kah-rah-**powsh**
scallops	*escalopes*	ish-kah-**loh**-pish
shrimp	*camarão*	kah-mah-**row**
sole	*linguad*	leen-goo-**ahd**
squid	*lulas*	**loo**-lahsh
swordfish	*espadarte*	ish-pah-**dar**-teh
tiger shrimp	*camarão tigre*	kah-mah-**row tee**-greh
trout	*truta*	**troo**-tah
tuna	*atum*	ah-**toon**
How much for a portion?	*Quanto para uma dose?*	**kwahn**-too **pah**-rah **oo**-mah **doh**-zeh
What's fresh today?	*O que há de bem fresco hoje?*	oo kee ah deh bayn **frehsh**-koo oh-zheh
Do you eat this part?	*Come-se esta parte?*	**koh**-meh-seh **ehsh**-tah **par**-teh
Just the head, please.	*Só a cabeça, por favor.*	soh ah kah-**beh**-sah poor fah-**vor**

In restaurants, seafood is sold by the "*KG*" (kilogram) or "*dose*" (portion). KG is dangerous. Ask, "*Quanto para uma dose?*" (How much for a portion?).

EATING

Seafood Specialties

arroz de marisco	ah-**rohsh** deh mah-**reesh**-koo	rich seafood rice dish, similar to Spain's *paella*
arroz de polvo	ah-**rohsh** deh **pohl**-voo	stew of octopus and rice
bacalhau cozido	bah-kahl-**yow** koh-**zee**-doo	boiled cod with green beans and carrots
bife de atum	**bee**-feh deh ah-**toon**	tuna steak often served with sautéed onions
caldeirada, açorda de marisco	kahl-day-**rah**-dah, ah-**sor**-dah deh mah-**reesh**-koo	bouillabaisse-like fish stew thickened with bread
cataplanas	kah-tah-**plah**-nahsh	hearty shellfish and ham stew
lulas grelhadas	**loo**-lahsh grehl-**yah**-dahsh	grilled squid
percebes	pehr-**seh**-behsh	boiled barnacles
porco à alentejana	**por**-koo ah ah-**lehn**-teh-zhah-nah	clams and pork with tomatoes and onion
sardinhas assadas	sar-**deen**-yahz ah-**sah**-dash	broiled sardines

Percebes (boiled barnacles) are sold as munchies on the street, in bars, and sometimes in restaurants. To eat a barnacle, peel off and discard the outer skin, then wash it down with beer.

EATING

Poultry

poultry	*aves*	**ah**-vish
chicken	*frango*	**frang**-goo
stewing chicken	*galinha*	gah-**leen**-yah
duck	*pato*	**pah**-too
turkey	*peru*	peh-**roo**
partridge	*perdiz*	pehr-**deesh**
How long has this been dead?	*À quanto tempo é que isto está morto?*	ah **kwahn**-too **tayn**-poo eh keh **eesh**-too ish-**tah mor**-too

Avoiding Mis-Steaks

alive	vivo	**vee**-voo
raw	crú	kroo
very rare	muito mal passado	**mween**-too mahl pah-**sah**-doo
rare	mal passado	mahl pah-**sah**-doo
medium	médio, no ponto	**may**-dee-oo, noo **pohn**-too
well-done	bem passado	bay<u>n</u> pah-**sah**-doo
very well-done	muito bem passado	**mween**-too bay<u>n</u> pah-**sah**-doo
almost burnt	quase queimada	**kwah**-zeh kay-**mah**-dah

Meat

meat	carne	**kar**-neh
beef	carne de vaca	**kar**-neh deh **vah**-kah
beef steak	bife	**bee**-feh
ribsteak	costela	kohsh-**teh**-lah
bunny	coelho	**kwayl**-yoo
cutlet	costeleta	koosh-teh-**lay**-tah
a wee goat	cabrito	kah-**bree**-too
ham	fiambre	fee-**ahm**-breh
lamb	borrego, carneiro	bor-**reh**-goo, kah-**nay**-roo
pork	porco	**por**-koo
roast beef	carne assada	**kar**-neh ah-**sah**-dah
sausage	salsicha	sahl-**see**-shah
smoked ham	presunto	preh-**zoon**-too
suckling pig	leitão	lay-**tow**
veal	vitela	vee-**teh**-lah

Meat, but...

These are the cheapest items on a menu for good reason.

brains	mioleira	mee-oh-**lay**-rah
kidney	rim	reeng

liver	*fígado*	**fee**-gah-doo
snails	*caracóis*	kah-rah-**koysh**
tongue	*lingua*	**leeng**-gwah
tripe	*tripas*	**tree**-pahsh

Main Course Specialties

coelho à caçador	**kwayl**-yoo ah kah-sah-**dor**	rabbit with carrots and potatoes
costeletas de porco à alentejana	kohsh-teh-**leh**-tahsh deh **por**-koo ah ah-**lehn**-teh-zhah-nah	pork chops with tomatoes and onions
cozida à portuguesa	koo-**zee**-dah ah por-too-**gay**-zah	boiled dinner with different meats, sausages, vegetables, rice, and beans
feijoada	**fay**-zhoh-ah-dah	pork and sausage with beans
frango no churrasco	**frang**-goo noo shoo-**rahsh**-koo	roasted chicken with hot and spicy piri-piri sauce
leitão assado	lay-**tow** ah-**sah**-doo	roast suckling pig
perna de cabrito	**pehr**-nah deh kah-**bree**-too	roasted leg of baby goat
rojões	roh-**zhohnsh**	crispy, fried pork

How It's Prepared

assorted	*diversos*	dee-**vehr**-soosh
baked	*no forno*	noo **for**-noo
boiled	*cozido*	koo-**zee**-doo
braised	*flamejado*	flah-meh-**zhah**-doo
broiled	*grelhado*	grehl-**yah**-doo
cold	*frio*	**free**-oo
cooked	*cozinhado*	koo-zeen-**yah**-doo
deep fried	*frito*	**free**-too
fillet	*filete*	fee-**leh**-teh
fresh	*fresco*	**frehsh**-koo
fried	*frito*	**free**-too
grilled	*grelhado*	grehl-**yah**-doo

homemade	caseiro	kah-**zay**-roo
hot	quente	**kayn**-teh
in cream sauce	com natas	koh<u>n</u> **nah**-tahsh
medium	meio passado	**may**-oo pah-**sah**-doo
microwave	microondas	mee-kroo-**ohn**-dahsh
mild	médio	**meh**-dee-oo
mixed	mista	**meesh**-tah
poached	escalfado	ish-kahl-**fah**-doo
rare	mal passado	mahl pah-**sah**-doo
raw	crú	kroo
roasted	assado	ah-**sah**-doo
sautéed	sautée	sow-**teh**
smoked	fumado	foo-**mah**-doo
sour	amargo	ah-**mar**-goo
Spanish-style	Espanhola	ish-pahn-**yoh**-lah
(peppers and tomatoes)		
spicy hot	picante	pee-**kahn**-teh
steamed	cozido ao vapor	koo-**zee**-doo ow vah-**por**
stuffed	recheado	reh-shee-**ah**-doo
sweet	doce	**doh**-seh
well-done	bem passado	bayn pah-**sah**-doo
with rice	com arroz	koh<u>n</u> ah-**rohsh**

Veggies

vegetables	legumes	lay-**goo**-mish
mixed veggies	verduras	vehr-**doo**-rahsh
	sortidas	sor-**tee**-dahsh
artichoke	alcachofra	ahl-kah-**shoh**-frah
asparagus	espargos	ish-**par**-goosh
beans	feijões	fay-**zhohnsh**
beets	beterraba	beh-teh-**rah**-bah
broccoli	brócolo	**broh**-koo-loo
cabbage	couve	**koh**-veh
carrots	cenoura	seh-**noh**-rah
cauliflower	couve-flor	**koh**-veh-flor
corn	milho	**meel**-yoo

EATING

cucumbers	*pepinos*	peh-**pee**-noosh
eggplant	*berinjela*	beh-reen-**zheh**-lah
French fries	*batatas fritas*	bah-**tah**-tahsh **free**-tahsh
garlic	*alho*	**ahl**-yoo
green beans	*feijões verdes*	fay-**zhohnsh vehr**-dish
lentils	*lentilhas*	lehn-**teel**-yahsh
mushrooms	*cogumelos*	koo-goo-**meh**-loosh
olives	*azeitonas*	ah-zay-**toh**-nahsh
onions	*cebolas*	seh-**boh**-lahsh
peas	*ervilhas*	ehr-**veel**-yahsh
pepper...	*pimento...*	pee-**mayn**-too
...green / hot / red	*...verde / picante / vermelho*	**vehr**-deh / pee-**kahn**-teh / vehr-**mehl**-yoo
pickle	*pepino de conserva*	peh-**pee**-noo deh kohn-**sehr**-vah
potatoes	*batatas*	bah-**tah**-tahsh
rice	*arroz*	ah-**rohsh**
spaghetti	*esparguete*	ish-par-**geh**-teh
spinach	*espinafre*	ish-pee-**nah**-freh
tomatoes	*tomates*	too-**mah**-tish
truffle	*trufa*	**troo**-fah
zucchini	*courgette*	koor-**zheh**-teh

You can usually get green beans and carrots (*feijões verdes e cenoura*) instead of the standard French fries by just asking. Another healthy vegetable side dish is *favas com azeite* (fava beans with olive oil).

Fruits

apple	*maçã*	mah-**sah**
apricot	*damasco*	dah-**mahsh**-koo
banana	*banana*	bah-**nah**-nah
berries	*bagas*	**bah**-gahsh
cantaloupe	*meloa*	meh-**low**-ah
cherry	*cereja*	seh-**ray**-zhah
date	*fruto seco*	**froo**-too **say**-koo

EATING

fig	figo	**fee**-goo
fruit	fruta	**froo**-tah
grapefruit	toranja	toh-**rahn**-zhah
grapes	uvas	**oo**-vahsh
honeydew melon	melão	meh-**low**
lemon	limão	lee-**mow**
orange	laranja	lah-**rahn**-zhah
peach	pêssego	**pay**-seh-goo
pear	pêra	**pay**-rah
pineapple	ananás	ah-nah-**nahsh**
plum	ameixa	ah-**may**-shah
prune	ameixa seca	ah-**may**-shah **say**-kah
raspberry	framboesa	frahm-**bway**-zah
strawberry	morango	moo-**rang**-goo
tangerine	tangerina	tahn-zheh-**ree**-nah
watermelon	melancia	meh-**lahn**-see-ah

Nuts to You

almond	amêndoa	ah-**mayn**-dwah
chestnut	castanha	kahsh-**tahn**-yah
coconut	coco	**koh**-koo
hazelnut	avelã	ah-veh-**lah**
peanut	amendoim	ah-mayn-**dweem**
pistachio	pistácio	peesh-**tah**-see-oo
walnut	noz	nohsh

Just Desserts

dessert	sobremesa	soo-breh-**may**-zah
cake	bolo	**boh**-loo
ice cream...	gelado...	zheh-**lah**-doo
...cone	...numa cone	**noo**-mah **koh**-neh
...cup	...numa chávena	**noo**-mah **shah**-veh-nah
scoop of	uma colher	**kool**-yehr
ice cream	de gelado	deh zheh-**lah**-doo
vanilla	baunilha	bow-**neel**-yah
chocolate	chocolate	shoo-koo-**lah**-teh

EATING

strawberry	*morango*	moo-**rang**-goo
fruit cup	*salada de fruta*	sah-**lah**-dah deh **froo**-tah
tart	*tarte*	**tar**-teh
whipped cream	*chântily*	**shahn**-tee-lee
chocolate mousse	*mousse de chocolate*	**moo**-seh deh shoo-koo-**lah**-teh
pudding	*pudim*	**poo**-deem
pastry	*pastelaria*	pahs-teh-lah-**ree**-ah
cookies	*bolos*	**boh**-loosh
candy	*rebuçados*	ray-boo-**sah**-doosh
low calorie	*poucas calorias*	**poh**-kahsh kah-loo-**ree**-ahsh
homemade	*caseiro*	kah-**zay**-roo
We'll split one.	*Vamos dividir um.*	**vah**-moosh dee-vee-**deer** oo<u>n</u>
Two forks / Two spoons, please.	*Dois garfos / Duas colheres, por favor.*	doysh **gar**-foosh / **doo**-ahsh **kool**-yeh-rish poor fah-**vor**
I shouldn't, but...	*Não devia, mas...*	no<u>w</u> deh-**vee**-ah mahsh
Exquisite!	*Requintado!*	ray-keen-**tah**-doo
It's heavenly!	*É divinal!*	eh dee-vee-**nahl**
Death by chocolate.	*Morro por chocolate.*	**moh**-roo poor shoo-koo-**lah**-teh
Better than sex.	*Melhor que sexo.*	mil-**yor** keh **sehk**-soo
A moment on the lips, forever on the hips.	*Um momento nos lábios, para sempre nos quadris.*	oo<u>n</u> moh-**mehn**-too noosh **lah**-bee-oosh **pah**-rah **sayn**-preh noosh kwah-**dreesh**

Dessert Specialties

arroz doce	ah-**rohsh doh**-seh	rice pudding
bolo podre	**boh**-loo **poh**-dreh	honey and cinnamon cake
fios de ovos	**fee**-oosh deh **oh**-voosh	sweet egg pudding
flan, pudim flan	flah<u>n</u>, **poo**-deem flah<u>n</u>	caramel custard
leite creme	**lay**-teh **kreh**-meh	cream custard

pastel de nata, pastel de Belém	**pahsh**-tehl deh **nah**-tah, **pahsh**-tehl deh beh-**layn**	cream custard tarts, called pastel de Belém in Belém and Lisbon, otherwise pastel de nata
queijadas	kay-**zhah**-dahsh	cheesecake
sonhos	**sohn**-yoosh	fried sweet dough, sprinkled with cinnamon and sugar
travesseiros	trah-veh-**say**-roosh	almond pastries
trouxas de ovos	**troo**-shahsh deh **oh**-voosh	sweet egg rolls

DRINKING

Water, Milk, and Juice

mineral water...	água mineral...	**ah**-gwah mee-neh-**rahl**
...with / without gas	...com / sem gás	kohn / sayn gahsh
tap water	água da torneira	**ah**-gwah dah tor-**nay**-rah
whole milk	leite gordo	**lay**-teh **gor**-doo
skim milk	leite magro	**lay**-teh **mah**-groo
fresh milk	leite fresco	**lay**-teh **frehsh**-koo
hot chocolate	leite com chocolate quente	**lay**-teh kohn shoo-koo-**lah**-teh **kayn**-teh
fruit juice	sumo de fruta	**soo**-moo deh **froo**-tah
100% juice	cem por cento sumo	sayn pehr **sayn**-too **soo**-moo
fresh-squeezed juice	sumo fresco	**soo**-moo **frehsh**-koo
orange juice (pure)	sumo de laranja (puro)	**soo**-moo deh lah-**rahn**-zhah (**poo**-roo)
apple juice	sumo de maçã	**soo**-moo deh mah-**sah**
lemonade	limonada	lee-moh-**nah**-dah
with / without...	com / sem...	kohn / sayn
...sugar	...açúcar	ah-**soo**-kar
...ice	...gelo	**zhay**-loo
glass / cup	copo / chávena	**koh**-poo / **shah**-veh-nah
small / large	pequena / grande	peh-**kay**-nah / **grahn**-deh
bottle	garrafa	gah-**rah**-fah

EATING

Key Phrases: Drinking

drink	*bebida*	beh-**bee**-dah
(mineral) water	*água (mineral)*	ah-gwah (mee-neh-**rahl**)
tap water	*água da torneira*	**ah**-gwah dah tor-**nay**-rah
milk	*leite*	**lay**-teh
juice	*sumo*	**soo**-moo
coffee	*café*	kah-**feh**
tea	*chá*	shah
wine	*vinho*	**veen**-yoo
beer	*cerveja*	sehr-**vay**-zhah
Cheers!	*Saúde!*	sah-**oo**-deh

Is this water safe to drink?	*Posso beber esta água?*	**pos**-soo beh-**behr** **ehsh**-tah **ah**-gwah

Tap water is free at restaurants—ask for *água da torneira.* If you like mineral water, your big decision is *com* or *sem gás* (with or without carbonation). *Com gás* is a taste well worth acquiring. The light, sturdy plastic water bottles are great to pack along and reuse as you travel.

Coffee and Tea

coffee...	*café...*	kah-**feh**
...black	*...prêto*	**pray**-too
...with milk	*...com leite*	koh<u>n</u> **lay**-teh
...with sugar	*...com açucar*	koh<u>n</u> ah-**soo**-kar
...American-style	*...estilo Americano*	ish-**tee**-loo ah-meh-ree-**kah**-noo
milk with a dash of coffee	*galão*	gah-**low**
coffee latte	*meia de leite*	**may**-ah deh **lay**-teh
espresso	*bica*	**bee**-kah
espresso with a touch of milk	*pingo*	**peen**-goo

EATING

espresso with milk	garoto	gah-**roh**-too
espresso with a touch of brandy	uma bica com uma pinga	**oo**-mah **bee**-kah koh<u>n</u> **oo**-mah **peen**-gah
decaffeinated	descaféinado	dish-kah-fay-**nah**-doo
instant coffee	Néscafe	**nehsh**-kah-feh
sugar	açúcar	ah-**soo**-kar
hot water	água quente	**ah**-gwah **kayn**-teh
tea / lemon	chá / limão	shah / lee-**mow**
tea bag	saquinho de chá	sah-**keen**-yoo deh shah
herbal tea	chá de ervas	shah deh **ehr**-vahsh
fruit tea	chá de frutas	shah deh **froo**-tahsh
small / large	pequeno / grande	peh-**kay**-noo / **grahn**-deh
Another cup.	Outra chávena.	**oh**-trah **shah**-veh-nah
Same price if I sit or stand?	É o mesmo preço se me sentar ou se estiver de pé?	eh oo **mehsh**-moo **preh**-soo seh meh sehn-**tar** oh seh ish-tee-**vehr** deh pay

Only tourists take milk with their coffee throughout the day. The Portuguese add milk only at breakfast.

Wine

I would like...	Gostaria...	goosh-tah-**ree**-ah
We would like...	Gostaríamos...	goosh-tah-**ree**-ah-moosh
...a glass...	...um copo...	oo<u>n</u> **koh**-poo
...a carafe...	...um jarro...	oo<u>n</u> **zhah**-roo
...a bottle...	...uma garrafa...	**oo**-mah gah-**rah**-fah
...a 5-liter jug...	...um garrafão...	oo<u>n</u> gah-rah-**fow**
...a barrel...	...um barril...	oo<u>n</u> bah-**reel**
...a vat...	...uma pipa...	**oo**-mah **pee**-pah
...of red wine	...de vinho tinto	deh **veen**-yoo **teen**-too
...of white wine	...de vinho branco	deh **veen**-yoo **brang**-koo
...of the region.	...da região.	dah rayzh-**yow**
...the wine list.	...a lista de vinhos.	ah **leesh**-tah deh **veen**-yoosh

EATING

Wine Words

wine	vinho	**veen**-yoo
select wine (good year)	vinho reserva	**veen**-yoo reh-**zehr**-vah
table wine	vinho de mesa	**veen**-yoo deh **may**-zah
cheap house wine	vinho da casa	**veen**-yoo dah **kah**-zah
local	local	loo-**kahl**
of the region	da região	dah rayzh-**yow**
red	tinto	**teen**-too
white	branco	**brang**-koo
rosé	rosé	roh-**zay**
sparkling	espumante	ish-poo-**mahn**-teh
light	leve	**leh**-veh
fruity	sabor a frutas	sah-**bor** ah **froo**-tahsh
sweet	doce	**doh**-seh
medium	médio	**meh**-dee-oo
semi-dry	meio seco	**may**-oo **say**-koo
dry	seco	**say**-koo
very dry	muito seco	**mween**-too **say**-koo
full-bodied	bem encorporado	bayn ayn-kor-por-**ah**-doo
mature	maduro	mah-**doo**-roo
cork	rolha	**rohl**-yah
corkscrew	saca-rolhas	sah-kah-**rohl**-yahsh
vineyard	vendimas	vehn-**dee**-mahsh
wine-tasting	provas de vinho	**proh**-vahsh deh **veen**-yoo
What is a good year (vintage)?	Qual foi um bom ano?	kwahl foy oon bohn **ah**-noo
What do you recommend?	O que é que recomenda?	oo keh eh keh ray-koo-**mayn**-dah

EATING

Portugal produces 55 percent of the world's cork. Cork oak grows well all over the country, especially on the Alentejo plains. The trees must be 25 years old before the first bark can be cut. After that, the trees are stripped every nine years and will produce for approximately one hundred years. Portuguese cork is valued for its lightness. Although cork can sometimes contaminate wine bottles, plastic substitutes still aren't serious competition for the natural plugs.

Wine Labels

These are the terms usually found on a Portuguese wine label.

DOC (denominação de origem controlada)	a wine that meets country-wide laws defining how and where quality wine is made
IPR (indicação de provêniência regulamentada)	a wine that meets quality control standards for regional wine
reserva	reserve or higher-quality wine, aged longer
casta	grape variety
Quinta	wine-producing estate
Zinha	vineyard
engarrafado na origem / Quinta	estate bottled
engarrafado por...	bottled by...
produzido por...	produced by...

For good, cheap wine, it's *vinho de casa* (house wine). A northern Portuguese specialty is *vinho verde* (green wine). This effervescent young wine, which goes well with shellfish, comes in red or white; while many argue that both are bad, the white is clearly better. From the island of Madeira comes a sweet, white, fortified wine called *Madeira*, better used for cooking than drinking. The same island produces a semi-sweet *verdelho* and a dry aperitif version called *sercial. Moscatel*, a sweet white from the Setubal region, is best with dessert or as an aperitif. Portugal also produces more rosé wine than other countries—the best known is *Mateus*, a sweet, bubbly wine. If you're looking for a drier, full-bodied red, try the wines from the Dão and Colares regions.

Beer

beer	cerveja	sehr-**vay**-zhah
from the tap	a copo	ah **koh**-poo
bottle	garrafa	gah-**rah**-fah
light / dark	leve / escura	**leh**-veh / ish-**koo**-rah
local / imported	local / importada	loo-**kahl** / ayn-poor-**tah**-dah

EATING

small / large	pequena / grande	peh-**kay**-nah / **grahn**-deh
small mug of draft beer (20 cl)	imperial	ay<u>n</u>-peh-ree-**ahl**
medium mug of draft beer (33 cl)	principe	**preen**-see-peh
large mug of draft beer (50 cl)	caneca	kah-**neh**-kah
one liter draft beer	girafe	zhee-**rah**-feh
thin glass of draft beer with no foam	fino	**fee**-noo
low-calorie	poucas calorias	**poh**-kahsh kah-loo-**ree**-ahsh
alcohol-free	sem alcool	say<u>n</u> **ahl**-kahl
cold	fresca	**frehsh**-kah
colder	mais fresca	mīsh **frehsh**-kah
beer garden	cervejaria	sehr-vay-zhah-**ree**-ah

Portuguese beer is stronger than its Spanish cousin—*Cuidado* (Be careful)! Sagres, Super Bock, and Cristal are the most popular lagers. For a meal with your beer, look for a *cervejaria* (beer garden).

Bar Talk

Want to go out for a drink?	Vamos tomar una bebida?	**vah**-moosh toh-**mar** **oo**-mah beh-**bee**-dah
I'll buy you a drink.	Pago a sua bebida.	**pah**-goo ah **soo**-ah beh-**bee**-dah
It's on me.	É por minha conta.	eh poor **meen**-yah **kohn**-tah
What would you like?	O que é que gostaria?	oo keh eh keh goosh-tah-**ree**-ah
I'd like a...	Queria...	keh-**ree**-ah
I don't drink alcohol.	Não bebo alcool.	no<u>w</u> **beh**-boo **ahl**-kahl
alcohol-free	sem alcool	say<u>n</u> **ahl**-kahl
What is the local specialty?	Qual é a especialidade local?	kwahl eh ah ish-peh-see-ah-lee-**dah**-deh loo-**kahl**

What's a good drink for a man / woman?	O que bebem os homens / as mulheres?	oo keh **beh**-bay<u>n</u> oosh **ah**-may<u>n</u>sh / ahsh mool-**yeh**-rish
Straight.	Puro.	**poo**-roo
With / Without...	Com / Sem...	koh<u>n</u> / say<u>n</u>
...alcohol.	...alcool.	**ahl**-kahl
...ice.	...gelo.	**zhay**-loo
One more.	Mais uma.	mīsh **oo**-mah
Cheers!	Saúde!	sah-**oo**-deh
Long live Portugal!	Vida longa Portugal!	**vee**-dah **loh<u>n</u>**-gah poor-too-**gahl**
I'm...	Estou...	ish-**toh**
...tipsy.	...tonto[a].	**tohn**-too
...drunk.	...bêbado[a].	**bay**-bah-doo
...hungover.	...com uma ressaca.	koh<u>n</u> **oo**-mah reh-**sah**-kah

In Lisbon, hole-in-the-wall bars sell *ginjinha* (zheen-**zheen**-yah), a sweet liqueur of cherry-like ginja berries, sugar, and schnapps.

Standard aperitifs are *martini com cerveja* (a type of vermouth topped with beer), *um branco seco* (a glass of dry white wine), and *água ardente* (firewater made from grape seeds). Favorite after-dinner drinks include *amêndoa amarga* (local amaretto), *armarguinha* (another sweet almond liqueur), *licor beirdo* (made from aromatic plants), and *bagaço* (firewater from grape husks).

Porto (port) is the famous fortified wine in a category of its own. Produced in northern Portugal, port takes its name from the city of Porto. The sweetest and cheapest versions are the red and ruby blends (from several different harvests); these young fortified wines are aged just three years. Tawny ports are semi-sweet red blends named after the color of the oak barrels they're aged in. Vintage port, the most valued, comes from a single high-quality harvest and is aged up to 20 years.

EATING

PICNICKING

At the Market

English	Portuguese	Pronunciation
Self-service?	Self-service?	"self-service"
Ripe for today?	Está maduro?	ish-**tah** mah-**doo**-roo
Does it need	Isto precisa	**eesh**-too preh-**see**-zah
to be cooked?	de ser cozinhado?	deh sehr koo-zeen-**yah**-doo
A little taste?	Um pouco de sabor?	oon **poh**-koo deh sah-**bor**
Fifty grams.	Cinquenta	seeng-**kwayn**-tah
	gramas.	**grah**-mahsh
One hundred grams.	Cem gramas.	sayn **grah**-mahsh
More. / Less.	Mais. / Menos.	mīsh / **may**-noosh
A piece.	Um pedaço.	oon peh-**dah**-soo
A slice.	Uma fatia.	**oo**-mah fah-**tee**-ah
Four slices.	Quatro fatias.	**kwah**-troo fah-**tee**-ahsh
Sliced (fine).	Cortadas (em	kor-**tah**-dahsh (ayn
	fatias finas).	fah-**tee**-ahsh **fee**-nahsh)
Half.	Metade.	meh-**tah**-deh
A small bag.	Um saco pequeno.	oon **sah**-koo peh-**kay**-noo
A bag, please.	Um saco, por favor.	oon **sah**-koo poor fah-**vor**
Will you make...	Pode fazer...	**pod**-eh fah-**zehr**...
for me / us?	para mim / nós?	**pah**-rah meeng / nohsh
...a sandwich	...uma sanduíche	**oo**-mah sahnd-**weesh**-eh
...two sandwiches	...duas	**doo**-ahsh
	sanduíches	sahnd-**weesh**-ish
To take out.	Levar para fora.	leh-**var pah**-rah **for**-ah
Can I / Can we	Posso / Podemos	**pos**-soo / poo-**day**-moosh
use the...?	usar o...?	oo-**zar** oo
...microwave	...microondas	mee-kroo-**ohn**-dahsh
May I borrow a...?	Pode-me	**pod**-eh-meh
	emprestar um...?	ayn-preh-**star** oon
Do you have a...?	Tem um...?	tayn oon
Where can I	A onde posso	ah **ohn**-deh **pos**-soo
buy / find a...?	compra /	kohn-**prar** /
	encontrar um...?	ayn-kohn-**trar** oon
...corkscrew	...saca-rolhas	sah-kah-**rohl**-yahsh
...can opener	...abre-latas	ah-breh-**lah**-tahsh

EATING

Is there a park nearby?	*Há algum parque perto?*	ah **ahl**-goon **par**-keh **pehr**-too
Where is a good place to picnic?	*Onde há um bom lugar para um piquenique?*	**ohn**-deh ah oon bohn loo-**gar pah**-rah oon **peek**-neek
Is picnicking allowed here?	*É permitido fazer piquenique aqui?*	eh pehr-mee-**tee**-doo fah-**zehr peek**-neek ah-**kee**

Picnic Prose

open air market	*mercado municipal*	mehr-**kah**-doo moo-nee-see-**pahl**
grocery store	*mercearia*	mehr-see-ah-**ree**-ah
supermarket	*supermercado*	soo-pehr-mehr-**kah**-doo
delicatessen	*charcutaria*	shehr-koo-teh-**ree**-ah
bakery	*padaria*	pah-dah-**ree**-ah
pastry shop	*pastelaria*	pahsh-teh-lah-**ree**-ah
sweets shop	*confeitaria*	kohn-fay-tah-**ree**-ah
picnic	*piquenique*	**peek**-neek
sandwich	*sanduíche, sande*	sahnd-**weesh**-eh, **sahn**-deh
bread (whole wheat)	*pão (de trigo)*	**pow** (deh **tree**-goo)
roll	*papo seco, pães*	**pah**-poo **seh**-koo, pay<u>n</u>sh
ham	*fiambre*	fee-**ahm**-breh
sausage	*salsicha*	sahl-**see**-shah
cheese	*queijo*	**kay**-zhoo
mustard...	*mostarda...*	moosh-**tar**-dah
mayonnaise...	*maionese...*	mah-yoh-**neh**-zeh
...in a tube	*...num tubo*	noom **too**-boo
yogurt	*yogurte*	yoo-**goor**-teh
fruit	*fruta*	**froo**-tah
box of juice	*pacote de sumo*	pah-**koh**-teh deh **soo**-moo
cold drinks	*bebidas frias*	beh-**bee**-dahsh **free**-ahsh

EATING

spoon / fork...	*colher / garfo...*	**kool**-yehr / **gar**-foo
...made of plastic	*...plástico*	**plahsh**-tee-koo
cup / plate...	*chávena / prato...*	**shah**-veh-nah / **prah**-too
...made of paper	*...de papel*	deh pah-**pehl**

You can shop at a *supermercado,* but smaller shops are more fun. Get bread for your *sanduíche* at a *padaria* and order meat and cheese by the gram at a *mercearia.* For a meal on the run on a bun, try a *prego no pão* (meat and egg roll) or a *tosta mista* (toasted cheese and ham sandwich).

MENU DECODER

PORTUGUESE/ENGLISH

This won't contain every word on your menu, but it'll help you get *mesilhões* (mussels) instead of *mioleira* (brains). An English/Portuguese Decoder follows.

a copo	from the tap
acepipes	appetizers
açorda	chowder
açúcar	sugar
água	water
água ardente	firewater
água da torneira	tap water
água mineral	mineral water
alcachofra	artichoke
alcool	alcohol
alentejana	with tomatoes and onions
alface	lettuce
alho	garlic
almoço	lunch
amargo	sour
amêijoas	clams
amêijoas à Bulhão Pato	small clams in wine, garlic, and cilantro broth

ameixa	plum
ameixa seca	prune
amêndoa	almond
amendoim	peanut
ananás	pineapple
anchovas	anchovies
aquecido	heated
arenque	herring
arroz	rice
arroz de marisco	seafood rice dish (*paella*)
arroz de polvo	octopus, rice stew
arroz doce	rice pudding
assado	roasted, broiled
atum	tuna
avelã	hazelnut
aves	poultry
azeitonas	olives
bacalhau	cod
bacalhau cozido	boiled cod with green beans and carrots
bagas	berries
banana	banana
batata	potato
batatas fritas	French fries
baunilha	vanilla
bebida	beverage
bem encorporado	full-bodied (wine)
bem passado	well-done (meat)
berinjela	eggplant
beterraba	beets
bica	espresso
bifana no pão	pork sandwich
bife	beef steak
bife de atum	tuna steak with onions
bola	scoop
bolaichas	crackers
bolo	cake

bolo podre	honey and cinnamon cake
bolos	cookies
borrego	lamb
branco	white
brócolos	broccoli
cabrito	baby goat
cachorro (quente)	hot dog
café	coffee
café com açucar	coffee with sugar
café com leite	coffee with milk
café estilo Americano	American-style coffee
café prêto	black coffee
caldeirada	fish stew
caldo verde	soup with potato, kale, and sausage
camarão	shrimp
camarão tigre	tiger shrimp
camarão-carne	fried pastry filled with meat
camarãoes com piri piri	sautéed shrimp with garlic and hot peppers
camarão-peixe	fried pastry filled with fish
caneca	large draft beer (50 cl)
canja	broth
caracóis	snails
caranguejo	crab
carapaus	scad (like mackerel)
carne	meat
carneiro	lamb
casa	house
caseiro	homemade
casta	grape variety
castanha	chestnut
cataplanas	shellfish and ham stew
cebola	onion
cenoura	carrots
cereja	cherry
cerveja	beer
chá	tea

chá de ervas	herbal tea
chá de frutas	fruit tea
chá gelado	iced tea
chântily	whipped cream
chávena	cup
chinês	Chinese
choco	cuttlefish
chouriço	smoked pork sausage
chouriço assado	grilled smoked pork sausage
coco	coconut
coelho	bunny
coelho à caçador	rabbit with carrots and potatoes
cogumelos	mushrooms
colher	spoon; scoop (ice cream)
com	with
comida	food
compota	jam
cone	cone
copo	glass
cortada	sliced
costela	ribsteak
costeleta	cutlet
costeletas de porco à alentejana	pork chops with tomatoes and onions
courgette	zucchini
couve	cabbage
couve-flor	cauliflower
cozida à portuguesa	Portuguese boiled dinner with meats and vegetables
cozido	boiled
cozido ao vapor	steamed
cozinhado	cooked
creme de camarão	pureed spicy shrimp soup
crepe de galinha / legumes	chicken / vegetable crêpe
crú	raw
da região	of the region
damasco	apricot

de	of
descaféinado	decaffeinated
diversos	assorted
doce	sweet
dose	portion
e	and
ementa	menu
ementa do dia	menu of the day
ementa turistica	tourist menu (fixed-price meal)
enguia	eel
entradas	appetizers
ervas	herbs
ervilhas	peas
escalfado	poached
escalopes	scallops
espadarte	swordfish
Espanhola	with peppers and tomatoes
espargos	asparagus
esparguete	spaghetti
especialidade	specialty
especialidade da casa	specialty of the house
espinafre	spinach
espumante	sparkling (wine)
estilo	style
estrelados	fried
faca	knife
factura	receipt
fatia	slice
feijoada	beans with pork and sausage
feijões	beans
feijões verdes	green beans
fiambre	ham
fígado	liver
figo	fig
filete	fillet
filetes	fried white fish
fino	thin glass of draft beer

fios de ovos	sweet egg pudding
flamejado	braised
flan	caramel custard
forno	baked
framboesa	raspberry
Francesinha	sandwich meat, cheese, tomato, and beer
frango	chicken
frango no churrasco	roasted chicken with piri-piri sauce
fresco	fresh
frio	cold
frito	fried or deep-fried
fruta	fruit
fruto seco	date
fumado	smoked
galão	milk with a dash of coffee
galinha	stewing chicken
gambas	prawns
gambas fritas com alho	sautéed garlic prawns
garfo	fork
garoto	espresso with milk
garrafa	bottle
gelado	ice cream; iced
geléia	jelly
gelo	ice
girafe	one-liter draft beer
gordura	fat
gostoso	tasty
grande	large
grelhado	grilled, broiled
guardanapo	napkin
imperial	small draft beer (20 cl)
importada	imported
incluido	included
jantar	dinner
jarro	carafe
lagosta	lobster
lagostins	crayfish

laranja	orange
legumes	vegetables
leitão	suckling pig
leitão assado	roast suckling pig
leite	milk
leite com chocolate quente	hot chocolate
leite creme	cream custard
leite fresco	fresh milk
leite gordo	whole milk
leite magro	skim milk
lentilhas	lentils
leve	light (wine)
limão	lemon
lingua	tongue
linguad	sole
lista	list
lulas	squid
lulas grelhadas	grilled squid
maçã	apple
maduro	mature (wine)
maionese	mayonnaise
mal passado	rare (meat)
manteiga	butter
manteiga de amendoim	peanut butter
margarina	margarine
marisco	seafood, shellfish
massa	pasta
médio	mild; medium (meat or wine)
meia de leite	coffee with equal portions milk
meia dose	half portion
meio seco	semi-dry (wine)
mel	honey
melancia	watermelon
melão	honeydew melon
meloa	cantaloupe
mesa	table
mexidos	scrambled

mexilhões	mussels
microondas	microwave
milho	corn
mioleira	brains
mista	mixed
molho	sauce, dressing
morango	strawberry
mostarda	mustard
mousse	chocolate mousse
muito	very
muito bem passado	very well-done (meat)
muito mal passado	very rare (meat)
muito seco	very dry (wine)
não	not
Néscafe	instant coffee
no forno	baked
no ponto	medium (meat)
noz	walnut
óleo	oil
omeleta	omelet
orgânico	organic
ostras	oysters
ou	or
ovo	egg
ovo cozido	boiled egg
ovo muito cozido	hard-boiled egg
ovo não muito cozido	soft-boiled egg
ovos estrelados	fried eggs
ovos mexidos	scrambled eggs
pães	roll
palhinha	straw
palito	toothpick
pão	bread
pão de trigo	whole wheat bread
papo seco	roll
para levar	"to go"
pargo	bream (fish)

pasta de atum	tuna paté
pastas	bread with sardine spread
pastel	small doughy snack (sweet or savory)
pastel de Belém (Lisbon), pastel de nata (elsewhere)	cream custard tart
pastelaria	pastry; pastry shop
pasties de bacalhau	cod fish cakes
pato	duck
pedaço	piece
peixe	fish
pepinos	cucumbers
pepinos de conserva	pickles
pequeno	small
pequeno almoço	breakfast
pêra	pear
percebes	barnacles
perdiz	partridge
perna de cabrito	roasted leg of baby goat
peru	turkey
pêssego	peach
petiscos	munchies (tapas)
picante	spicy hot
pimenta	pepper (seasoning)
pimento	bell pepper
pimento picante	hot pepper
pimento verde	green pepper
pimento vermelho	red pepper
pingo	espresso with a touch of milk
pistácio	pistachio
polvo	octopus
porção	portion
porco	pork
porco à alentejana	clams and pork with tomatoes
porto	port (fortified wine)
poucas calorias	low calorie
prato	plate
prato do dia	special of the day

prato misto	combination plate
prego no pão	meat and fried egg roll
presunto	smoked ham
principe	medium draft beer (33 cl)
pudim	pudding
pudim flan	caramel custard
puro	pure
queijadas	cheesecake
queijo	cheese
queijo di serra	sheep cheese
queijo fresco	fresh goat cheese
quente	hot (temperature)
Quinta	vineyard
rebuçados	candy
recheado	stuffed
recibo	receipt
refeição	meal
região	local
requeijão	ricotta-style cheese
rim	kidney
rojões	crispy-fried pork
rolha	cork
rosé	rosé (wine)
sacarina	artificial sweetener
saca-rolhas	corkscrew
sal	salt
salada	salad
salada de alface	green salad
salada de atum	salad with tuna, potatoes, and egg
salada de ovo	egg salad
salada de pimento	salad with green peppers and grilled sardines
salada de polvo	salad with octopus
salada mista	mixed salad
salada Russa	Russian salad (tuna and mayo)
salame	salami
salgados	savory pastries

salmão	salmon
salsicha	sausage
sande	sandwich
sanduíche	sandwich
santola recheada	stuffed spider crab
sapateira	Dungeness crab
saquinho de chá	tea bag
sardinhas	sardines
sardinhas assadas	broiled sardines
seco	dry (wine)
sem	without
separado	on the side
sobremesa	dessert
sonhos	fried sweet dough, sprinkled with cinnamon and sugar
sopa	soup
sopa de alentejana	soup with egg, bread, and herbs
sopa de mariscos	shellfish soup
sopa de pedra	vegetable soup with sausage
sopa de peixe	fish soup
sopa de tomate com ovo	tomato soup with poached egg
sumo	juice
talheres	silverware
tangerina	tangerine
tarte	tart
tinto	red
tixa aplicada	cover charge
tomate	tomato
toranja	grapefruit
torrada	toast
torrado	toasted
tosta mista	toasted ham and cheese sandwich
toucinho	bacon
travesseiros	almond pastries
trigo	wheat
tripas	tripe
trouxas de ovos	sweet egg rolls

trufa	truffle
truta	trout
uvas	grapes
vaca	beef
vapor	steamed
vendimas	vineyard
verde	green
vinagre	vinegar
vinho	wine
vinho da casa	cheap house wine
vinho de mesa	table wine
vinho reserva	select wine (good year)
vitela	veal
yogurte	yogurt

ENGLISH/PORTUGUESE

English / Portuguese

MENU DECODER

alcohol	alcool
almond	amêndoa
anchovies	anchovas
and	e
appetizers	entradas, petiscos, acepipes
apple	maçã
apricot	damasco
artichoke	alcachofra
artificial sweetener	sacarina
asparagus	espargos
assorted	diversos
bacon	toucinho
baked	(no) forno
banana	banana
barnacles	percebes
beans	feijões
beans, green	feijões verdes
beef	vaca
beef steak	bife
beer	cerveja
beer, draft, large (50 cl)	caneca
beer, draft, medium (33 cl)	principe
beer, draft, one liter	girafe
beer, draft, small (20 cl)	imperial
beer, draft, thin glass	fino
beer, from the tap	a copo
beets	beterraba
bell pepper	pimento
berries	bagas
beverage	bebida
boiled	cozido
boiled egg	ovo cozido
bottle	garrafa
brains	mioleira
braised	flamejado

bread	pão
bread, whole wheat	pão de trigo
breakfast	pequeno almoço
bream (fish)	pargo
broccoli	brócolos
broiled	grelhado
broth	canja
butter	manteiga
cabbage	couve
cake	bolo
candy	rebuçados
cantaloupe	meloa
carafe	jarro
caramel custard	(pudim) flan
carrots	cenoura
cauliflower	couve-flor
cheese	queijo
cheese, goat	queijo fresco
cheese, ricotta-style	requeijão
cheese, sheep	queijo di serra
cheeseburger	cheeseburger
cheesecake	queijadas
cherry	cereja
chestnut	castanha
chicken	frango
chicken, stewing	galinha
Chinese	chinês
chocolate mousse	mousse
chocolate, hot	leite com chocolate quente
chowder	açorda
clams	amêijoas
coconut	coco
cod	bacalhau
coffee	café
coffee with equal portions milk	meia de leite
coffee with lots of milk	galão
coffee with milk	café com leite

English / Portuguese

MENU DECODER

coffee with sugar	café com açúcar
coffee, American-style	café estilo Americano
coffee, black	café prêto
coffee, espresso	bica
coffee, espresso with a touch of milk	pingo
coffee, espresso with milk	garoto
coffee, instant	Néscafe
cold	frio
combination plate	prato misto
cone	cone
cooked	cozinhado
cookies	bolos
cork	rolha
corkscrew	saca-rolhas
corn	milho
cover charge	tixa aplicada
crab	caranguejo
crab, Dungeness	sapateira
crackers	bolaichas
crayfish	lagostins
cream custard	leite creme
cream custard tarts	pastel de nata; pastel de Belém (in Belém and Lisbon)
cream, whipped	chântily
cucumbers	pepinos
cup	chávena
custard, caramel	flan, pudim flan
custard, cream	leite creme
cutlet	costeleta
cuttlefish	choco
date	fruto seco
decaffeinated	descaféinado
dessert	sobremesa
dinner	jantar
dressing	molho
dry (wine)	seco

duck	pato
Dungeness crab	sapateira
eel	enguia
egg	ovo
egg salad	salada de ovo
egg, boiled	ovo cozido
egg, hard-boiled	ovo muito cozido
egg, soft-boiled	ovo não muito cozido
eggplant	berinjela
eggs, fried	ovos estrelados
eggs, scrambled	ovos mexidos
espresso	bica
espresso with a touch of milk	pingo
espresso with milk	garoto
fat	gordura
fig	figo
fillet	filete
firewater	água ardente
fish	peixe
food	comida
fork	garfo
French fries	batatas fritas
fresh	fresco
fried	frito; estrelado (eggs)
fried eggs	ovos estrelados
fried white fish	filetes
from the tap	a copo
fruit	fruta
fruit tea	chá de frutas
full-bodied (wine)	bem encorporado
garlic	alho
glass	copo
goat (baby)	cabrito
goat cheese	queijo fresco
grapefruit	toranja
grapes	uvas
green	verde

green beans	feijões verdes
green pepper	pimento verde
green salad	salada de alface
grilled	grelhado
half portion	meia dose
ham	fiambre
ham, smoked	presunto
hamburger	hamburger
hard-boiled egg	ovo muito cozido
hazelnut	avelã
heated	aquecido
herbal tea	chá de ervas
herbs	ervas
herring	arenque
homemade	caseiro
honey	mel
honeydew melon	melão
hot (temperature)	quente
hot (spicy)	picante
hot chocolate	leite com chocolate quente
hot dog	cachorro (quente)
hot pepper	pimento picante
house	casa
house wine	vinho da casa
ice	gelo
ice cream	gelado
iced	gelado
iced tea	chá gelado
imported	importada
included	incluido
instant coffee	Néscafe
jam	compota
jelly	geléia
juice	sumo
kidney	rim
knife	faca
lamb	borrego, carneiro

large	grande
lemon	limão
lentils	lentilhas
lettuce	alface
light (wine)	leve
list	lista
liver	fígado
lobster	lagosta
local	local, (da) região
low calorie	poucas calorias
lunch	almoço
margarine	margarina
mature (wine)	maduro
mayonnaise	maionese
meal	refeição
meat	carne
meat, medium	médio, no ponto
meat, rare	mal passado
meat, raw	crú
meat, very rare	muito mal passado
meat, very well-done	muito bem passado
meat, well-done	bem passado
medium (meat)	médio, no ponto
medium (wine)	médio
melon, honeydew	melão
menu	ementa
menu of the day	ementa do dia
menu, tourist (fixed-price meal)	ementa turistica
microwave	microondas
mild	médio
milk	leite
milk, fresh	leite fresco
milk, skim	leite magro
milk, whole	leite gordo
mineral water	água mineral
mixed	mista

mixed salad	salada mista
mousse, chocolate	mousse
munchies (tapas)	petiscos
mushrooms	cogumelos
mussels	mexilhões
mustard	mostarda
napkin	guardanapo
not	não
octopus	polvo
of	de
oil	óleo
olives	azeitonas
omelet	omeleta
on the side	separado
onion	cebola
or	ou
orange	laranja
organic	orgânico
oysters	ostras
partridge	perdiz
pasta	massa
pastry	pastelaria
peach	pêssego
peanut	amendoim
peanut butter	manteiga de amendoim
pear	pêra
peas	ervilhas
pepper (seasoning)	pimenta
pepper, bell	pimento
pepper, green	pimento verde
pepper, hot	pimento picante
pepper, red	pimento vermelho
pickles	pepinos de conserva
piece	pedaço
pig, suckling	leitão
pineapple	ananás
pistachio	pistácio

plate	prato
plum	ameixa
poached	escalfado
pork	porco
pork sandwich	bifana no pão
port (fortified wine)	porto
portion	dose, porção
potato	batata
poultry	aves
prawns	gambas
prune	ameixa seca
pudding	pudim
pudding, rice	arroz doce
pure	puro
rabbit	coelho
rare (meat)	mal passado
raspberry	framboesa
raw	crú
receipt	recibo, factura
red (wine)	tinto
red pepper	pimento vermelho
ribsteak	costela
rice	arroz
rice pudding	arroz doce
roasted	assado
roll	papo seco, pães
rosé (wine)	rosé
salad	salada
salad, egg	salada de ovo
salad, green	salada de alface
salad, mixed	salada mista
salad, Russian (tuna and mayo)	salada Russa
salami	salame
salmon	salmão
salt	sal
sandwich	sanduíche, sande

sandwich, pork	bifana no pão
sardines	sardinhas
sauce	molho
sausage	salsicha
scad (like mackerel)	carapaus
scallops	escalopes
scoop	bola
scoop (ice cream)	colher
scrambled	mexidos
scrambled eggs	ovos mexidos
seafood	marisco
semi-dry (wine)	meio seco
sheep cheese	queijo di serra
shellfish	marisco
shrimp	camarão
shrimp, tiger	camarão tigre
side, on the	separado
silverware	talheres
skim milk	leite magro
slice	fatia
sliced	cortada
small	pequeno
smoked	fumado
smoked ham	presunto
snails	caracóis
soft-boiled egg	ovo não muito cozido
sole	linguad
soup	sopa
sour	amargo
spaghetti	esparguete
sparkling (wine)	espumante
special of the day	prato do dia
specialty	especialidade
specialty of the house	especialidade da casa
spicy hot	picante
spinach	espinafre
spoon	colher
squid	lulas

steak, beef	bife
steak, tuna	bife de atum
steamed	(cozido ao) vapor
stew, fish	caldeirada
straw	palhinha
strawberry	morango
stuffed	recheado
style	estilo
suckling pig	leitão
sugar	açúcar
sweet	doce
sweetener, artificial	sacarina
swordfish	espadarte
table	mesa
table wine	vinho de mesa
tangerine	tangerina
tap water	água da torneira
tap, from the	a copo
tart	tarte
tasty	gostoso
tea	chá
tea bag	saquinho de chá
tea, herbal	chá de ervas
tea, iced	chá gelado
tiger shrimp	camarão tigre
"to go"	para levar
toast	torrada
toasted	torrado
tomato	tomate
tongue	lingua
toothpick	palito
tripe	tripas
trout	truta
truffle	trufa
tuna	atum
turkey	peru
vanilla	baunilha
veal	vitela

vegetable	legumes
very	muito
very dry (wine)	muito seco
very rare (meat)	muito mal passado
very well-done (meat)	muito bem passado
vinegar	vinagre
vineyard	vendimas, quinta, zinha
walnut	noz
water	água
water, mineral	água mineral
water, tap	água da torneira
watermelon	melancia
well-done (meat)	bem passado
wheat	trigo
whipped cream	chântily
white	branco
whole milk	leite gordo
wine	vinho
wine, dry	vinho seco
wine, fortified (port)	porto
wine, full-bodied	vinho bem encorporado
wine, house	vinho da casa
wine, light	vinho leve
wine, mature	vinho maduro
wine, medium	vinho médio
wine, red	vinho tinto
wine, rosé	vinho rosé
wine, select (good year)	vinho reserva
wine, semi-dry	vinho meio seco
wine, sparkling	vinho espumante
wine, table	vinho de mesa
wine, very dry	vinho muito seco
wine, white	vinho branco
with	com
without	sem
yogurt	yogurte
zucchini	courgette

ACTIVITIES

SIGHTSEEING

Where?

Where is...?	Onde é...?	**ohn**-deh eh
...the best view	...a melhor vista	ah mil-**yor veesh**-tah
...the main square	...a praça principal	ah **prah**-sah preen-see-**pahl**
...the old town center	...a parte da cidade velha	ah **par**-teh dah see-**dah**-deh **vehl**-yah
...the museum	...o museu	oo moo-**zeh**-oo
...the castle	...o castelo	oo kahsh-**teh**-loo
...the ruins	...as ruínas	ahsh roo-**ee**-nahsh
...an amusement park	...o parque de diversões	oo **par**-keh deh dee-vehr-**sowsh**
...the tourist information office	...a informação turistica	ah een-for-mah-**sow** too-**reesh**-tee-kah
...the toilet	...a casa de banho	ah **kah**-zah deh **bahn**-yoo
...the entrance / exit	...a entrada / saída	ah ayn-**trah**-dah / sah-**ee**-dah
Is there a festival nearby?	Há um festival aqui perto?	ah oon fehsh-tee-**vahl** ah-**kee pehr**-too

At the Sight

Do you have...?	Tem...?	tay**n**
...information...	...informações...	een-for-mah-**sowsh**

125

Key Phrases: Sightseeing

Where is...?	*Onde é...?*	**ohn**-deh eh
How much is it?	*Quanto custa?*	**kwahn**-too **koosh**-tah
What time does this open / close?	*A que horas é que abre / fecha?*	ah kee **oh**-rahsh eh keh **ah**-breh / **fay**-shah
Do you have a guided tour?	*Tem uma visita guiada?*	tayn **oo**-mah vee-**zee**-tah gee-**ah**-dah
When is the next tour in English?	*Quando é a próxima visita guiada em inglês?*	**kwahn**-doo eh ah **proh**-see-mah vee-**zee**-tah gee-**ah**-dah ayn een-**glaysh**

...a guidebook...	*...um guia...*	oon **gee**-ah
...in English	*...em inglês*	ayn een-**glaysh**
Is it free?	*É grátis?*	eh **grah**-teesh
How much is it?	*Quanto custa?*	**kwahn**-too **koosh**-tah
Is the ticket good all day?	*O bilhete é bom para o dia inteiro?*	oo beel-**yeh**-teh eh bohn **pah**-rah oo **dee**-ah een-**tay**-roo
Can I get back in?	*Posso reentrar?*	**pos**-soo reh-ayn-**trar**
What time does this open / close?	*A que horas é que abre / fecha?*	ah kee **oh**-rahsh eh keh **ah**-breh / **fay**-shah
What time is the last entry?	*A que horas é a última entrada?*	ah kee **oh**-rahsh eh ah **ool**-tee-mah ayn-**trah**-dah

Please

PLEASE let me in.	*POR FAVOR, deixe-me entrar.*	poor fah-**vor day**-sheh-meh ayn-**trar**
PLEASE let us in.	*POR FAVOR, deixe-nos entrar.*	poor fah-**vor day**-sheh-nooz ayn-**trar**
I've traveled all the way from ___.	*Estou a viajar de muito longe ___.*	ish-**toh** ah vee-ah-**zhar** deh **mween**-too **lohn**-zheh

ACTIVITIES

We've traveled all the way from ___.	Nós estamos a viajar de muito longe ___.	nohsh ish-**tah**-moosh ah vee-ah-**zhar** deh **mween**-too **lohn**-zheh
I must leave tomorrow.	Tenho que partir amanhã.	**tayn**-yoo keh par-**teer** ah-ming-**yah**
We must leave tomorrow.	Temos que partir amanhã.	**tay**-moosh keh par-**teer** ah-ming-**yah**
I promise I'll be fast.	Prometo que sou rápido[a].	proo-**may**-too keh soh **rah**-pee-doo
We promise we'll be fast.	Prometemos que seremos rápidos.	proo-meh-**teh**-moosh keh seh-**reh**-moosh **rah**-pee-doosh
It was my mother's dying wish that I see this.	Era o ultimo desejo da minha mãe, que eu visse isto.	**eh**-rah oo **ool**-tee-moo deh-**zeh**-zhoo dah **meen**-yah **mayn**-eh keh **eh**-oo **vee**-seh **eesh**-too
I've always wanted to see this.	Eu sempre quiz ver isto.	**eh**-oo **sehm**-preh keesh vehr **eesh**-too
We've always wanted to see this.	Nós sempre quizemos ver isto.	nohsh **sehm**-preh kee-**zeh**-moosh vehr **eesh**-too

Tours

Do you have...?	Tem...?	tay<u>n</u>
...an audioguide...	...um audio guia...	oo<u>n</u> **ow**-dee-oo **gee**-ah
...a guided tour...	...uma visita guiada...	**oo**-mah vee-**zee**-tah gee-**ah**-dah
...a city walking tour...	...passeio a pé pela cidade...	pah-**say**-oo ah peh **peh**-lah see-**dah**-deh
...in English	...em inglês	ay<u>n</u> een-**glaysh**
When is the next tour in English?	Quando é a próxima visita guiada em inglês?	**kwahn**-doo eh ah **proh**-see-mah vee-**zee**-tah gee-**ah**-dah ay<u>n</u> een-**glaysh**
Is it free?	É grátis?	eh **grah**-teesh
How much is it?	Quanto custa?	**kwahn**-too **koosh**-tah
How long does it last?	Quanto tempo leva?	**kwahn**-too **tayn**-poo **leh**-vah

| Can I join a tour in progress? | Posso juntar-me ao grupo em processo? | **pos**-soo zhoon-**tar**-meh ow **groo**-poo ay<u>n</u> proh-**say**-soo |
| Can we join a tour in progress? | Podemos juntar-nos ao grupo em processo? | poo-**day**-moosh zhoon-**tar**-nooz ow **groo**-poo ay<u>n</u> proh-**say**-soo |

On entrance signs, *adultos* is the price an adult pays, an *obra* is an exhibit, a *visita guiada* is a guided tour, and the words "*Você está aqui*" on a map mean "You are here."

Discounts

You may be eligible for discounts at tourist sites, hotels, or on buses and trains—ask.

Is there a discount for...?	Tem desconto para...?	tay<u>n</u> dish-**kohn**-too **pah**-rah
...youths	...jovens	**zhah**-vay<u>n</u>sh
...students	...estudantes	ish-too-**dahn**-tish
...families	...famílias	fah-**meel**-yahsh
...seniors	...idosos	id-**oh**-zoosh
...groups	...grupos	**groo**-poosh
I am...	Tenho...	**tayn**-yoo
He / She is...	Ele / Ela tem...	**eh**-leh / **eh**-lah tay<u>n</u>
... ___ years old.	... ___ anos.	___ **ah**-noosh
I am...	Sou...	soh
He / She is...	Ele / Ela é...	**eh**-leh / **eh**-lah eh
...extremely old.	...velhinho.	vehl-**yeen**-hoo

In the Museum

Where is...?	Onde é...?	**ohn**-deh eh
I'd like to see...	Gostaria de ver...	goosh-tah-**ree**-ah deh vehr
We'd like to see...	Gostaríamos de ver...	goosh-tah-**ree**-ah-moosh deh vehr
Photo / Video O.K?	Foto / Vídeo O.K.?	**foh**-too / **vee**-day-oo "O.K."
No flash / tripod.	Não flash / tripé.	now flahsh / tree-**peh**

I like it.	Eu gosto.	**eh**-oo **gohsh**-too
It's so...	É tão...	eh tow
...beautiful.	...lindo.	**leen**-doo
...ugly.	...feio.	**fay**-oo
...strange.	...estranho.	ish-**trahn**-yoo
...boring.	...aborrecido.	ah-boh-reh-**see**-doo
...interesting.	...interessante.	een-teh-reh-**sahn**-teh
...thought-provoking.	...provocante.	proh-voh-**kahn**-teh
...B.S.	...porcaria.	por-kah-**ree**-ah
I don't get it.	Não percebo.	now pehr-**seh**-boo
Is it upside down?	Está aõ contrario?	ish-**tah** ow kohn-**trah**-ree-oo
Who did this?	Quem fez isto?	kayn fehz **eesh**-too
How old is this?	Quantos anos tem isto?	**kwahn**-toosh **ah**-noosh tayn **eesh**-too
Wow!	Fiche!	**fee**-sheh
My feet hurt!	Os meus pés estão cansados!	oosh **meh**-oosh pehsh ish-**tow** kahn-**sah**-doosh
I'm exhausted!	Estou estoirado[a]!	ish-**toh** ish-toy-**rah**-doo
We're exhausted! (m / f)	Estamos estoirados[as]!	ish-**tah**-moosh ish-toy-**rah**-doosh

Art and Architecture

art	arte	**ar**-teh
artist	artista	ar-**teesh**-tah
painting	pintura	peeng-**too**-rah
self portrait	auto-retrato	ow-too-reh-**trah**-too
sculptor	escultor[a]	ish-kool-**tor**
sculpture	escultura	ish-kool-**too**-rah
architect	arquiteto	ar-kee-**teh**-too
architecture	arquitetura	ar-kee-teh-**too**-rah
original	original	oo-ree-zhee-**nahl**
restored	restaurado	rish-too-**rah**-doo
B.C.	A.C.	ah say
A.D.	D.C.	day say
century	secúlo	seh-**koo**-loo

style	*estilo*	ish-**tee**-loo
copy by ___	*copiado por ___*	koo-pee-**ah**-doo poor
after the style of ___	*como o estilo de ___*	**koh**-moo oo ish-**tee**-loo deh
from the school of ___	*da escola de ___*	dah ish-**koh**-lah deh
abstract	*abstrato*	ahb-**shtrah**-too
ancient	*antigo*	ahn-**tee**-goo
Art Nouveau	*arte nova*	**ar**-teh **noh**-vah
Baroque	*barroco*	bah-**roh**-koo
classical	*clássico*	**klah**-see-koo
Gothic	*gótico*	**got**-ee-koo
Impressionist	*impressio- nista*	eem-preh-see-oo-**neesh**-tah
medieval	*mediaval*	meh-dee-ah-**vahl**
Modern art	*arte moderna*	**ar**-teh moh-**dehr**-nah
Moorish	*mouro*	**moh**-roo
Renaissance	*renascimento*	reh-nahsh-see-**mayn**-too
Romanesque	*românico*	roo-**mah**-nee-koo
Romantic	*romântico*	roo-**mahn**-tee-koo
Manueline	*Manuelino*	mah-neh-weh-**lee**-noo

Portugal's golden age of trade and exploration gave birth to a lavish, flamboyant Gothic style called "Manueline," named after King Manuel of the early 16th century.

Castles and Palaces

castle	*castelo*	kahs-**teh**-loo
palace	*palácio*	pah-**lah**-see-oo
kitchen	*cozinha*	koh-**zeen**-yah
cellar	*celeiro*	seh-**lay**-roo
dungeon	*masmorra*	mahs-**moh**-rah
moat	*fosso*	**foh**-soo
fortified walls	*fortificação*	for-tee-fee-kah-**sow**
tower	*torre*	**tor**-reh
fountain	*fonte*	**fohn**-teh
garden	*jardim*	zhar-**deeng**

ACTIVITIES

king	*rei*	ray
queen	*raínha*	rah-**een**-yah
knight	*cavaleiro*	kah-vah-**lay**-roo

Religious Words

cathedral	*catedral*	kah-teh-**drahl**
church	*igreija*	ee-**gray**-zhah
monastery	*monestério*	moo-nish-**teh**-ree-oo
mosque	*mesquita*	mehsh-**kee**-tah
synagogue	*sinagoga*	see-nah-**goh**-gah
chapel	*capela*	kah-**peh**-lah
altar	*altar*	ahl-**tar**
bells	*sinos*	**see**-noosh
choir	*coral*	koo-**rahl**
cloister	*mosteiro*	moo-**shtay**-roo
cross	*cruz*	kroosh
crypt	*caixão*	kī-**show**
dome	*cúpula*	**koo**-poo-lah
organ	*orgão*	or-**gow**
pulpit	*púlpito*	**pool**-pee-too
relic	*rélica*	**reh**-lee-kah
treasury	*tesoraria*	teh-zoh-**rah**-ree-ah
saint	*santo[a]*	**sahn**-too
God	*Deus*	**deh**-oosh
Christian	*Cristão*	kreesh-**tow**
Protestant	*Protestante*	proh-tish-**tayn**-teh
Catholic	*Católico[a]*	kah-**tal**-ee-koo
Jewish	*Judeu*	**zhoo**-deh-oo
Muslim	*Muçulmano[a]*	moo-sool-**mah**-noo
agnostic	*agnóstico[a]*	ahg-**nash**-tee-koo
atheist	*ateu*	ah-**teh**-oo
When is the mass / service?	*Quando é a missa / serviço?*	**kwahn**-doo eh ah **mee**-sah / sehr-**vee**-soo
Are there concerts in the church?	*Dão concertos na igreija?*	dow kohn-**sehr**-toosh nah ee-**gray**-zhah

SHOPPING

Portuguese Shops

Where is a...?	Onde é um...?	**ohn**-deh eh oo<u>n</u>
antique shop	antiquário	ahn-tee-**kwah**-ree-oo
art gallery	galeria de arte	gah-leh-**ree**-ah deh **ar**-teh
bakery	padaria	pah-dah-**ree**-ah
barber shop	barbeiro	bar-**bay**-roo
beauty salon	cabelareiro	kah-beh-lah-**ray**-roo
book shop	livraria	leev-rah-**ree**-ah
camera shop	loja fotográfica	**lah**-zhah foh-toh-**grah**-fee-kah
cell phone shop	loja de telemóveis	**lah**-zhah deh teh-leh-**mow**-veh-eesh
clothing boutique	loja de roupa	**lah**-zhah deh **roh**-pah
coffee shop	café	kah-**feh**
delicatessen	charcutaria	shehr-koo-teh-**ree**-ah
department store	grande armazen	**grahn**-deh ar-mah-**zayn**
flea market	feira	**fay**-rah
flower market	mercado de flores	mehr-**kah**-doo deh **floh**-rish
grocery store	mercearia	mehr-see-ah-**ree**-ah
hardware store	casa de ferragens	**kah**-zah deh feh-rah-**zhayn**
Internet café	café Internet	kah-**feh een**-tehr-neht
jewelry shop	joalheria	zhoo-ahl-yeh-**ree**-ah
launderette	lavandaria	lah-vahn-dah-**ree**-ah
newsstand	quiosque	kee-**ahsh**-keh
office supplies	papelaria	pah-peh-lah-**ree**-ah
open air market	mercado municipal	mehr-**kah**-doo moo-nee-see-**pahl**
optician	oculista	ok-oo-**leesh**-tah
pastry shop	pastelaria	pahsh-teh-lah-**ree**-ah
pharmacy	farmácia	far-**mah**-see-ah
photocopy shop	casa de fotocopias	**kah**-zah deh foo-too-koh-**pee**-ahsh

ACTIVITIES

Key Phrases: Shopping

Where can I buy...?	*Onde compro...?*	**ohn**-deh **kohn**-proo
Where is a...?	*Onde é um...?*	**ohn**-deh eh oon
...grocery store	*...mercearia*	mehr-see-ah-**ree**-ah
...department store	*...grande armazen*	**grahn**-deh ar-mah-**zayn**
...Internet café	*...café Internet*	kah-**feh een**-tehr-neht
...launderette	*...lavandaria*	lah-vahn-dah-**ree**-ah
...pharmacy	*...farmácia*	far-**mah**-see-ah
How much is it?	*Quanto custa?*	**kwahn**-too **koosh**-tah
I'm just browsing.	*Estou só a olhar.*	ish-**toh** sah ah ohl-**yar**

shopping mall	*centro comercial*	**sayn**-troo koo-mehr-see-**ahl**
souvenir shop	*loja de lembranças*	**lah**-zhah deh layn-**brang**-sahsh
supermarket	*supermercado*	soo-pehr-mehr-**kah**-doo
sweets shop	*confeitaria*	kohn-fay-tah-**ree**-ah
toy store	*loja de brinquedos*	**lah**-zhah deh breeng-**kay**-doosh
travel agency	*agência de viagens*	ah-**zhayn**-see-ah deh vee-**ah**-zhaynsh
used bookstore	*loja de livros usados*	**lah**-zhah deh **leev**-rooz oo-**zah**-doosh
...with books in English	*...com livros em ingles*	kohn **leev**-rooz ayn een-**glaysh**
wine shop	*loja de vinhos*	**lah**-zhah deh **veen**-yoosh

In Portugal, most shops close for lunch from about 13:00 until 15:00, and all day on Sundays.

Shop Till You Drop

opening hours	*horário*	oh-**rah**-ree-oo
sale	*saldo*	**sahl**-doo
Where can I buy...?	*Onde compro...?*	**ohn**-deh **kohn**-proo

English	Portuguese	Pronunciation
Where can we buy...?	Onde compramos...?	**ohn**-deh kohn-**prah**-moosh
How much is it?	Quanto custa?	**kwahn**-too **koosh**-tah
I'm / We're just browsing.	Estou / Estamos só a olhar.	ish-**toh** / ish-**tah**-moosh soh ah ohl-**yar**
I'd like...	Gostaria...	goosh-tah-**ree**-ah
Do you have...?	Tem...?	tayn
...more	...mais	mīsh
...something cheaper	...alguma coisa mais barato	ahl-**goo**-mah **koy**-zah mīsh bah-**rah**-too
Better quality, please.	Melhor qualidade, por favor.	mil-**yor** kwah-lee-**dah**-deh poor fah-**vor**
genuine / imitation	genuino / imitação	zheh-noo-**ee**-noo / eem-mee-tah-**sow**
Can I / Can we see more?	Posso / Podemos ver mais?	**pos**-soo / poo-**day**-moosh vehr mīsh
This one.	Este aqui.	**ehsh**-teh ah-**kee**
Can I try it on?	Posso exprimentar?	**pos**-soo ish-pree-mayn-**tar**
Do you have a mirror?	Tem um espelho?	tayn oon ish-**payl**-yoo
Too...	Muito...	**mween**-too
...big.	...grande.	**grahn**-deh
...small.	...pequeno.	peh-**kay**-noo
...expensive.	...caro.	**kah**-roo
It's too...	É muito...	eh **mween**-too
...short / long.	...curto / longo.	**koor**-too / **lon**-goo
...tight / loose.	...apertado / largo.	ah-pehr-**tah**-doo / **lar**-goo
...dark / light.	...escuro / claro.	ehsh-**koo**-roo / **klah**-roo
What is this made of?	Isto é feito de quê?	**eesh**-too eh **fay**-too deh kay
Is it machine washable?	Posso lavar á máquina?	**pos**-soo lah-**var** ah **mah**-kee-nah
Will it shrink?	Vai encolher?	vī ayn-kohl-**yehr**
Will it fade in the wash?	A côr sai na lavagem?	ah kor sī nah lah-**vah**-zhayn

Credit card O.K.?	Cartão de crédito O.K.?	kar-**tow** deh **kreh**-dee-too "O.K."
Can you ship this?	Pode enviar isto?	**pod**-eh ayn-vee-**ar** **eesh**-too
Tax-free?	Livre de impostos?	**lee**-vreh deh eem-**pohsh**-toosh
I'll think about it.	Vou pensar.	voh payn-**sar**
What time do you close?	A que horas é que fecha?	ah kee **oh**-rahsh eh keh **fay**-shah
What time do you open tomorrow?	A que horas é que abre amanhã?	ah kee **oh**-rahsh eh keh **ah**-breh ah-ming-**yah**

Street Markets

Did you make this?	Foi você que fez isto?	foy voh-**say** keh fehz **eesh**-too
Is that your best price?	É o seu melhor preço?	eh oo **seh**-oo mil-**yor** **pray**-soo
Cheaper?	Mais barato?	mīsh bah-**rah**-too
My last offer.	A minha última oferta.	ah **meen**-yah **ool**-tee-mah oo-**fehr**-tah
Good price.	Bom preço.	bohn **pray**-soo
I'll take it.	Eu levo.	**eh**-oo **leh**-voo
We'll take it.	Nós levamos.	nohsh leh-**vah**-moosh
I'm nearly broke.	Estou quase sem dinheiro.	ish-**toh kwah**-zeh sayn deen-**yay**-roo
We're nearly broke.	Estamos quase sem dinheiro.	ish-**tah**-moosh **kwah**-zeh sayn deen-**yay**-roo
My male friend...	O meu amigo...	oo **meh**-oo ah-**mee**-goo
My female friend...	A minha amiga...	ah **meen**-yah ah-**mee**-gah
My husband...	O meu marido...	oo **meh**-oo mah-**ree**-doo
My wife...	A minha mulher...	ah **meen**-yah mool-**yehr**
...has the money.	...tem o dinheiro.	tayn oo deen-**yay**-roo

At street markets, it's common to bargain.

Clothes

For...	Para...	pah-rah
...a male / female baby.	...um menino / uma menina bebé.	oon meh-**nee**-noo / **oo**-mah meh-**nee**-nah bay-**bay**
...a child (m / f)	...um menino / uma menina.	oon meh-**nee**-noo / **oo**-mah meh-**nee**-nah
...a teenager (m / f)	...um rapaz / uma rapariga.	oon rah-**pahsh** / **oo**-mah rah-pah-**ree**-gah
...a man.	...um homem.	oon **oh**-mayn
...a woman.	...uma senhora.	**oo**-mah sehn-**yoh**-rah
bathrobe	robe	**roh**-beh
bib	babete	bah-**beh**-teh
belt	cinto	**seen**-too
bra	soutien	**soo**-tee-ayn
clothing	roupas	**roh**-pahsh
dress	vestido	vehsh-**tee**-doo
flip-flops	sandálias de dedo	sahn-**dah**-lee-ahsh deh **deh**-doo
gloves	luvas	**loo**-vahsh
hat	chapéu	chah-**pow**
jacket	casaco	kah-**zah**-koo
jeans	ganga	**gahn**-gah
nightgown	camisa de dormir	kah-**mee**-zah deh dor-**meer**
nylons	meia de vidro, collants	**may**-ah deh **veed**-roo, koh-**lahnts**
pajamas	pijamas	pee-**zhah**-mahsh
pants	calças	**kahl**-sahsh
raincoat	capa de chuva	**kah**-pah deh **shoo**-vah
sandals	sandálias	sahn-**dah**-lee-ahsh
scarf	lenço	**lehn**-soo
shirt...	camisa...	kah-**mee**-zah
...long-sleeved	...manga-longa	mayn-gah-**lohn**-gah
...short-sleeved	...manga-curta	mayn-gah-**koor**-tah
...sleeveless	...sem mangas	sayn **mayn**-gahsh

ACTIVITIES

shoelaces	cordão de sapatos	kor-**dow** deh sah-**pah**-toosh
shoes	sapatos	sah-**pah**-toosh
shorts	calções	kahl-**sowsh**
skirt	saia	**sah**-ee-ah
sleeper (for baby)	pijama	pee-**zhah**-mah
slip	combinação	koh<u>n</u>-bee-nah-**sow**
slippers	chinélos	shee-**neh**-loosh
socks	meias	**meh**-ee-ahs
sweater	camisolas	kah-**mee**-zoh-lahsh
swimsuit	fato de banho	**fah**-too deh **bahn**-yoo
tennis shoes	tenis	**teh**-nees
T-shirt	T-shirt	"T-shirt"
underwear	roupas de interior	**roh**-pahsh deh in-teh-ree-**oor**
vest	colete	koh-**leh**-teh

Colors

black	prêto	**pray**-too
blue	azul	**ah**-zool
brown	castanho	kah-**shtayn**-yoo
gray	cinzento	seen-**zehn**-too
green	verde	**vehr**-deh
orange	laranja	lah-**rayn**-zhah
pink	rosa	**roh**-zah
purple	roxo	**roh**-shoh
red	vermelho, encarnado	vehr-**mehl**-yoo, ehn-kar-**nah**-doo
white	branco	**brang**-koo
yellow	amarelo	ah-mah-**reh**-loo
dark / light	escuro / claro	ehsh-**koo**-roo / **klah**-roo
Lighter...	Mais claro...	mīsh **klah**-roo
Brighter...	Mais brilhante...	mīsh breel-**yahn**-teh
Darker...	Mais escuro...	mīsh ehsh-**koo**-roo
...shade.	...tonalidade.	toh-nah-lee-**dah**-deh

Materials

brass	*latão*	lah-**tow**
bronze	*bronze*	**brohn**-zeh
ceramic	*ceramica*	seh-**rah**-mee-kah
copper	*cobre*	**koh**-breh
cotton	*algodão*	ahl-goh-**dow**
glass	*vidro*	**veed**-roo
gold	*ouro*	**oh**-roo
lace	*renda*	**rehn**-dah
leather	*pele*	**peh**-leh
linen	*linho*	**leen**-yoh
marble	*mármore*	**mar**-mor-eh
metal	*metal*	meh-**tahl**
nylon	*nylon*	**ni**-lohn
paper	*papel*	pah-**pehl**
pewter	*estanho*	ehsh-**tahn**-yoo
plastic	*plástico*	**plahsh**-tee-koo
polyester	*poliester*	poh-lee-**ehsh**-tehr
porcelain	*porcelana*	por-seh-**lah**-nah
silk	*seda*	**seh**-dah
silver	*prata*	**prah**-tah
velvet	*veludo*	veh-**loo**-doo
wood	*madeira*	mah-**day**-rah
wool	*lã*	lahn

Jewelry

bracelet	*bracelete*	brah-seh-**leh**-teh
brooch	*broche*	**broh**-sheh
earrings	*brincos*	**breen**-koosh
jewelry	*jóias*	**zhoh**-ee-ahsh
necklace	*côlar*	**koh**-lar
ring	*anel*	**ah**-nehl
Is this...?	*Isto é...?*	**eesh**-too eh
...sterling silver	*...de prata*	deh **prah**-tah
...real gold	*...de ouro*	deh **oh**-roo
...stolen	*...roubado*	roh-**bah**-doo

ACTIVITIES

SPORTS

Bicycling

bicycle	*bicicleta*	bee-see-**kleh**-tah
mountain bike	*bicicleta de montanha*	bee-see-**kleh**-tah deh mohn-**tahn**-yah
I'd like to rent a bicycle.	*Gostaria de alugar uma bicicleta.*	goosh-tah-**ree**-ah deh ah-loo-**gar oo**-mah bee-see-**kleh**-tah
We'd like to rent two bicycles.	*Gostaríamos de alugar duas bicicletas.*	goosh-tah-**ree**-ah-moosh deh ah-loo-**gar doo**-ahsh bee-see-**kleh**-tahsh
How much per...?	*Quanto é por...?*	**kwahn**-too eh poor
...hour	*...hora*	**oh**-rah
...half day	*...meio-dia*	may-oo-**dee**-ah
...day	*...dia*	**dee**-ah
Is a deposit required?	*É preciso depósito impresindível?*	eh preh-**see**-zoo deh-**poh**-zee-too eem-preh-seen-**dee**-vehl
deposit	*depósito*	deh-**poh**-zee-too
helmet	*capacete*	kah-pah-**seh**-teh
lock	*aluquete*	ah-loo-**keh**-teh
air / no air	*ar / não há ar*	ar / no<u>w</u> ah ar
tire	*pneu*	**pehn**-yoo
pump	*bomba*	**bohm**-bah
map	*mapa*	**mah**-pah
How many gears?	*Quantas mudanças?*	**kwahn**-tahsh **moo**-dahn-sahsh
What is a...	*O que é uma...*	oo keh eh **oo**-mah...
route of about ___ kilometers?	*rota de cerca de ___ kilómetros?*	**roo**-tah deh **sehr**-kah deh ___ kee-**loo**-meh-troosh
...good	*...bom*	boh<u>n</u>
...scenic	*...bonita*	boh-**nee**-tah
...interesting	*...interessante*	een-teh-reh-**sahn**-teh
...easy	*...fácil*	**fah**-seel

English	Portuguese	Pronunciation
How many minutes / hours by bicycle?	Quantos minutos / horas de bicicleta?	**kwahn**-toosh mee-**noo**-toosh / **oh**-rahsh deh bee-see-**kleh**-tah
I (don't) like hills.	Eu (não) gosto de subídas.	**eh**-oo (now) **gohsh**-too deh soo-**bee**-dahsh
I brake for bakeries.	Paro em todas as padarias.	**pah**-roo ayn **toh**-dahsh ahsh pah-dah-**ree**-ahsh

For more on route-finding, see page 46 in the Traveling chapter.

Swimming and Boating

English	Portuguese	Pronunciation
Where can I / can we rent a...?	Onde posso / podemos alugar um...?	**ohn**-deh **pos**-soo / poh-**day**-moosh ah-loo-**gar** oon
...paddleboat	...gaivota	gī-**voh**-tah
...rowboat	...barco a rêmo	**bar**-koo ah **ray**-moo
...boat	...barco	**bar**-koo
...sailboat	...veleiro	veh-**lay**-roo
How much per...?	Quanto é por...?	**kwahn**-too eh poor
...hour	...hora	**oh**-rah
...half day	...meio-dia	may-oo-**dee**-ah
...day	...dia	**dee**-ah
beach	praia	**pri**-ah
nude beach	praia de nudismo	**pri**-ah deh noo-**deezh**-moo
Where's a good beach?	Onde fica uma boa praia?	**ohn**-deh **fee**-kah **oo**-mah **boh**-ah **pri**-ah
Is it safe for swimming?	É seguro nadar?	eh seh-**goo**-roo nah-**dar**
flip-flops	sandálias	sahn-**dah**-lee-ahsh
pool	piscina	pee-**shee**-nah
snorkel and mask	tubo e máscara para mergulho	**too**-boo ee **mahsh**-kah-rah **pah**-rah mehr-**gool**-yoo
sunglasses	óculos de sol	**oh**-koo-loosh deh sool
sunscreen	crème proteção solar	**kreh**-meh proh-teh-**sow** soh-**lar**
surfboard	prancha	**prayn**-shah

surfer	surfista	**soor**-fee-shtah
swimsuit	fato de banho	**fah**-too deh **bahn**-yoo
towel	toalha	too-**ahl**-yah
waterskiing	esqui aquático	ish-**kee** ah-**kwah**-tee-koo
windsurfing	windsurfing	"windsurfing"

In Portugal, nearly any beach is topless. For a nude beach, keep your eyes peeled for a *praia de nudismo*.

Sports Talk

sports	desporto	dish-**por**-too
game	jogo	**zhoh**-goo
team	equipe	eh-**kee**-peh
championship	campeonato	kahm-peh-oo-**nah**-too
soccer	futebol	foo-teh-**bohl**
basketball	basquetebol	bash-keht-**bohl**
hockey	hóquei	**oh**-kay
American football	futebol	foo-teh-**bohl**
	americano	ah-meh-ree-**kah**-noo
baseball	basebol	bayz-**bohl**
tennis	ténis	**teh**-neesh
golf	golfe	"golf"
skiing	esquiar	ish-kee-**ar**
gymnastics	ginastica	zheen-**ahsh**-tee-kah
jogging	correr	koh-**rehr**
Olympics	Olímpicos	oh-**leem**-pee-koosh
medal...	medalha...	meh-**dahl**-yah
...gold / silver / bronze	...de ouro / de prata / de bronze	deh **oh**-roo / deh **prah**-tah / deh **brohn**-zeh
What is your favorite sport / athlete / team?	Qual é o seu desporto / atleta / equipe favorito?	kwahl eh oo **seh**-oo dish-**por**-too / aht-**leh**-tah / eh-**kee**-peh fah-voh-**ree**-too
Where can I see a game?	Onde posso ver um jogo?	**ohn**-deh **pos**-soo vehr oon **zhoh**-goo
Where's a good place to jog?	A onde há um bom sitio para correr?	ah **ohn**-deh ah oon bohn **see**-tee-oo **pah**-rah koh-**rer**

ENTERTAINMENT

What's happening tonight?	O que se passa esta noite?	oo keh seh **pah**-sah **ehsh**-tah **noy**-teh
What do you recommend?	O que é que recomenda?	oo keh eh keh ray-koo-**mayn**-dah
Where is it?	Onde é?	**ohn**-deh eh
How do I / do we get there?	Como chego / chegamos lá?	**koh**-moo **shay**-goo / shay-**gah**-moosh lah
Is it free?	É gratis?	eh **grah**-teesh
Are there seats available?	Há mais assentos?	ah mīz ah-**sehn**-toosh
Where can I buy a ticket?	Onde posso comprar um bilhete?	**ohn**-deh **pos**-soo kohn-**prar** oon beel-**yeh**-teh
Do you have tickets for today / tonight?	Há bilhetes para hoje / hoje a noite?	ah beel-**yeh**-tish **pah**-rah **oh**-zheh / **oh**-zheh ah **noy**-teh
When does it start?	Quando começa?	**kwahn**-doo koh-**meh**-sah
When does it end?	Quando termina?	**kwahn**-doo tehr-**mee**-nah
Where's the best place to dance nearby?	Onde é o melhor lugar para dançar por aqui?	**ohn**-deh eh oo mil-**yor** loo-**gar pah**-rah dah<u>n</u>-**sar** poor ah-**kee**
Where do people stroll?	Onde se pode passear?	**ohn**-deh seh **pod**-eh pah-seh-**ar**

Fado is Portugal's mournful style of folk singing. An evening absorbed in these fishermen's "blues" can leave you with sorrow creases. A good show is powerful stuff.

Entertaining Words

movie...	filme...	**feel**-meh
...original version	...versão original	vehr-**sow** oo-ree-zhee-**nahl**
...in English	...em inglês	ayn een-**glaysh**
...with subtitles	...com legendas	koh<u>n</u> leh-**zhayn**-dahsh
...dubbed	...dobrado	doo-**brah**-doo

ACTIVITIES

music...	*música...*	**moo**-zee-kah
...live	*...ao vivo*	ow **vee**-voo
...classical	*...clássico*	**klah**-see-koo
...folk	*...folclore*	fool-**klah**-reh
...opera	*...ópera*	**oh**-peh-rah
...symphony	*...simfonia*	seeng-foh-**nee**-ah
...choir	*...coral*	koo-**rahl**
rock / jazz / blues	*rock / jazz / blues*	"rock" / zhahz / bloosh
singer	*cantor[a]*	kahn-**tor**
concert	*concerto*	koh<u>n</u>-**sehr**-too
show	*espetáculo*	ish-peh-**tah**-koo-loo
(folk) dancing	*dança (folclórica)*	**dah<u>n</u>**-sah (fool-**klah**-ree-kah)
cockfight	*briga de galo*	**bree**-gah deh **gah**-loo
disco	*disco*	**deesh**-koo
bar with live music	*bar com música ao vivo*	bar koh<u>n</u> **moo**-zee-kah ow **vee**-voo
nightclub	*nightclub, bar*	"nightclub," bar
(no) cover charge	*(não) entrada*	(no<u>w</u>) ay<u>n</u>-**trah**-dah
sold out	*vendido*	vehn-**dee**-doo

CONNECT

PHONING

English	Portuguese	Pronunciation
I'd like to buy a...	Quero compar um...	**kay**-roo kohn-**prar** oon
...telephone card.	...cartão telefónico.	kar-**tow** teh-leh-**foh**-nee-koo
...cheap international telephone card.	...cartão telefónico económico para chamadas internacionais.	kar-**tow** teh-leh-**foh**-nee-koo eh-koo-**noh**-mee-koo **pah**-rah shah-**mah**-dahsh een-tehr-nah-see-oh-**nīsh**
Where is the nearest phone?	Onde é o próximo telefone?	**ohn**-deh eh oo **proh**-see-moo teh-leh-**foh**-neh
It doesn't work.	Não funciona.	now foon-see-**oh**-nah
May I use your phone?	Posso utilizar o seu telefone?	**pos**-soo oo-tee-lee-**zar** oo **seh**-oo teh-leh-**foh**-neh
Can you talk for me?	Pode falar por mim?	**pod**-eh fah-**lar** poor meeng
It's busy.	Está ocupado.	ish-**tah** oo-koo-**pah**-doo
Will you try again?	Pode tentar novamente?	**pod**-eh tayn-**tar** noo-vah-**mayn**-teh
Hello. (answering the phone)	Está.	ish-**tah**
My name is ___.	Chamo-me ___.	**shah**-moo-meh
Sorry, I speak only a little Portuguese.	Desculpe, eu so falo um pouquinho português.	dish-**kool**-peh **eh**-oo soh **fah**-loo oon poh-**keen**-yoo poor-too-**gaysh**
Speak slowly and clearly.	Fale devagar e claramente.	**fah**-leh deh-vah-**gar** eh klah-rah-**mayn**-teh

144

Wait a moment.	*Espere um momento.*	ehsh-**peh**-reh oo<u>n</u> moo-**mayn**-too

In this book, you'll find the phrases you need to reserve a hotel room (page 50) or a table at a restaurant (page 67). To spell your name over the phone, use the code alphabet on page 52.

Make your calls using a handy phone card. These are sold at post offices, train stations, *quiosques* (newsstands), *tabacarias* (tobacco shops), and machines near phone booths. There are two kinds of phone cards:

1) an insertable card (*cartão telefónico*) that you slide into a phone in a phone booth, and...

2) a cheaper-per-minute international phone card (with a scratch-off PIN code) that you can use from any phone, usually even from your hotel room. To get a PIN card, ask for a *cartão telefónico económico para chamadas internacionais.*

At phone booths, you'll encounter these words on the phone: *introduzir o cartão* (insert the card), *marque o numero* (dial your number), and *importancia restante* (the amount of money left on your card). At any time while you're dialing, you may hear a brusque recording: "*Esse numero não existe*" (The number you're dialing does not work). You can also make phone calls from easy-to-use metered phones in post offices, telephone offices. For more tips, see "Let's Talk Telephones" on page 255 in the appendix.

Telephone Words

telephone	*telefone*	teh-leh-**foh**-neh
telephone card	*cartão telefónico*	kar-**tow** teh-leh-**foh**-nee-koo
cheap telephone card with a	*cartão telefónico económico*	kar-**tow** teh-leh-**foh**-nee-koo eh-koo-**noh**-mee-koo
PIN code	*para chamadas internacionais*	**pah**-rah shah-**mah**-dahsh een-tehr-nah-see-oh-**nīsh**
PIN code	*código pessoal*	**koh**-dee-goo peh-soh-**ahl**
phone booth	*telefone publico*	teh-leh-**foh**-neh **poob**-lee-koo
out of service	*desligado*	dish-lee-**gah**-doo

metered phone	telefone com contador	teh-leh-**foh**-neh koh<u>n</u> koh<u>n</u>-tah-**dor**
post office	correios	koo-**ray**-oosh
phone office	puesto telefónico	**pway**-shtoo teh-leh-**foh**-nee-koo
operator	telefonista	teh-leh-foh-**neesh**-tah
international assistance	assistência internacional	ah-seesh-**tayn**-see-ah een-tehr-nah-see-oo-**nahl**
international call	chamada internacional	shah-**mah**-dah een-tehr-nah-see-oo-**nahl**
collect call	chamada para pagar	shah-**mah**-dah **pah**-rah pah-**gar**
credit card call	chamada com cartão de crédito	shah-**mah**-dah koh<u>n</u> kar-**tow** deh **kreh**-dee-too
toll-free call	chamada taxa grátis	shah-**mah**-dah **tah**-shah **grah**-teesh
fax	fax	fahks
country code	código do país	**kod**-ee-goo doo pah-**eesh**
area code	código da área	**kod**-ee-goo dah **ah**-ray-ah
extension	extenção	ish-tehn-**sow**
telephone book	lista telefónica	**leesh**-tah teh-leh-**foh**-nee-kah
yellow pages	páginas amarelas	**pah**-zhee-nahsh ah-mah-**reh**-lahsh

Cell Phones

Where is a cell phone shop?	Onde é a loja que vende telemoveis?	**ohn**-deh eh ah **lah**-zhah keh **vehn**-deh teh-leh-**moh**-veh-ish
I'd like / We'd like...	Queria / Queríamos...	keh-**ree**-ah / keh-**ree**-ah-moosh
...a cell phone.	...um telemóvel.	oo<u>n</u> teh-leh-**moh**-vehl
...a chip.	...um cartão.	oo<u>n</u> kar-**tow**
...to buy more time.	...carregar o cartão.	kah-reh-**gar** oo kar-**tow**
How do you...?	Como se...?	**koh**-moo seh
...make calls	...faz uma chamada	fahz **oo**-mah shah-**mah**-dah

CONNECT

...receive calls	...receber chamadas	reh-seh-**behr** shah-**mah**-dahsh
Will this work outside this country?	*Posso usar fôra do país?*	**pos**-soo oo-**zar** **foh**-rah doo pah-**eesh**
Where can I buy a chip for this service / phone?	*Onde posso comprar um cartão para este serviço / telefone?*	**ohn**-deh **pos**-soo kohn-**prar** oon kar-**tow** **pah**-rah **ehsh**-teh sehr-**vee**-soo / teh-leh-**foh**-neh

Many travelers now buy cell phones in Europe to make both local and international calls. You'll pay under €100 for a "locked" phone that works only in the country you buy it in (includes about €20 worth of calls). You can buy additional time at a newsstand or cell phone shop. An "unlocked" phone is more expensive, but it works all over Europe: when you cross a border, buy a SIM card at a cell phone shop and insert the pop-out chip, which comes with a new phone number. Pricier tri-band phones (*telefone de linha tripula*) also work in North America.

EMAIL AND THE WEB

Email

My email address is ___.	*Meu endereço eletrônico é ___.*	**meh**-oo ayn-deh-**ray**-soo eh-leh-**troh**-nee-koo eh
What's your email address?	*Qual é o seu endereço eletrônico?*	kwahl eh oo **seh**-oo ayn-deh-**ray**-soo eh-leh-**troh**-nee-koo
Can I use this computer to check my email?	*Posso usar este computador para verificar o meu email?*	**pos**-soo oo-**zar ehsh**-teh kohm-poo-tah-**dor pah**-rah veh-ree-fee-**kar** oo **meh**-oo ee-mayl
Where can I / can we access the Internet?	*Onde posso / podemos usar a Internet?*	**ohn**-deh **pos**-soo / poh-**day**-mooz oo-**zar** ah **een**-tehr-neht

Where is an Internet café?	A onde é o café Internet?	ah **ohn**-deh eh oo kah-**feh een**-tehr-neht
How much for... minutes?	Quanto é por... minutos?	**kwahn**-too eh poor mee-**noo**-toosh
...10	...dez	dehsh
...15	...quinze	**keen**-zeh
...30	...trinta	**treen**-tah
...60	...sessenta	seh-**sayn**-tah
Help me, please.	Por favor ajude-me.	poor **fah**-vor ah-**zhoo**-deh-meh
How do I...?	Como...?	**koh**-moo
...start this	...ligo	**lee**-goo
...send a file	...mando uma página	**mahn**-doo **oo**-mah **pah**-zhee-nah
...print out a file	...emprimo uma página	ayn-**pree**-moo **oo**-mah **pah**-zhee-nah
...make this symbol	...faço este símbolo	**fah**-soo **ehsh**-teh **seeng**-boh-loo
...type @	...escrevo arrôba	ish-**kreh**-voo ah-**roh**-bah
This isn't working.	Isto está avariado.	**eesh**-too ish-**tah** ah-vah-ree-**ah**-doo

Web Words

email	email	ee-mayl
email address	endereço eletrônico	ayn-deh-**ray**-soo eh-leh-**troh**-nee-koo
website	local da Web	loh-**kahl** dah wehb
Internet	Internet	**een**-tehr-neht
surf the Web	navegar a Web	nah-veh-**gar** ah wehb
download	transferência	traynsh-feh-**rayn**-see-ah
@ sign	arrôba	ah-**roh**-bah
dot	ponto	**pohn**-too
hyphen (-)	hífen	**hee**-fehn
underscore (_)	sublinhar	soob-leen-**yar**
Wi-Fi	Wi-Fi	**wee**-fee

CONNECT

Key Phrases: Email and the Web

email	*email*	**ee**-mayl
Internet	*Internet*	**een**-tehr-neht
Where is the	*A onde é o*	ah **ohn**-deh eh oo
nearest	*próximo*	**proh**-see-moo
Internet café?	*café Internet?*	kah-**feh een**-tehr-neht
I'd like to check	*Gostaria ver*	goosh-tah-**ree**-ah vehr
my email.	*o meu email.*	oo **meh**-oo **ee**-mayl

On Screen

abrir	open		guardar	save
eliminar	delete		imprimir	print
enviar	send		escrever	write
escrever	write		mensagem	message
ficheiro	file		voltar	reply

MAILING

Where is the post office?	*Onde é os correios?*	**ohn**-deh eh oosh koo-**ray**-oosh
Which window for...?	*Que janela para...?*	keh zhah-**neh**-lah **pah**-rah
Is this the line for...?	*Esta é a fila para...?*	**ehsh**-tah eh ah **fee**-lah **pah**-rah
...stamps	*...selos*	**say**-loosh
...packages	*...embrulhos*	ayn-**brool**-yoosh
To the United States...	*Para os Estados Unidos...*	**pah**-rah ooz ish-**tah**-doosh oo-**nee**-doosh
...by air mail.	*...por avião.*	poor ahv-**yow**
...by surface mail.	*...de barco.*	deh **bar**-koo
...slow and cheap.	*...sem pressa e barato.*	say<u>n</u> **preh**-sah eh bah-**rah**-too

How much is it?	Quanto custa?	**kwahn**-too **koosh**-tah
How much to send a letter / postcard to...?	Quanto custa para mundar uma carta / um cartão postal para...?	**kwahn**-too **koosh**-tah **pah**-rah moon-**dar** **oo**-mah **kar**-tah / oo<u>n</u> kar-**tow** poosh-**tahl** **pah**-rah
I need stamps for ___ postcards to...	Preciso de selos para ___ cartões postais para...	preh-**see**-zoo deh **say**-loosh **pah**-rah ___ kar-**towsh** poosh-**tish pah**-rah
...America	...América	ah-**meh**-ree-kah
...Canada	...Canadá	kah-nah-**dah**
Pretty stamps, please.	Selos bonitos, por favor.	**say**-loosh boh-**nee**-toosh, poor fah-**vor**
I always choose the slowest line.	Eu sempre escolho a bicha mais lenta.	**eh**-oo **sehm**-preh ehsh-**kohl**-yoh ah **bee**-shah mīsh **lehn**-tah
How many days will it take?	Quantos dias é que demora?	**kwahn**-toosh **dee**-ahs eh keh deh-**moh**-rah

Handy Postal Words

post office	correios	koo-**ray**-oosh
stamp	selo	**say**-loo
postcard	cartão postal	kar-**tow** poosh-**tahl**
letter	carta	**kar**-tah
envelope	envelope	ay<u>n</u>-veh-**loh**-peh
package	embrulho	ay<u>n</u>-**brool**-yoo
box...	caixa...	**kī**-shah
...cardboard	...cartolina	kar-toh-**lee**-nah
string	fio	**fee**-oo
tape	adesivo	ah-deh-**zee**-voo
mailbox	caixa postal	**kī**-shah poosh-**tahl**
air mail	por avião	poor ahv-**yow**
express	expresso	ish-**preh**-soo
surface mail	de barco	deh **bar**-koo
slow and cheap	sem pressa e barato	say<u>n</u> **preh**-sah eh bah-**rah**-too

CONNECT

book rate	o livro da	oo **leev**-roo dah
	tabela de	tah-**beh**-lah deh
	preços	**preh**-soosh
weight limit	limite de peso	lee-**mee**-teh deh **pay**-zoo
registered	registrado	ray-zheesh-**trah**-doo
insured	seguro	say-**goo**-roo
fragile	frágil	**frah**-zheel
contents	conteúdo	koh<u>n</u>-teh-**oo**-doo
customs	alfândega	ahl-**fahn**-deh-gah
sender	remetente	reh-meh-**tayn**-teh
destination	destino	dish-**tee**-noo
to / from	para / de	**pah**-rah / deh
address	endereço	ay<u>n</u>-deh-**ray**-soo
zip code	código postal	**kod**-ee-goo poosh-**tahl**
general delivery	Despacho Geral	dehsh-**pah**-shoo zheh-**rahl**

In Portugal, you can often get stamps at a *quiosque* (newsstand) or *tabacaria* (tobacco shop). As long as you know which stamps you need, this is a great convenience.

HELP!

Help!	Socorro!	soo-**koh**-roo
Help me!	Ajude-me!	ah-**zhoo**-deh-meh
Call a doctor!	Chame um doutor!	**shah**-meh oon doh-**tor**
Call...	Chame...	**shah**-meh
...the police.	...a polícia.	ah poo-**lee**-see-ah
...an ambulance.	...a ambulância.	ah ayn-boo-**lahn**-see-ah
...the fire department.	...os bombeiros.	oosh bohn-**bay**-roosh
I'm lost.	Estou perdido[a].	ish-**toh** pehr-**dee**-doo
We're lost.	Estamos perdidos[as].	ish-**tah**-moosh pehr-**dee**-doosh
Thank you for your help.	Obrigado[a] por a sua ajuda.	oh-bree-**gah**-doo poor ah **soo**-ah ah-**zhoo**-dah
You are very kind.	Você é muito gentil.	voh-**say** eh **mween**-too zhayn-**teel**

Theft and Loss

Stop, thief!	Pare, ladrão!	**pah**-reh lah-**drow**
I have been robbed.	Fui roubado[a].	fwee roh-**bah**-doo
We have been robbed.	Fomos roubados[as].	**foh**-moosh roh-**bah**-doosh
A thief took...	Um ladrão levou...	oon lah-**drow** leh-**voh**
Thieves took...	Ladrões levaram...	lah-**drowsh** leh-**vah**-rayn
I've lost my...	Perdi o meu...	**pehr**-dee oo **meh**-oo
...money.	...dinheiro.	deen-**yay**-roo

Key Phrases: Help!

accident	*acidente*	ah-see-**dayn**-teh
emergency	*emergência*	ee-mehr-**zhayn**-see-ah
police	*polícia*	poo-**lee**-see-ah
Help!	*Socorro!*	soo-**koh**-roo
Call a doctor /	*Chame um doutor /*	**shah**-meh oon doh-**tor** /
the police!	*a policia!*	ah poo-**lee**-see-ah
Stop, thief!	*Pare, ladrão!*	**pah**-reh lah-**drow**

...passport.	*...passaporte.*	pah-sah-**por**-teh
...ticket.	*...bilhete.*	beel-**yeh**-teh
...baggage.	*...bagagem.*	bah-**gah**-zhayn
I've lost my...	*Perdi a minha...*	**pehr**-dee ah **meen**-yah
...purse.	*...bolsa.*	**bohl**-sah
...wallet.	*...carteira.*	kar-**tay**-rah
...faith in	*...fé na*	feh nah
humankind.	*humanidade.*	oo-mah-nee-**dah**-deh
We've lost...	*Perdemos...*	pehr-**deh**-moosh
...our money.	*...o nosso dinheiro.*	oo **noh**-soo deen-**yay**-roo
...our passports.	*...nossos*	**noh**-soosh
	passaportes.	pah-sah-**por**-tish
...our tickets.	*...nossos bilhetes.*	**noh**-soosh beel-**yeh**-tish
...our baggage.	*...nossa bagagem.*	**noh**-sah bah-**gah**-zhayn
I want to contact	*Quero contactar*	**kay**-roo kohn-tahk-**tar**
my embassy.	*a minha*	ah **meen**-yah
	embaixada.	ayn-bī-**shah**-dah
I need to file	*Quero fazer uma*	**kay**-roo fah-**zehr oo**-mah
a police report	*ocorrência na*	oh-koh-**rayn**-see-ah nah
for my insurance.	*policia para*	poo-**lee**-see-ah **pah**-rah
	o meu seguro.	oo **meh**-oo seh-**goo**-roo

See page 256 in the appendix for information on the American and
Canadian embassies in Lisbon.

Helpful Words

ambulance	*ambulância*	ayn-boo-**lahn**-see-ah
accident	*acidente*	ah-see-**dayn**-teh
injured	*ferido*	feh-**ree**-doo
emergency	*emergência*	ee-mehr-**zhayn**-see-ah
emergency room	*sala de emergência*	**sah**-lah deh ee-mehr-**zhayn**-see-ah
fire	*fogo*	**foh**-goo
police	*polícia*	poo-**lee**-see-ah
smoke	*fumo*	**foo**-moo
thief	*ladrão*	lah-**drow**
pickpocket	*carteirista*	kar-tay-**rish**-tah

Help for Women

Leave me alone.	*Deixe-me em paz.*	**day**-sheh-meh ayn pahsh
I want to be alone.	*Quero estar só.*	**keh**-roo ish-**tar** soh
I'm not interested.	*Não estou interessada.*	now ish-**toh** een-teh-reh-**sah**-dah
I'm married.	*Sou casada.*	soh kah-**zah**-dah
I'm a lesbian.	*Sou lésbia.*	soh **lehzh**-bee-ah
I have a contagious disease.	*Tenho uma doença contagiosa.*	**tayn**-yoo **oo**-mah doo-**ayn**-sah kohn-tah-zhee-**oh**-zah
You are bothering me.	*Você está a incomodar-me.*	voh-**say** ish-**tah** ah een-koh-moh-**dar**-meh
This man is bothering me.	*Este senhore está a incomodar-me.*	**ehsh**-teh sin-**yoh**-reh ish-**tah** ah een-koh-moh-**dar**-meh
You are intrusive.	*Você é curioso.*	voh-**say** eh koo-ree-**oh**-zoh
Don't touch me.	*Não me toque.*	now meh **toh**-keh
You're disgusting.	*Tu dás-me nojo.*	too **dahsh**-meh **noh**-zhoo
Stop following me.	*Pare de me seguir.*	**pah**-reh deh meh seh-**geer**
Stop it!	*Pare com isso!*	**pah**-reh kohn **ee**-soo
Enough!	*Chega!*	**shay**-gah
Go away.	*Vá-se embora.*	**vah**-seh ayn-**boh**-rah

Get lost!	*Desapareça!*	day-zah-pah-**ray**-sah
Drop dead!	*Quero que morra!*	**keh**-roo keh **moh**-rah
I'll call the police!	*Vou chamar a polícia!*	voh shah-**mar** ah poo-**lee**-see-ah

SERVICES

Laundry

Is a... laundry nearby?	Há uma... lavanderia por perto?	ah **oo**-mah... lah-vahn-dah-**ree**-ah poor **pehr**-too
...self-service	...self-service	"self-service"
...full-service	...serviço completo	sehr-**vee**-soo koh<u>n</u>-**pleh**-too
Help me, please.	Por favor ajude-me.	poor fah-**vor** ah-**zhoo**-dah-meh
How does this work?	Como funciona?	**koh**-moo foon-see-**oh**-nah
Where is the soap?	Onde está o sabão?	**ohn**-deh ish-**tah** oo sah-**bow**
Are these yours?	São seus?	sow **seh**-oosh
This stinks.	Cheira muito mal	**shay**-rah **mween**-too mahl
Smells like...	Cheira como...	**shay**-rah **koh**-moo
...spring time.	...primavera.	pree-mah-**veh**-rah
...a locker room.	...um gabinet.	oo<u>n</u> gah-bee-**neht**
...cheese.	...queijo.	**kay**-zhoo
I need change.	Preciso de troco.	pray-**see**-zoo deh **troh**-koo
Same-day service?	No mesmo dia?	noo **mehsh**-moo **dee**-ah
By when do I need to drop off my clothes?	Quando é que tenho de deixar as minhas roupas?	**kwahn**-doo eh keh **tayn**-yoo deh day-**shar** ahsh **meen**-yahsh **roh**-pahsh

When will my clothes be ready?	Quando é que as minhas roupas estão prontas?	**kwahn**-doo eh keh ahsh **meen**-yahsh roh-pahsh ish-**tow prohn**-tahsh
Dried?	Secas?	**say**-kahsh
Folded?	Dobradas?	doo-**brah**-dahsh
Hey there, what's spinning?	O que está a rodar?	oo keh ish-**tah** ah roh-**dar**

Clean words

full-service laundry	serviço completo lavandaria	sehr-**vee**-soo kohn-**pleh**-too lah-vahn-dah-**ree**-ah
self-service laundry	self-service lavandaria	"self-service" lah-vahn-dah-**ree**-ah
wash / dry	lavar / secar	lah-**var** / say-**kar**
washer / dryer	máquina de lavar roupa / secador	**mah**-kee-nah deh lah-**var** **roh**-pah / **seh**-kah-dor
detergent	detergente	deh-tehr-**zhayn**-teh
token	ficha	**fee**-shah
whites	roupa branca	**roh**-pah **brahng**-kah
colors	roupa de cor	**roh**-pah deh kor
delicates	roupa delicada	**roh**-pah deh-lee-**kah**-dah
handwash	lavar à mão	lah-**var** ah mow

Haircuts

Where is a barber / hair salon?	Onde é o barbeiro / cabelereiro?	**ohn**-deh eh oo bar-**bay**-roo / kah-beh-lah-**ray**-roo
I'd like...	Eu queria...	**eh**-oo keh-**ree**-ah
...a haircut.	...um cortar o cabelo.	oon kor-**tar** oo kah-**beh**-loo
...a permanent.	...uma permanente.	**oo**-mah pehr-mah-**nayn**-teh
...just a trim.	...cortar só as pontas.	kor-**tar** soh ahsh **pohn**-tahsh
Cut about this much off.	Corte este tanto.	**kor**-teh **ehsh**-teh **tayn**-too
Cut my bangs here.	Cortar a minha franja.	kor-**tar** ah **meen**-yah **frayn**-zhah
Longer / Shorter here.	Mais longo / Mais curto aqui.	mīsh **lon**-goo / mīsh **koor**-too ah-**kee**

I'd like my hair...	Eu gosto do meu cabelo...	**eh**-oo **gohsh**-too doo **meh**-oo kah-**beh**-loo
...short.	...curto.	**koor**-too
...colored.	...tingido.	teen-**zhee**-doo
...shampooed.	...lavado.	lah-**vah**-doo
...blow dried.	...seco.	**seh**-koo
It looks good.	Está bom.	ish-**tah** boh<u>n</u>

Repair

These handy lines can apply to any repair, whether it's a ripped rucksack, bad haircut, or crabby camera.

This is broken.	Isto está avariado.	**eesh**-too ish-**tah** ah-vah-ree-**ah**-doo
Can you fix it?	Pode reparar isto?	**pod**-eh reh-pah-**rar** **eesh**-too
Just do the essentials.	Faça só o que for preciso.	**fah**-sah soh oo keh for preh-**see**-zoo
How much will it cost?	Quanto vai custar?	**kwahn**-too vī koosh-**tar**
When will it be ready?	Quando é que vai estar pronto?	**kwahn**-doo eh keh vī ish-**tar** **prohn**-too
I need it by ___.	Preciso até ___.	preh-**see**-zoo ah-**teh**
We need it by ___.	Precisamos até ___.	preh-see-**zah**-moosh ah-**teh**
Without it, I'm...	Sem isto eu estou...	say<u>n</u> **eesh**-too **eh**-oo ish-**toh**
...lost.	...perdido[a].	pehr-**dee**-doo
...stuck.	...aflito[a].	ah-**flee**-too
...toast.	...frito.	**free**-too

Filling Out Forms

Sr. / Sra. / Menina	Mr. / Mrs. / Miss
nome	first name
apelido	last name
endereço	address
rua	street
cidade	city

estado	state
pais	country
nacionalidade	nationality
origem / destino	origin / destination
idade	age
dia de nascimento	date of birth
lugar de nascimento	place of birth
sexo	sex
homem	male
mulher	female
casado / casada	married man / married woman
solteiro / solteira	single man / single woman
profissão	profession
adulto	adult
criança / rapaz / rapariga	child / boy / girl
crianças	children
familia	family
assinatura	signature
data	date

When filling out dates, do it European-style: day/month/year.

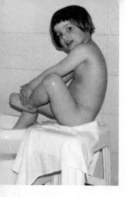

HEALTH

I am sick.	*Estou doente.*	ish-**toh** doo-**ayn**-teh
I feel (very) sick.	*Sinto-me (muito) mal.*	**seeng**-too-meh (**mween**-too) mahl
My husband / My wife...	*Meu marido / Minha mulher...*	**meh**-oo mah-**ree**-doo / **meen**-yah mool-**yehr**
My son / My daughter...	*Meu filho / Minha filha...*	**meh**-oo **feel**-yoo / **meen**-yah **feel**-yah
My male friend / My female friend...	*Meu amigo / Minha amiga...*	**meh**-oo ah-**mee**-goo / **meen**-yah ah-**mee**-gah
...feels (very) sick.	*...sente-se (muito) mal.*	**sehn**-teh-seh (**mween**-too) mahl
It's urgent.	*É urgente.*	eh oor-**zhayn**-teh
I need / We need to see a doctor...	*Eu preciso / Nós precisamos ver um doutor...*	**eh**-oo preh-**see**-zoo / nohsh preh-see-**zah**-moosh vehr oon doh-**tor**
...who speaks English.	*...que fale inglês.*	keh **fah**-leh een-**glaysh**
Please call a doctor.	*Por favor telefone ão doutor.*	poor fah-**vor** teh-leh-**foh**-neh ow doh-**tor**
Could a doctor come here?	*Um doutor pode vir cá?*	oon doh-**tor** pod-eh veer kah
I am...	*Sou...*	soh
He / She is...	*Ele / Ela é...*	**eh**-leh / **eh**-lah eh
...allergic to penicillin / sulfa.	*...alérgico[a] a pinicilina / sulfa.*	ah-**lehr**-zhee-koo ah pee-nee-see-**lee**-nah / **sool**-fah

160

I am diabetic.	Sou diabético[a].	soh dee-ah-**beh**-tee-koo
I have cancer.	Eu tenho cancer.	**eh**-oo tayn-yoo **kan**-sehr
I had a heart attack ___ years ago.	Tive um ataque do coração á ___ anos átraz.	**tee**-veh oon ah-**tah**-keh doo koo-rah-**sow** ah ___ **ah**-nooz **ah**-trahsh
It hurts here.	Dói aqui.	doy ah-**kee**
I feel faint.	Sinto-me tonta.	**seeng**-too-meh **tohn**-tah
It hurts to urinate.	Dói a urinar.	doy ah oo-ree-**nar**
I have body odor.	Tenho cheiro corporal.	**tayn**-yoo **shay**-roo kor-poo-**rahl**
I'm going bald.	Estou a ficar caréca.	ish-**toh** ah fee-**kar** kah-**reh**-kah
Is it serious?	É grave?	eh **grah**-veh
Is it contagious?	É contagioso?	eh kohn-tah-zhee-**oh**-zoo
Aging sucks.	Envelhecer é muito chato.	ehn-vehl-yeh-**sehr** eh **mween**-too **shah**-too
Take one pill every ___ hours for ___ days before / with meals.	Tome um comprimido a cada ___ horas por ___ dias antes / com as refeições.	**toh**-meh oon kohn-pree-**mee**-doo ah **kah**-dah ___ **oh**-rahsh poor ___ **dee**-ahsh **ahn**-tish / kohn ahsh reh-fay-**sowsh**
I need a receipt for my insurance.	Preciso do recibo para o meu seguro.	preh-**see**-zoo doo reh-**see**-boo **pah**-rah oo **meh**-oo seh-**goo**-roo

Ailments

I have...	Tenho...	**tayn**-yoo
He / She has...	Ele / Ela tem...	**eh**-leh / **eh**-lah tayn
I / We need medication for...	Preciso / Precisamos de medicamentos para...	preh-**see**-zoo / preh-see-**zah**-moosh deh meh-dee-kah-**mayn**-toosh **pah**-rah
...arthritis.	...artrite.	**art**-ree-teh
...asthma.	...asma.	**ahzh**-mah
...athlete's foot (fungus).	...pé de atleta (fungo).	peh deh aht-**leh**-tah (**foong**-goo)

HEALTH

HEALTH

Key Phrases: Health

doctor	*doutor[a], médico[a]*	doh-**tor**, **may**-dee-koo
hospital	*hospital*	ohsh-pee-**tahl**
pharmacy	*farmácia*	far-**mah**-see-ah
medicine	*medicina*	meh-dee-**zee**-nah
I am sick.	*Estou doente.*	ish-**toh** doo-**ayn**-teh
I need a doctor	*Eu preciso*	**eh**-oo preh-**see**-zoo
(who speaks	*ver um doutor*	vehr oon doh-**tor**
English).	*(que fale inglês).*	(keh **fah**-leh een-**glaysh**)
It hurts here.	*Doi aqui.*	doy ah-**kee**

...bad breath.	*...mau halito.*	mow ah-**lee**-too
...blisters.	*...bolhas.*	**bohl**-yahsh
...bug bites.	*...picadelas de insectos.*	pee-kah-**deh**-lahsh deh een-**sehk**-toosh
...a burn.	*...uma queimadura.*	**oo**-mah kay-mah-**doo**-rah
...chest pains.	*...uma dor no peito.*	**oo**-mah dor noo **pay**-too
...chills.	*...arrepios.*	ah-reh-**pee**-oosh
...a cold.	*...uma constipação.*	**oo**-mah kohnsh-tee-pah-**sow**
...congestion.	*...congestão.*	kohn-zhish-**tow**
...constipation.	*...prisão de ventre.*	pree-**zow** deh **vayn**-treh
...a cough.	*...uma tosse.*	**oo**-mah **tos**-seh
...cramps.	*...dor, cãibra.*	dor, **kayn**-brah
...diabetes.	*...diabetes.*	dee-ah-**beh**-tish
...diarrhea.	*...diarréia.*	dee-ah-**ray**-ah
...dizziness.	*...tonturas.*	tohn-**too**-rahsh
...earache.	*...dor de ouvido.*	dor deh **oh**-vee-doo
...epilepsy.	*...epilepcia.*	eh-pee-**lehp**-see-ah
...a fever.	*...febre.*	**feh**-breh
...the flu.	*...uma gripe.*	**oo**-mah **gree**-peh
...food poisoning.	*...envenanamento alimentar.*	ayn-vehn-ahn-ah-**mayn**-too ah-lee-mayn-**tar**
...the giggles.	*...gargalhadas.*	gar-gahl-**yah**-dahsh

...hay fever.	...febre dos fenos.	feh-breh doosh feh-noosh
...a headache.	...uma dor de cabeça.	oo-mah dor deh kah-beh-sah
...a heart condition.	...problema no coração.	proo-blay-mah noo koo-rah-sow
...hemorrhoids.	...hemorróidas.	eh-moh-rah-dahsh
...high blood pressure.	...tensão alta.	tayn-sow ahl-tah
...indigestion.	...uma indigestão.	oo-mah een-dee-zhish-tow
...an infection.	...uma infecção.	oo-mah een-fehk-sow
...inflammation.	...inflamação.	een-flah-mah-sow
...a migraine.	...uma enxaqueca.	oo-mah ayn-shah-keh-kah
...nausea.	...náusea.	now-zeh-ah
...pneumonia.	...pneumonia.	pehn-yoo-moh-nee-ah
...a rash.	...uma erupção.	oo-mah ee-roop-sow
...sinus problems.	...sinosite.	see-noh-zee-teh
...a sore throat.	...uma dor de garganta.	oo-mah dor deh gar-gahn-tah
...a stomachache.	...uma dor de estômago.	oo-mah dor deh ish-toh-mah-goo
...sunburn.	...queimadura solar.	kay-mah-doo-rah soh-lar
...a swelling.	...um inchado.	oon een-shah-doo
...a toothache.	...uma dor de dente.	oo-mah dor deh dayn-teh
...a urinary infection.	...uma infecção urinaria.	oo-mah een-fehk-sow oo-ree-nah-ree-ah
...a venereal disease.	...uma doença venéria.	oo-mah doo-ayn-sah veh-neh-ree-ah
...vicious sunburn.	...queimadura solar grave.	kay-mah-doo-rah soh-lar grah-veh
...vomiting.	...vómitos.	vah-mee-toosh
...worms.	...vermes.	vehr-mish

Women's Health

menstruation	menstruação	mayn-shtroo-ah-sow
menstrual cramps	cólicas	kol-ee-kahsh
period	menstruação, período	mehn-shtroo-ah-sow, peh-ree-oh-doo

HEALTH

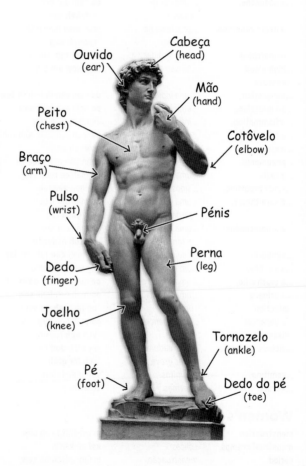

Ouvido (ear)

Cabeça (head)

Mão (hand)

Peito (chest)

Cotôvelo (elbow)

Braço (arm)

Pulso (wrist)

Pénis

Perna (leg)

Dedo (finger)

Joelho (knee)

Tornozelo (ankle)

Pé (foot)

Dedo do pé (toe)

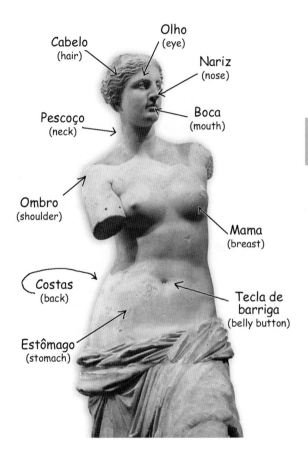

Cabelo
(hair)

Olho
(eye)

Nariz
(nose)

Pescoço
(neck)

Boca
(mouth)

Ombro
(shoulder)

Mama
(breast)

Costas
(back)

Tecla de
barriga
(belly button)

Estômago
(stomach)

HEALTH

pregnancy (test)	(teste de) gravidez	(**tehsh**-teh deh) grah-vee-**dehsh**
miscarriage	abôrto natural	ah-**bor**-too nah-too-**rahl**
abortion	abôrto	ah-**bor**-too
birth control pills	pilula anti-concepcional	peel-**oo**-lah ahn-tee-koh<u>n</u>-sehp-see-oh-**nahl**
diaphragm	diafragma	dee-ah-**frahg**-mah
I'd like to see a female...	Eu quero ver uma...	**eh**-oo **kay**-roo vehr **oo**-mah
...doctor.	...doutora.	doh-**toh**-rah
...gynecologist.	...enicologista.	eh-nee-koh-loh-**zhee**-stah
I've missed a period.	Faltou o meu período.	**fahl**-toh oo **meh**-oo peh-**ree**-oh-doo
My last period started on ___.	O meu ultimo período começou em ___.	oo **meh**-oo **ool**-tee-moo peh-**ree**-oh-doo koh<u>n</u>-meh-**soh** ay<u>n</u>
I am / She is... pregnant.	Eu estou / Ela está gravida...	**eh**-oo ish-**toh** / **eh**-lah ish-**stah grah**-vee-dah
...___ months	...de ___ mesês.	deh ___ **meh**-zaysh

Parts of the Body

ankle	tornozelo	tor-noo-**zeh**-loo
arm	braço	**brah**-soo
back	costas	**kosh**-tahsh
bladder	bexiga	beh-**shee**-gah
breast	mama	**mah**-mah
buttocks	traseiro	trah-**zay**-roo
chest	peito	**pay**-too
ear	ouvido	**oh**-vee-doo
elbow	cotôvelo	koo-**toh**-veh-loo
eye	olho	**ohl**-yoo
face	rosto	**rohsh**-too
finger	dedo	**deh**-doo
foot	pé	peh
hair	cabelo	kah-**beh**-loo
hand	mão	mo<u>w</u>

head	cabeça	kah-**beh**-sah
heart	coração	koo-rah-**sow**
intestines	intestino	een-tish-**tee**-noo
knee	joelho	zhoo-**ehl**-yoo
leg	perna	**pehr**-nah
lung	pulmão	pool-**mow**
mouth	boca	**boh**-kah
navel	umbigo	oo<u>n</u>-**bee**-goo
neck	pescoço	pehsh-**koh**-soh
nose	nariz	**nah**-reesh
penis	pénis	**peh**-neesh
rectum	recto	**rehk**-too
shoulder	ombro	**ohn**-broo
stomach	estômago	ish-**toh**-mah-goo
teeth	dentes	**dehn**-tish
testicles	testículos	tish-**tee**-koo-loosh
throat	garganta	gar-**gahn**-tah
toe	dedo do pé	**deh**-doo doo peh
urethra	uretra	oo-**reht**-rah
uterus	útero	**oo**-teh-roo
vagina	vagina	vah-**zhee**-nah
waist	cintura	seen-**too**-rah
wrist	pulso	**pool**-soo

HEALTH

Healthy Words

24-hour pharmacy	farmácia aberta vinte e quatro horas	far-**mah**-see-ah ah-**behr**-tah **veen**-teh ee **kwah**-troo **oh**-rahsh
bleeding	sangrar	sang-**grar**
blood	sangue	**sang**-geh
contraceptives	contracepçaõ	koh<u>n</u>-trah-sehp-**sow**
dentist	dentista	day<u>n</u>-**teesh**-tah
doctor	doutor[a], médico[a]	doh-**tor**, **may**-dee-koo
health insurance	seguro de saúde	say-**goo**-roo deh sah-**oo**-deh
hospital	hospital	ohsh-pee-**tahl**
medical clinic	clinica médica	**klee**-nee-kah **may**-dee-kah

medicine	medicina	meh-dee-**zee**-nah
nurse	enfermeira	ayn-fehr-**may**-rah
pain	dor	dor
pharmacy	farmácia	far-**mah**-see-ah
pill	comprimido	koh<u>n</u>-pree-**mee**-doo
prescription	receita médica	reh-**say**-tah **may**-dee-kah
refill	encher	ayn-**shehr**
unconscious	inconciente	een-koh<u>n</u>-see-**ehn**-teh
X-ray	raio X	**ray**-oo sheesh

First-Aid Kit

antacid	remédio	reh-**meh**-dee-oo
	para azia	**pah**-rah ah-**zee**-ah
antibiotic	antibiótico	ahn-tee-bee-**oh**-tee-koo
aspirin	aspirina	ahsh-pee-**ree**-nah
aspirin	comprimido para	koh<u>n</u>-pree-**mee**-do **pah**-rah
substitute	as dores	ash **doh**-rehsh
bandage	gaze	**gah**-zeh
Band-Aids	pensos	**payn**-soosh
cold medicine	remédio para	reh-**meh**-dee-oo **pah**-rah
	constipação	koh<u>n</u>sh-tee-pah-**sow**
cough drops	rebuçados	reh-boo-**sah**-doosh
	da tosse	dah **tos**-seh
decongestant	descongestio-	dish-koh<u>n</u>-zhish-tee-oh-
	nante	**nahn**-teh
disinfectant	desinfetante	dehz-een-feh-**tahn**-teh
first-aid cream	creme	**kreh**-meh
	desinfetante	dehz-een-feh-**tahn**-teh
gauze / tape	gaze / adesivo	**gah**-zeh / ah-deh-**zee**-voo
	médico	**may**-dee-koo
laxative	laxativo	lak-sah-**tee**-voo
medicine for	remédio para	reh-**meh**-dee-oo **pah**-rah
diarrhea	a diarréia	ah dee-ah-**ray**-ah
moleskin	sinal	see-**nahl**
painkiller	comprimidos	koh<u>n</u>-pree-**mee**-doosh
	para as dores	**pah**-rah ahsh **doh**-rish
Preparation H	Preparação H	preh-pah-rah-**sow** eh-**gah**

HEALTH

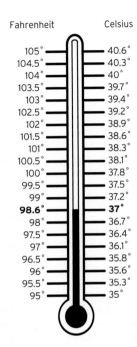

HEALTH

support bandage	*ligadora*	lee-gah-**doo**-rah
thermometer	*termometro*	tehr-**mow**-may-troo
Vaseline	*vasilina*	vah-zee-**lee**-nah
vitamins	*vitaminas*	vee-tah-**mee**-nahsh

Contacts and Glasses

glasses	*ocúlos*	oo-**koo**-loosh
sunglasses	*ocúlos de sol*	oo-**koo**-loosh deh sohl
prescription	*receita*	reh-**say**-tah
contact lenses...	*lentes de contacto...*	**lehn**-tish deh koh<u>n</u>-**tahk**-too

...soft	...flexibeis	fleh-**shee**-baysh
...hard	...rigidas	ree-**zhee**-dahsh
solution...	solução...	soo-loo-**sow**
...cleaning	...de limpeza	deh leem-**pay**-zah
...soaking	...para molhar	**pah**-rah mool-**yar**
all-purpose solution	solução para limpeza e tratamento	soo-loo-**sow pah**-rah leem-**pay**-zah ee trah-tah-**mayn**-too
20/20 vision	visão vinte sobre vinte	vee-**zow** veen-teh **soh**-breh veen-teh
I've lost / I've swallowed my contact lens.	Perdi / Engoli minha lente de contacto.	pehr-**dee** / ayn-goo-**lee meen**-yah **lehn**-teh deh kohn-**tahk**-too

Toiletries

comb	pente	**payn**-teh
conditioner (for hair)	condicionador (para o cabelo)	kohn-dee-see-oh-nah-**door** (**pah**-rah oo kah-**behl**-oo)
condoms	preservativos	pray-zehr-vah-**tee**-voosh
dental floss	fio dental	**fee**-oo dayn-**tahl**
deodorant	desodorizante	deh-zoo-dor-ee-**zayn**-teh
facial tissue	lenços de papel	**layn**-soosh deh pah-**pehl**
hairbrush	escova do cabelo	ish-**koh**-vah doo kah-**beh**-loo
hand lotion	creme para as mãos	**kreh**-meh **pah**-rah ahsh **mowsh**
lip salve	batão de cierio	bah-**tow** deh see-**yay**-roo
mirror	espelho	ish-**payl**-yoo
nail clipper	cortas-unhas	**kor**-tah **oon**-yahsh
razor	lâmina	**lah**-mee-nah
sanitary napkins	pensos higiénicos	**payn**-soosh ee-zhee-**ehn**-ee-koosh
scissors	tesoura	teh-**zoh**-rah
shampoo	shampoo	"shampoo"
shaving cream	creme de barbear	**kreh**-meh deh bar-**behr**
soap	sabão	sah-**bow**

sunscreen	protector solar	proo-tehk-**tor** soo-**lar**
tampons	tampões	tah<u>n</u>-**powsh**
	higiénicos	ee-zhee-**ehn**-ee-koosh
tissues	lenços de papel	**layn**-soosh deh pah-**pehl**
toilet paper	papel	pah-**pehl**
	higiénico	ee-zhee-**ehn**-ee-koo
toothbrush	escova de	ish-**koh**-vah deh
	dentes	**dayn**-tish
toothpaste	pasta dos	**pahsh**-tah doosh
	dentes,	**dayn**-tish,
	dentifrice	day<u>n</u>-tee-**free**-seh
tweezers	pinça	**peen**-sah

HEALTH

Makeup

blush	blush	"blush"
eye shadow	sombra	**soh<u>n</u>**-brah
eyeliner	lápis para os	**lah**-peesh **pah**-rah ooz
	olhos,	**ohl**-yoosh,
	delineador	deh-leen-eh-ah-**door**
face cleanser	produto para	proh-**doo**-too **pah**-rah
	a limpeza	ah leem-**pay**-zah
	do rosto	doo **rohsh**-too
face powder	pó para o rosto	poh **pah**-rah oo **rohsh**-too
foundation	base	**bah**-zeh
lipstick	baton	bah-**toh<u>n</u>**
makeup	maquiagem	mah-kee-**ah**-zhay<u>n</u>
mascara	rimel	**ree**-mehl
moisturizer...	hidratante...	eed-rah-**tahn**-teh
...with sunblock	...com proteção	koh<u>n</u> proh-tehk-**sow**
	solar	soh-**lar**
nail polish	verniz para	vehr-**neezh pah**-rah
	as unhas	ahz **oon**-yahsh
nail polish remover	acetona	ah-seh-**toh**-nah
perfume	perfume	pehr-**foo**-meh

For Babies

baby	bebé	bay-**bay**
baby food	comida para bebés	koo-**mee**-dah **pah**-rah bay-**baysh**
bib	babete	bah-**beh**-teh
bottle	bibron	beeb-**rohn**
diaper(s)	fralda(s)	**frahl**-dah(sh)
diaper wipes	lenço húmido para fraldas	**layn**-soo **oo**-mee-doo **pah**-rah **frahl**-dahsh
diaper ointment	creme para fraldas	**kreh**-meh **pah**-rah **frahl**-dahsh
formula...	alimento suplementar...	ah-lee-**mehn**-too soo-pleh-mehn-**tar**
...powdered	...em pó	ay<u>n</u> poh
...liquid	...em líquido	ay<u>n</u> **lee**-kee-doo
...soy	...em soja	ay<u>n</u> **soh**-zhah
medication for...	medicação para...	meh-dee-kah-**sow pah**-rah
...diaper rash	...assadura das fraldas	ah-sah-**doo**-rah dahsh **frahl**-dahsh
...teething	...dentição	dehn-tee-**sow**
nipple	bico do peito	**bee**-koo doo **pay**-too
pacifier	chupeta	shoo-**pay**-tah
Will you refrigerate this?	Pode por no frigorifico?	**pod**-eh poor noo free-goh-**ree**-fee-koo
Will you warm... for a baby?	Pode aquecer... para o bebé?	**pod**-eh ah-keh-**sehr**... **pah**-rah oo bay-**bay**
...this	...isto	**eesh**-too
...some water	...um pouco de água	oo<u>n</u> **poh**-koo deh **ah**-gwah
...some milk	...um pouco de leite	oo<u>n</u> **poh**-koo deh **lay**-teh
Not too hot, please.	Não muito quente, por favor.	no<u>w</u> **mween**-too **kay<u>n</u>**-teh poor fah-**vor**

More Baby Things

backpack to carry baby	saco para levar o bebé nas costas	**sah**-koo **pah**-rah leh-**vahr** oo bay-**bay** nahsh **kosh**-tahsh
booster seat	suporte para cadeira	soo-**por**-teh **pah**-rah kah-**day**-rah
car seat	cadeira de carro para o bebé	kah-**day**-rah deh **kah**-roo **pah**-rah oo bay-**bay**
high chair	cadeira alta	kah-**day**-rah **ahl**-tah
playpen	parque	**par**-keh
stroller	carrinho de bebê	kar-**een**-yoo deh bay-**bay**

CHATTING

English	Portuguese	Pronunciation
My name is ___.	Chamo-me ___.	**shah**-moo-meh
What's your name?	Como se chama?	**koh**-moo seh **shah**-mah
Pleased to meet you.	Prazer em conhecer.	**p**rah-**zehr** ayn koh**n**-yeh-**sehr**
This is ___. (informal)	Esta é ___.	**ehsh**-tah eh
This is ___. (formal)	Apregento-lhe ___.	ah-preh-**zhehn**-tool-yeh
How are you?	Como está?	**koh**-moo ish-**tah**
Very well, thanks.	Muito bem, obrigado[a].	**mween**-too bay**n** oh-bree-**gah**-doo
Where are you from?	De onde é que você é?	deh **ohn**-deh eh keh voh-**say** eh
What city?	De que cidade?	deh keh see-**dah**-deh
What country?	De que pais?	deh keh pah-**eesh**
What planet?	De que planeta?	deh keh plah-**nay**-tah
I am...	Sou...	soh
...American.	...Americano[a].	ah-meh-ree-**kah**-noo
...Canadian.	...Canadiano[a].	kah-nah-dee-**ah**-noo
...a pest.	...terrível.	teh-**ree**-vehl
Where are you going?	Onde vai?	**ohn**-deh vī
I'm going to ___.	Vou para ___.	voh **pah**-rah
We're going to ___.	Vamos para ___.	**vah**-moosh **pah**-rah
Will you take my / our photo?	Pode tirar a minha foto / a nossa foto?	**pod**-eh tee-**rar** ah **meen**-yah **foh**-too / ah **noh**-sah **foh**-too

174

Key Phrases: Chatting

My name is ___.	Chamo-me ___.	**shah**-moo-meh ___
What's your name?	Como se chama?	**koh**-moo seh **shah**-mah
Pleased to	Prazer em	prah-**zehr** ayn
meet you.	conhecer.	kohn-yeh-**sehr**
Where are	De onde é que	deh **ohn**-deh eh keh
you from?	você é?	voh-**say** eh
I'm from ___.	Eu sou de ___.	**eh**-oo soh de ___
Where are	Onde vai?	**ohn**-deh vī
you going?		
I'm going to ___.	Vou para ___.	voh **pah**-rah
I like...	Gosto...	**gohsh**-too
Do you like...?	Você gosta...?	voh-**say gohsh**-tah
Thank you	Muito	**mween**-too
very much.	obrigado[a].	oh-bree-**gah**-doo
Have a good trip!	Boa-viagem!	boh-ah-vee-**ah**-zhayn

Can I take a	Posso tirar-lhe	**pos**-soh tee-**rar**-leh
photo of you?	uma foto?	**oo**-mah **foh**-too
Smile!	Sorria!	soh-**ree**-ah

Nothing More Than Feelings...

I am / You are...	Eu estou /	**eh**-oo ish-**toh** /
	Você está...	voh-**say** ish-**tah**
He is / She is...	Ele está /	**eh**-leh ish-**tah** /
	Ela está...	**eh**-lah ish-**tah**
...happy.	...feliz.	feh-**leesh**
...sad.	...triste.	**treesh**-teh
...tired.	...cansado[a].	kahn-**sah**-doo
...thirsty.	...com sede.	kohn **say**-deh
...hungry.	...com fome.	kohn **fah**-meh
...lucky.	...afortunado[a].	ah-for-too-**nah**-doo
...homesick.	...com saudades	kohn soh-**dah**-dish
	de casa.	deh **kah**-zah

| ...cold. | ...com frio. | koh<u>n</u> **free**-oh |
| ...hot. | ...com calor. | koh<u>n</u> kah-**lor** |

Who's Who

My... (male / female)	O meu / A minha...	oo **meh**-oo / ah **meen**-yah
...male friend / female friend.	...amigo / amiga.	ah-**mee**-goo / ah-**mee**-gah
...boyfriend / girlfriend.	...namorado / namorada.	nah-moo-**rah**-doo / nah-moo-**rah**-dah
...husband / wife.	...marido / mulher.	mah-**ree**-doo / mool-**yehr**
...son / daughter.	...filho / filha.	**feel**-yoo / **feel**-yah
...brother / sister.	...irmão / irmã.	eer-**mow** / eer-**mayn**
...father / mother.	...pai / mãe.	pī / **mayn**-eh
...uncle / aunt.	...tio / tia.	**tee**-oo / **tee**-ah
...nephew / niece.	...sobrinho / sobrinha.	soo-**breen**-yoo / soo-**breen**-yah
...male / female cousin.	...primo / prima.	**pree**-moo / **pree**-mah
...grandpa / grandma.	...avô / avó.	ah-**voh** / ah-**vah**
...grandson / granddaughter.	...neto / neta.	**nay**-too / **nay**-tah

Family

Are you married? (asked of a man)	É casado?	eh kah-**zah**-doo
Are you married? (asked of a woman)	É casada?	eh kah-**zah**-dah
Do you have children?	Tem algumas crianças?	tay<u>n</u> ahl-**goo**-mahsh kree-**ahn**-sahsh
How many boys / girls?	Quantos rapazes / raparigas?	**kwahn**-toosh rah-**pah**-zish / rah-pah-**ree**-gahsh
Do you have photos?	Tem fotos?	tay<u>n</u> **foh**-toosh
How old is your child?	Que idade tem a sua criança?	keh ee-**dah**-deh tay<u>n</u> ah **soo**-ah kree-**ahn**-sah

| Beautiful child! | Linda criança! | **leen**-dah kree-**ahn**-sah |
| Beautiful children! | Lindas crianças! | **leen**-dahsh kree-**ahn**-sahsh |

Work

What is your occupation?	Qual é a sua profissão?	kwahl eh ah **soo**-ah proo-fee-**sow**
Do you like your work?	Gosta do seu trabalho?	**gohsh**-tah doo **seh**-oo trah-**bahl**-yoo
I work...	Eu trabalho...	**eh**-oo trah-**bahl**-yoo
I'm studying to work...	Estou a estudar para trabalhar...	ish-**toh** ah ish-too-**dar** **pah**-rah trah-bahl-**yar**
I used to work...	Trabalhava...	trah-bahl-**yah**-vah
I want a job...	Quero um emprego...	**kay**-roo oon ayn-**preh**-goo
...in accounting.	...em contabilidade.	ayn kohn-tah-bee-lee-**dah**-deh
...in the medical field.	...no campo médico.	noo **kahm**-poo **may**-dee-koo
...in social services.	...em serviços sociais.	ayn sehr-**vee**-soosh soh-see-**ish**
...in the legal profession.	...em profição juridical.	ayn proh-fee-**sow** zhoo-ree-dee-**kahl**
...in banking.	...no banco.	noo **bang**-koo
...in business.	...nos negócios.	noosh neh-**gah**-see-oosh
...in government.	...no governo.	noo goh-**vehr**-noo
...in engineering.	...em engenharia.	ayn ayn-zhehn-yah-**ree**-ah
...in public relations.	...em relações publicas.	ayn reh-lah-**sowsh** **poob**-lee-kahsh
...in science.	...no campo da ciência.	noo **kahm**-poo dah see-**ayn**-see-ah
...in teaching.	...na educação.	nah ee-doo-kah-**sow**
...in the computer field.	...na área dos computadores.	nah **ah**-reh-ah doosh kohm-poo-tah-**dor**-ish
...in the travel industry.	...no turismo.	noo too-**reezh**-moo

...in the arts.	...nas artes.	nahz **ar**-tehsh
...in journalism.	...no jornalismo.	noo zhoor-nah-**leezh**-moo
...in a restaurant.	...no restaurante.	noo rish-toh-**rahn**-teh
...in a store.	...numa loja.	**noo**-mah **lah**-zhah
...in a factory.	...numa fabrica.	**noo**-mah **fah**-bree-kah
I am...	Estou...	ish-**toh**
...unemployed.	...desempregado[a].	dehz-ayn-preh-**gah**-doo
...retired.	...reformado[a].	reh-for-**mah**-doo
I'm a professional traveler.	Sou viajante professional.	soh vee-ah-**zhahn**-teh proo-feh-see-oo-**nahl**
Do you have a...?	Você tem um...?	voh-**say** tayn oon
Here is my / our...	Aqui está o meu / nosso...	ah-**kee** ish-**tah** oo **meh**-oo / **noh**-soo
...business card	...cartão	kar-**tow**
...email address	...endereço eletrônico	ayn-deh-**ray**-soo eh-leh-**troh**-nee-koo

Chatting with Children

What's your name?	Como te chamas?	**koh**-moo teh **shah**-mahsh
My name is ___.	Chamo-me ___.	**shah**-moo-meh
How old are you?	Que idade tens?	keh ee-**dah**-deh taynsh
Do you have brothers and sisters?	Tens irmãos e irmãs?	taynsh eer-**mowsh** ee eer-**mahsh**
Do you like school?	Gostas da escola?	**gohsh**-tahsh dah ish-**koh**-lah
What are you studying?	O que é que estuda?	oo keh eh keh ish-**too**-dah
I'm studying...	Estou a estudar...	ish-**toh** ah ish-too-**dar**
What's your favorite subject?	Qual é a tua disciplina preferida?	kwahl eh oo **too**-ah dee-shee-**plee**-nah pray-feh-**ree**-dah
Do you have pets?	Tens animais de estimação?	taynsh ah-nee-**mish** deh ish-tee-mah-**sow**
I have / We have a...	Eu tenho / Nós temos um...	**eh**-oo tayn-yoo / nohsh **teh**-moosh oon

CHATTING

English	Portuguese	Pronunciation
...cat / dog / fish / bird.	...gato / cão / peixe / pássaro	**gah**-too / ko<u>w</u> / **pay**-sheh / **pah**-sah-roo
What is this?	O que é isto?	oo keh eh **eesh**-too
Will you teach me...?	Ensina-me...?	ay<u>n</u>-**see**-nah-meh
Will you teach us...?	Ensina-nos...?	ay<u>n</u>-**see**-nah-nohsh
...some Portuguese words	...algumas palavras em português	ahl-**goo**-mahsh pah-**lah**-vrahz ay<u>n</u> poor-too-**gaysh**
...a simple Portuguese song	uma canção portuguêsa	**oo**-mah kah<u>n</u>-**sow** poor-too-**gay**-zah
Guess which country I live in / we live in.	Adivinha em que país eu vivo / nós vivemos.	ah-dee-**veen**-yah ay<u>n</u> keh pah-**eez** eh-oo **vee**-voo / nohsh vee-**veh**-moosh
How old am I?	Quantos anos tenho?	**kwahn**-toosh **ah**-noosh **tayn**-yoo
I'm ___ years old.	Tenho ___ anos.	**tayn**-yoo ___ **ah**-noosh
Want to hear me burp?	Queres ouvir-me a arrotar?	**keh**-rish oh-**veer**-meh ah ah-roo-**tar**
Teach me a fun game.	Ensina-me um jogo engraçado.	ay<u>n</u>-**see**-nah-meh oon **zhoh**-goo ay<u>n</u>-grah-**sah**-doo
Got any candy?	Tens um rebuçado?	tay<u>n</u>sh oon reh-boo-**sah**-doo
Want to thumb wrestle?	Queres um braço de força?	**keh**-rehz oon **brah**-soo deh **for**-sah
Gimme five.	Dá-me cinco.	**dah**-meh **seeng**-koo

If you do break into song, you'll find the words for "Happy Birthday" on page 23 and the national anthem on page 253.

Travel Talk

English	Portuguese	Pronunciation
I am / Are you...?	Estou / Está...?	ish-**toh** / ish-**tah**
...on vacation	...de férias	deh **feh**-ree-ahsh
...on business	...em negócios	ay<u>n</u> neh-**gos**-ee-oosh
How long have you been traveling?	Á quanto tempo é que tem estado a viajar?	ah **kwahn**-too **tayn**-poo eh keh tay<u>n</u> ish-**tah**-doo ah vee-ah-**zhar**

CHATTING

day / week	*dia / semana*	**dee**-ah / seh-**mah**-nah
month / year	*mês / ano*	maysh / **ah**-noo
When are you going home?	*Quando é que vai voltar para casa?*	**kwahn**-doo eh keh vī vohl-**tar** pah-rah **kah**-zah
This is my first time in ___.	*Esta é a minha primeira vêz em ___.*	**ehsh**-tah eh ah **meen**-yah pree-**may**-rah vaysh ayn
This is our first time in ___.	*Esta é a nossa primeira vêz em ___.*	**ehsh**-tah eh ah **noh**-sah pree-**may**-rah vaysh ayn
It is (not) a tourist trap.	*(Não) é uma armadilha para turista.*	(now) eh **oo**-mah ar-mah-**deel**-yah **pah**-rah too-**reesh**-tah
I'm happy here.	*Estou contente aqui.*	ish-**toh** kohn-**tehn**-teh ah-**kee**
This is paradise.	*Isto é um paraiso.*	**eesh**-too eh oon pah-rah-**ee**-zoo
Portugal is wonderful.	*Portugal é maravilhoso.*	poor-too-**gahl** eh mah-rah-veel-**yoh**-zoo
The Portuguese are friendly / boring / rude.	*Os portuguêses são simpáticos / chatos / rudes.*	oosh poor-too-**gay**-zish sow seeng-**pah**-tee-koosh / **shah**-toosh / **roo**-dish
So far...	*Até agora...*	ah-**teh** ah-**goh**-rah
Today...	*Hoje...*	**oh**-zheh
...I have seen / we have seen ___ and ___.	*...eu vi / nós vimos ___ e___.*	**eh**-oo vee / nohsh **vee**-moosh ___ ee ___
Next...	*Depois...*	day-**pwaysh**
Tomorrow...	*Amanhã...*	ah-ming-**yah**
...I will see / we will see ___.	*...eu vou ver / nós vamos ver ___.*	**eh**-oo voh vehr / nohsh **vah**-moosh vehr
Yesterday...	*Ontem...*	**ohn**-tayn
...I saw / we saw ___.	*...eu vi / nós vimos ___.*	**eh**-oo vee / nohsh **vee**-moosh
My / Our vacation is ___ days long, starting in ___ and ending in ___.	*Minhas / Nossas férias são de ___ dias, começando em ___ até ___.*	**meen**-yahsh / **noh**-sahsh **feh**-ree-ahsh sow deh ___ **dee**-ahsh koh-meh-**sayn**-doo ayn ___ ah-**teh**

To travel is to live.	A maneira de viver é viajar.	ah mah-**nay**-rah deh vee-**vehr** eh vee-ah-**zhar**
Travel is enlightening.	Viajar é agradável.	vee-ah-**zhar** eh ah-grah-**dah**-vehl
I wish all (American) politicians traveled.	Desejo que todos os (americanos) politicos tivessem viajado.	deh-**zeh**-zhoo keh **toh**-dooz ooz (ah-meh-ree-**kah**-noosh) poh-**lee**-tee-koosh tee-**veh**-say<u>n</u> vee-ah-**zhah**-doo
Have a good trip!	Boa-viagem!	boh-ah-vee-**ah**-zhay<u>n</u>

Map Musings

Use the following maps and phrases to delve into family history and explore travel dreams.

I live here.	Eu vivo aqui.	**eh**-oo **vee**-voo ah-**kee**
We live here.	Vivimos aqui.	vee-**vee**-moosh ah-**kee**
I was born here.	Eu nasci aqui.	**eh**-oo **nahsh**-see ah-**kee**
My ancestors came from ___.	Os meus antepassados vieram de ___.	oosh **meh**-oosh ahn-teh-pah-**sah**-doosh vee-**eh**-rahm deh
I've traveled to ___.	Já viajei a ___.	zhah vee-ah-**zhay** ah
We've traveled to ___.	Já viajamos a ___.	zhah vee-ah-**zhah**-mooz ah
Next I'll go to ___.	Em seguida irei ___.	ay<u>n</u> sehg-**ee**-dah ee-**ray**
Next we'll go to ___.	Em seguida iremos ___.	ay<u>n</u> sehg-**ee**-dah ee-**ray**-moosh
I'd like / We'd like to go to ___.	Gostaria / Gostaríamos de ir para ___.	goosh-tah-**ree**-ah / goosh-tah-**ree**-ah-moosh deh eer **pah**-rah
Where do you live?	A onde vive?	ah **ohn**-deh **vee**-veh
Where were you born?	A onde nasceu?	ah **ohn**-deh nahsh-**seh**-oo
Where did your ancestors come from?	De onde vieram os vossos antepassados?	deh **ohn**-deh vee-**eh**-rahm oosh **voh**-soosh ahn-teh-pah-**sah**-doosh

Portugal

Europe

The United States

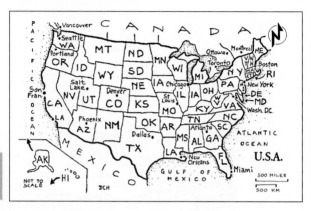

The World

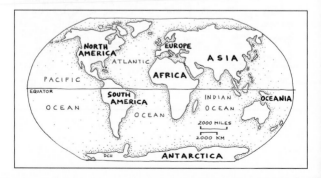

CHATTING

Where have you traveled?	A onde tem viajado?	ah **ohn**-deh tay<u>n</u> vee-ah-**zhah**-doo
Where are you going?	A onde vai?	ah **ohn**-deh vī
Where would you like to go?	A onde gostaria de ir?	ah **ohn**-deh goosh-tah-**ree**-ah deh eer

Favorite Things

What's your favorite...?	Qual é o seu... favorito?	kwahl eh oo **seh**-oo... fah-voo-**ree**-too
...hobby	...passatempo	pah-sah-**tayn**-poo
...ice cream	...gelado	zheh-**lah**-doo
...male singer	...cantor	kahn-**tor**
...male movie star	...actor	ah-**tor**
...male artist	...artista	ar-**teesh**-tah
...male author	...escritor	ish-kree-**tor**
...movie	...filme	**feel**-meh
...(kind of) book	...(tipo de) livro	(**tee**-poo deh) **leev**-roo
...sport	...desporto	dish-**por**-too
...vice	...vício	**vee**-see-oo
What's your favorite...?	Qual é o sea... favorita?	kwahl eh oo **seh**-ah... fah-voo-**ree**-tah
...food	...comida	koo-**mee**-dah
...art	...arte	**ar**-teh
...music	...música	**moo**-zee-kah
...female singer	...cantora	kahn-**toh**-rah
...female movie star	...actriz	ah-**treesh**
...female artist	...artista	ar-**teesh**-tah
...female author	...escritora	ish-kree-**toh**-rah
Can you recommend a good...?	Pode recomendar um bom...?	**pod**-eh reh-koh-may<u>n</u>-**dar** oo<u>n</u> boh<u>n</u>
...Portuguese CD	...CD em português	say day ay<u>n</u> poor-too-**gaysh**
...Portuguese book translated in English	...livro português traduzido em inglês	**lee**-vroo poor-too-**gaysh** trah-doo-**zee**-doo ay<u>n</u> een-**glaysh**

Weather

What will the weather be like tomorrow?	*Qual é o tempo para amanhã?*	kwahl eh oo **tayn**-poo **pah**-rah ah-ming-**yah**
sunny / cloudy	*sol / nublado*	sohl / noo-**blah**-doo
hot / cold	*quente / frio*	**kayn**-teh / **free**-oo
muggy / windy	*úmido / vento*	**oo**-mee-doo / **vayn**-too
rain / snow	*chuva / neve*	**shoo**-vah / **neh**-veh
Should I bring a jacket?	*Preciso trazer um casaco?*	preh-**see**-zoo trah-**zehr** oon kah-**zah**-koo

Thanks a Million

Thank you very much.	*Muito obrigado[a].*	**mween**-too oh-bree-**gah**-doo
You are...	*Você é...*	voh-**say** eh
...kind.	*...simpatico[a].*	seeng-**pah**-tee-koo
...wonderful.	*...maravilhoso[a].*	mah-rah-veel-**yoh**-zoo
...generous.	*...generouso[a].*	zheh-neh-**roh**-zoo
You spoil me / us.	*Mimou me / nos.*	**mee**-moh meh / nohsh
You've been a great help.	*Você foi uma grande ajuda.*	voh-**say** foy **oo**-mah **grahn**-deh ah-**zhoo**-dah
I will remember you...	*Vou lembrar-me de você...*	voh lehm-**brar**-meh deh voh-**say**
We will remember you...	*Vamos lembrar-nos de você...*	**vah**-moosh lehm-**brar**-noosh deh voh-**say**
...always.	*...sempre.*	**sayn**-preh
...until Tuesday.	*...até terça-feira.*	ah-**teh** tehr-sah-**fay**-rah

Responses for All Occasions

I like that.	*Gosto disto.*	**gohsh**-too **deesh**-too
We like that.	*Gostamos disto.*	goosh-**tah**-moosh **deesh**-too
I like you.	*Gosto de si.*	**gohsh**-too deh see
We like you.	*Gostamos de si.*	goosh-**tah**-moosh deh see
Fantastic!	*Fantástico!*	fahn-**tahsh**-tee-koo

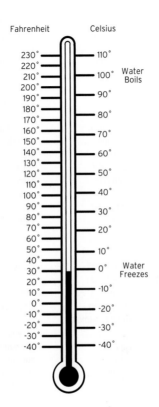

	Fahrenheit	Celsius	
	230°	110°	
	220°		
	210°	100°	Water Boils
	200°		
	190°	90°	
	180°	80°	
	170°		
	160°	70°	
	150°		
	140°	60°	
	130°		
	120°	50°	
	110°		
	100°	40°	
	90°		
	80°	30°	
	70°	20°	
	60°		
	50°	10°	
	40°		
	30°	0°	Water Freezes
	20°		
	10°	-10°	
	0°		
	-10°	-20°	
	-20°	-30°	
	-30°		
	-40°	-40°	

What a nice place.	*Que sítio bonito.*	keh **see**-tee-oo boh-**nee**-too
Perfect.	*Perfeito.*	pehr-**fay**-too
Funny.	*Cómico.*	**kom**-ee-koo
Interesting.	*Interessante.*	een-teh-reh-**sahn**-teh
Really?	*A sério?*	ah **seh**-ree-oo
Wow!	*Fiche!*	**fee**-sheh

English	Portuguese	Pronunciation
Congratulations!	*Parabéns!*	pah-rah-**baynsh**
Well done!	*Bem feito!*	bayn **fay**-too
You're welcome.	*Não tem de quê.*	now tayn deh kay
Bless you! (after sneeze)	*Santinho!*	sahn-**teen**-yoo
What a pity.	*É uma pena.*	eh **oo**-mah **pay**-nah
That's life.	*É a vida.*	eh ah **vee**-dah
No problem.	*Não tem problema.*	now tayn proo-**blay**-mah
O.K.	*Está bem.*	ish-**tah** bayn
This is the good life!	*Esta é a boa vida!*	**ehsh**-tah eh ah **boh**-ah **vee**-dah
Have a good day!	*Tenha um bom dia!*	**tehn**-yah oon bohn **dee**-ah
Good luck!	*Boa-sorte!*	boh-ah-**sor**-teh
Let's go!	*Vamos!*	**vah**-moosh

Smoking

Do you smoke?	*Você fuma?*	voh-**say foo**-mah
Do you smoke pot?	*Você fuma ervas?*	voh-**say foo**-mah **ehr**-vahsh
I (don't) smoke.	*(Não) fumo.*	(now) **foo**-moo
We (don't) smoke.	*(Não) fumamos.*	(now) foo-**mah**-moosh
lighter	*esqueiro*	ish-**kay**-roo
cigarettes	*cigarros*	see-**gah**-roosh
marijuana	*erva, marijuana*	**ehr**-vah, mah-ree-**zhwah**-nah
hash	*hashishe*	ah-**shee**-sheh
joint	*baseado*	bah-zeh-**ah**-doo
stoned	*drogado[a]*	droh-**gah**-doo
Wow!	*Fiche!*	**fee**-sheh

Conversing with Animals

English	Portuguese	Pronunciation
rooster / cock-a-doodle-doo	*galo / co-coro-cocó*	**gah**-loo / koo-koo-roo-koo-**kah**
bird / tweet tweet	*pássaro / piu piu*	**pah**-sah-roo / pee-**oo** pee-**oo**

CHATTING

cat / meow	gato / miau	**gah**-too / **mee**-ow
dog / woof woof	cão / ão ão	ko<u>w</u> / ow ow
duck / quack quack	pato / quac quac	**pah**-too / kwahk kwahk
cow / moo	vaca / moo	**vah**-kah / moo
pig / oink oink (or just snort)	porco / orn orn	**por**-koo / orn orn

Profanity

People make animal noises, too. These words will help you understand what the more colorful locals are saying.

bastard	bastardo	bahsh-**tar**-doo
bitch	puta	**poo**-tah
breasts	mamas	**mah**-mahsh
penis	pénis	**peh**-neesh
shit	merda	**mehr**-dah
drunk	bêbado	**bay**-bah-doo
imbecile	parvo	**par**-voo
jerk	palerma	pah-**lehr**-mah
stupid	estúpido[a]	ish-**too**-pee-doo
Did someone fart?	Alguem deu um peido?	**ahl**-gay<u>n</u> **deh**-oo oo<u>n</u> **pay**-doo
I burped.	En arrotei.	ay<u>n</u> ah-**roh**-tay
This sucks.	Isto é chato.	**eesh**-too eh **shah**-too
Go to hell!	Vá para o inferno!	vah **pah**-rah oo een-**fehr**-noo
Shove it up your ass.	Enfia no rabo.	ehn-**fee**-ah noh **rah**-boo
Bullshit.	Merda.	**mehr**-dah
You are...	Vôce é...	voh-**say** eh
Don't be...	Não seja...	no<u>w</u> **seh**-zhah
...a son of a bitch.	...um filho da puta.	oo<u>n</u> **feel**-yoo dah **poo**-tah
...an idiot.	...um idióta.	oo<u>n</u> ee-dee-**ow**-dah
...a creep.	...um estranho.	oo<u>n</u> ish-**tray<u>n</u>**-yoo
...a cretin.	...um cretino.	oo<u>n</u> kreh-**tee**-noo
...a pig.	...um porco.	oo<u>n</u> **por**-koo

Sweet Curses

My goodness.	*Meu deus.*	**meh**-oo **deh**-oosh
Goodness gracious.	*Deus nos vale.*	**deh**-oosh noosh **vah**-leh
Oh, my gosh.	*Ó nossa.*	oo **noh**-sah
Shoot.	*Força.*	**for**-sah
Darn it!	*Caramba!*	kah-**rahm**-bah

CREATE YOUR OWN CONVERSATION

Using these lists, you can have deep (or ridiculous) conversations with the locals.

Who

I / you	*eu / você*	**eh**-oo / voh-**say**
he / she	*ele / ela*	**eh**-leh / **eh**-lah
we / they	*nós / eles*	nohsh / **eh**-lish
my / your...	*meus / seus...*	**meh**-oosh / **seh**-oosh
...parents / children	*...pais / crianças*	pīsh / kree-**ahn**-sahsh
men / women	*homens / mulheres*	**ah**-maynsh / mool-**yeh**-rish
rich / poor	*rico[a] / pobre*	**ree**-koo / **poh**-breh
young / middle-aged / old	*jovem / meia-idade / idoso[a]*	**zhah**-vayn / **may**-ah-ee-**dah**-deh / ee-**doh**-zoo
Portuguese	*Portugueses*	poor-too-**gay**-zish
Spanish	*Espanhóis*	ish-pahn-**yoysh**
Austrians	*Austriacos*	owsh-tree-**ah**-koosh
Belgians	*Belgas*	**behl**-gahsh
British	*Britânicos*	bree-**tah**-nee-koosh
Czechs	*Checos*	**cheh**-koosh
French	*Franceses*	frahn-**say**-zish
Germans	*Alemães*	ah-leh-**maynsh**
Irish	*Irlandês*	eer-lahn-**daysh**
Italians	*Italianos*	ee-tahl-**yah**-noosh
Moroccans	*Marroquinos*	mah-roo-**kee**-noosh

CHATTING

Swiss	Suiços	**swee**-soosh
Europeans	Europeus	eh-oo-roh-**pee**-oosh
EU	UE (União	oo eh (oo-nee-**ow**
(European Union)	Europeia)	eh-oo-roh-**peh**-ee-ah)
Americans	Americanos	ah-meh-ree-**kah**-noosh
liberals	liberais	lee-**beh**-raysh
conservatives	conservadores	kohn-sehr-vah-**doh**-rish
radicals	radicais	rah-**dee**-kaysh
terrorists	terroristas	teh-roh-**reesh**-tahsh
politicians	políticos	poo-**lee**-tee-koosh
big business	negócio grande	neh-**gos**-ee-oo **grahn**-deh
multinational	companhias	kohn-pahn-**yee**-ahsh
corporations	multinacionais	mool-tee-nah-see-oh-**nīsh**
military	militares	mee-lee-**tah**-rish
mafia	máfia	"mafia"
refugees	refigiados	reh-fee-zhee-**ah**-doosh
travelers	vijantes	vee-**zhan**-tish
God	Deus	**deh**-oosh
Christians	cristãos	kreesh-**towsh**
Catholics	católicos	kah-**tal**-ee-koosh
Protestants	protestantes	proh-tish-**tayn**-tehsh
Jews	judeus	**zhoo**-deh-oosh
Muslims	mussulmanos	moo-sool-**mah**-noosh
everyone	todas as	**toh**-dahsh ahsh
	pessoas	peh-**soh**-ahsh

CHATTING

What

buy / sell	comprar / vender	koh<u>n</u>-**prar** / vay<u>n</u>-**dar**
have / lack	ter / faltar	tehr / fahl-**tar**
help / abuse	ajudar / abusar	ah-zhoo-**dar** / ah-boo-**zar**
learn / fear	aprender / temer	ah-prayn-**dehr** / teh-**mehr**
love / hate	amar / odiar	ah-**mar** / oo-dee-**ar**
prosper / suffer	prósperar / sofrer	prahsh-peh-**rar** / soof-**rehr**
take / give	tirar / dar	tee-**rar** / dar
want / need	querer / precisar	keh-**rehr** / preh-see-**zar**
work / play	trabalhar / brincar	trah-bahl-**yar** / breen-**kar**

Why

(anti-)	(contra-)	(**kohn**-trah-)
globalization	globalização	gloh-bah-lee-zah-**sow**
class warfare	luta de classes	**loo**-tah deh **klah**-shish
corruption	corrupção	koo-roop-**sow**
democracy	democracia	deh-moo-krah-**see**-ah
education	instrucão	eensh-troo-**sow**
family	familia	fah-**meel**-yah
food	comida	koo-**mee**-dah
global perspective	perspectiva	persh-pehk-**tee**-vah
	mundial	moo<u>n</u>-dee-**ahl**
guns	pistolas	peesh-**toh**-lahsh
happiness	felicidade	feh-lee-see-**dah**-deh
health	saúde	sah-**oo**-deh
hope	esperança	ish-peh-**rahn**-sah
imperialism	imperialismo	eem-peh-ree-ah-**leezh**-moo
lies	mentiras	may<u>n</u>-**tee**-rahsh
love / sex	amor / sexo	ah-**mor** / **sehk**-soo
marijuana	marijuana	mah-ree-**zhwah**-nah
money / power	dinheiro /	deen-**yay**-roo /
	poder	poo-**dehr**
pollution	poluição	pool-wee-**sow**
racism	racismo	rah-**seesh**-moo
regime change	mudança de	moo-**dahn**-sah deh
	regime	reh-**zhee**-meh
relaxation	descanso	dish-**kahn**-soo
religion	religião	ray-lee-**zhow**
respect	respeito	rish-**pay**-too
taxes	taxas	**tahsh**-ahsh
television	televisão	teh-leh-vee-**zow**
violence	violência	vee-oo-**layn**-see-ah
war / peace	guerra / paz	**geh**-rah / pahsh
work	trabalho	trah-**bahl**-yoo

You Be the Judge

(no) problem	(não) á problema	(no<u>w</u>) ah proo-**blay**-mah
(not) good	(não) bom	(no<u>w</u>) boh<u>n</u>

(not) dangerous	(não) perigoso	(now) peh-ree-**goh**-zoo
(not) fair	(não) justo	(now) **zhoosh**-too
(not) guilty	(não) culpado	(now) kool-**pah**-doo
(not) powerful	(não) poderoso	(now) poo-deh-**roh**-zoo
(not) stupid	(não) estúpido	(now) ish-**too**-pee-doo
(not) happy	(não) feliz	(now) feh-**leesh**
because / for	porque / para	**poor**-keh / **pah**-rah
and / or / from	e / ou / de	ee / oh / deh
too much	demasiado	deh-mah-zee-**ah**-doo
(never) enough	(nunca é) suficiente	(**noon**-kah eh) soo-fee-see-**ayn**-teh
same	mesmo	**mehsh**-moo
better / worse	melhor / pior	mil-**yor** / pee-**or**
here / everywhere	aqui / em toda parte	ah-**kee** / ayn **toh**-dah **par**-teh

Beginnings and Endings

I like...	Gosto...	**gohsh**-too
We like...	Nós gostamos...	nohsh goosh-**tah**-moosh
I don't like...	Não gosto...	now **gohsh**-too
We don't like...	Não gostamos...	now goosh-**tah**-moosh
Do you like...?	Você gosta...	voh-**say gohsh**-tah
In the past...	No passado...	noo pah-**sah**-doo
When I was younger, I thought...	Quando eu era jovem, pensava...	**kwahn**-doo **eh**-oo **eh**-rah **zhah**-vayn payn-**sah**-vah
Now, I think...	Agora penso...	ah-**goh**-rah **payn**-soo
I am / Are you...?	Eu sou / Você é...?	**eh**-oo soh / voh-**say** eh
...an optimist / pessimist	...um optimista / pessimista	oon **ohp**-tee-meesh-tah / **peh**-see-meesh-tah
I (don't) believe...	(Não) acredito...	(now) ah-**kreh**-dee-too
Do you believe...?	Acredita...?	ah-kreh-**dee**-tah
...in God	...em Deus	ayn **deh**-oosh
...in life after death	...em vida depois da morte	ayn **vee**-dah day-**pwaysh** dah **mor**-teh
...in extra-terrestrial life	...que existe vida em outros planetas	keh ee-**zeesh**-teh **vee**-dah ayn **oh**-troosh plah-**nay**-tahsh

...in Santa Claus	...no Pai-Natal	noo pī-nah-**tahl**
Yes. / No.	Sim. / Não.	seeng / no<u>w</u>
Maybe. / I don't know.	Talvez. / Não sei.	**tahl**-vaysh / no<u>w</u> say
What's most important in life?	O que é a coisa mais importante na vida?	oo keh eh ah **koy**-zah mīsh eem-poor-**tahn**-teh nah **vee**-dah
The problem is...	O problema é...	oo proo-**blay**-mah eh
The answer is...	A resposta é...	ah rish-**pohsh**-tah eh
We have solved the world's problems.	Nós resolvemos os problemas do mundo.	nohsh reh-zool-**vay**-moosh oosh proo-**blay**-mahsh doo **moon**-doo

A PORTUGUESE ROMANCE

Words of Love

I / me / you / we	eu / mim / tú / nós	**eh**-oo / meeng / too / nohsh
flirt	namorar	nah-moo-**rar**
kiss	beijo	**bay**-zhoo
hug	abraço	ah-**brah**-soo
love	amor	ah-**mor**
make love	fazer amor	fah-**zehr** ah-**mor**
condom	preservativo	preh-zehr-vah-**tee**-voo
contraceptive	contraceptivo	koh<u>n</u>-trah-sehp-**tee**-voo
safe sex	sexo seguro	**sehk**-soo say-**goo**-roo
sexy	sexy	"sexy"
romantic	romântico	roh-**mahn**-tee-koo
my tender love	minha ternura	**meen**-yah tehr-**noo**-rah
my darling (male / female)	meu querido / minha querida	**meh**-oo keh-**ree**-doo / **meen**-yah keh-**ree**-dah
my angel	meu anjo	**meh**-oo **ahn**-zhoo
baby	bebé	bay-**bay**
my soft thing (male / female)	meu fofinho / minha fofinha	**meh**-oo foh-**feen**-yoo / **meen**-yah foh-**feen**-yah

CHATTING

Ah, Amor

What's the matter?	Que se passa?	keh seh **pah**-sah
Nothing.	Nada.	**nah**-dah
I am / Are you...?	Sou / És...?	soh / ehs
...straight	...normal	nor-**mahl**
...gay	...gay	"gay"
...bisexual	...bissexual	bee-sehk-**swahl**
...undecided	...indeciso[a]	een-day-**see**-zoo
...prudish	...puritano[a]	poo-ree-**tah**-noo
...horny	...excitado[a]	ish-see-**tah**-doo
We are on our honeymoon.	Nós estamos em lua de mel.	nohsh ish-**tah**-moosh ayn **loo**-ah deh mehl
I have...	Tenho...	**tayn**-yoo
...a boyfriend.	...um namorado.	oon nah-moo-**rah**-doo
...a girlfriend.	...uma namorada.	**oo**-mah nah-moo-**rah**-dah
I'm married.	Sou casado[a].	soh kah-**zah**-doo
I'm married but...	Sou casado[a] mas...	soh kah-**zah**-doo mahsh
I'm not married.	Não sou casado[a].	now soh kah-**zah**-doo
Do you have a boyfriend / girlfriend?	Tens namorado / namorada?	taynsh nah-moo-**rah**-doo / nah-moo-**rah**-dah
I'm adventurous.	Sou aventureiro[a].	soh ah-vehn-too-**ray**-roo
I'm lonely.	Sinto-me só.	**seeng**-too-meh soh
I'm lonely tonight.	Estou sozinho[a] hoje a noite.	ish-**toh** soh-**zeen**-yoo **oh**-zheh ah **noy**-teh
I'm rich and single.	Sou rico[a] e solteiro[a].	soh **ree**-koo ee sool-**tay**-roo
Do you mind if I sit here?	Importa-se se eu me sento aqui?	eem-**por**-tah-seh seh **eh**-oo meh **sehn**-too ah-**kee**
Would you like a drink?	Queres beber algo?	**keh**-rish beh-**behr** **ahl**-goo
Will you go out with me?	Queres sair comigo?	**keh**-rish sah-**eer** kohn-**mee**-goo
Would you like to go out tonight for...?	Queres sair hoje á noite por...?	**keh**-rish sah-**eer** **oh**-zheh ah **noy**-teh poor
...a walk	...um passeio	oon pah-**say**-oo

...dinner	...um jantar	oon zhan-**tar**
...a drink	...um copo	oon **koh**-poo
Where's the best place to dance nearby?	Onde é o melhor lugar para dançar por aqui?	**ohn**-deh ay oo mil-**yor** loo-**gar pah**-rah dahn-**sar** poor ah-**kee**
Do you want to dance?	Queres dançar?	**keh**-rish dahn-**sar**
Again?	Outra vez?	**oh**-trah vehz
Let's have a wild and crazy night!	Vamos nos divertir hoje a noite!	**vah**-moosh noosh dee-vehr-**teer oh**-zheh ah **noy**-teh
I have no diseases.	Não tenho nenhuma doença.	now **tayn**-yoo neen-**yoo**-mah doo-**ayn**-sah
I have many diseases.	Tenho muitas doenças.	**tayn**-yoo **mween**-tahsh doo-**ayn**-sahsh
I have only safe sex.	Só faço sexo com proteção.	soh **fah**-soo **sehk**-soo kohn proh-teh-**sow**
Can I take you home? (f / m)	Posso leva-la[o] para casa?	**pos**-soo **leh**-vah-lah **pah**-rah **kah**-zah
Why not?	Porque não?	poor-**kay** now
How can I change your mind?	Oque posso fazer para você mudar de idéia?	**oh**-keh **pos**-soo fah-**zehr pah**-rah voh-**say** moo-**dar** deh ee-**day**-yah
Kiss me.	Dê-me um beijo.	**deh**-meh oon **bay**-zhoo
May I kiss you?	Posso beijar?	**pos**-soo bay-**zhar**
Can I see you again?	Quando é que o / a posso ver?	**kwahn**-doo eh keh oo / ah **pos**-soo vehr
Your place or mine?	Na sua casa ou na minha?	nah **soo**-ah **kah**-zah oh nah **meen**-yah
How does this feel?	Como te fáz sentir?	**koh**-moo teh fahsh sehn-**teer**
Is this an aphrodisiac?	É isto um afrodisíaco?	eh **eesh**-too oon ah-froo-dee-**zee**-ah-koo
This is (not) my first time.	(Não) é a minha primeira vez.	(now) eh ah **meen**-yah pree-**may**-rah vaysh
You are my most beautiful souvenir.	Você é a minha melhor recordação.	voh-**say** ay ah **meen**-yah mil-**yor** reh-kor-dah-**sow**

Do you do this often?	*Faz isto regularmente?*	fahsh **eesh**-too reh-goo-lar-**mayn**-teh
Is my breath O.K.?	*Tenho bom hálito?*	**tayn**-yoo boh<u>n</u> **ah**-lee-too
Let's just be friends.	*Vamos ser só amigos.*	**vah**-moosh sehr soh ah-**mee**-goosh
I'll pay for my share.	*Pagarei a minha parte.*	pah-gah-**ray** ah **meen**-yah **par**-teh
Would you like a massage for...?	*Gostaria de uma massagem para...?*	goosh-tah-**ree**-ah deh **oo**-mah mah-**sah**-zhay<u>n</u> **pah**-rah
...your back	*...as tuas costas*	ahsh **too**-ahsh **kosh**-tahsh
...your feet	*...os seus pés*	oosh **seh**-oosh pehsh
Why not?	*Porquê não?*	poor-**kay** now
Try it.	*Exprimente.*	ish-pree-**mayn**-teh
It tickles.	*Isso faz cócegas.*	**ee**-soo fahsh **kah**-see-gahsh
Oh my God!	*Ó meu Deus!*	ah **meh**-oo **deh**-oosh
I love you.	*Eu amo-te.*	**eh**-oo **ah**-moo-teh
Darling, will you marry me?	*Querida, queres casar comigo?*	keh-**ree**-dah **keh**-rish kah-**zar** koo-**mee**-goo

DICTIONARY

PORTUGUESE/ENGLISH

You'll see some adjectives and nouns listed like this: *agressivo[a]*.
Use the *a* ending (pronounced "ah") if you're talking about a
female (including yourself).

A

á	at
á moda de casa	homemade
abaixo	down; below
aberto[a]	open (adj)
abertor de latas	can opener
abôrto	abortion
abôrto natural	miscarriage
Abril	April
abrir	open (v)
abstrato	abstract
abusar	abuse (v)
acabado	over (finished)
acesso a Internet	Internet access
acetona	nail polish remover
acidente	accident
acima	above
acordar	wake up
acordo, de	agree
adega	cellar
adesivo	tape (adhesive); Band-Aid
adeus	goodbye
adulto[a]	adult
advogado[a]	lawyer
aérea, linha	airline
aéreo, correio	air mail
aeroporto	airport
agência de viagens	travel agency
agnóstico[a]	agnostic
agora	now
Agosto	August
agrafador	stapler
agressivo[a]	aggressive
água	water
água da torneira	tap water

água mineral	mineral water
água potável	drinkable water
água, queda de	waterfall
agulha	needle
ajuda	help (n)
ajudar	help (v)
albergue de juventude	youth hostel
alcool	alcohol
alcunha	nickname
aldeia	village
aleijado[a]	handicapped
Alemanha	Germany
alergias	allergies
alérgico[a]	allergic
alfândega	customs
alfinete	pin
alfinete de segurança	safety pin
algodão	cotton
alguma coisa	something
alguns	some
alicate	pliers
alimento suplementar	baby formula
almoço	lunch
almoço, pequeno	breakfast
almofada	pillow
alta, tensão	high blood pressure
alto[a]	tall; high
alugar	rent (v)
amanhã	tomorrow
amante	lover
amar	love (v)
amarelo[a]	yellow
ambulância	ambulance
amigo[a]	friend
amizade	friendship
amor	love (n)
andar	walk (v); story (floor)
animal de estimação	pet (n)
aniversário	birthday
ano	year
antepassado[a]	ancestor
antes	before
antibiótico	antibiotic
antigo[a]	ancient
antiguidades	antiques
antiquário	antiques shop
ao lado	next door to
apanhar	catch (v)
apartamento	apartment
aperitivos	appetizers
apontamento	appointment
apontar	point (v)
aprender	learn
apressar	hurry (v)
apretado[a]	tight
aproximadamente	approximately
aqui	here
ar	air
ar condicionado	air-conditioned
arco íris	rainbow
armários	lockers
arranha	spider
arranjar	fix (v)
arrepios	chills
arrôba	"at" sign (@)
arte	art
arte nova	Art Nouveau
artesanato	crafts
artista	artist
artrite	arthritis

Portuguese / English

DICTIONARY

árvore	tree	banco	bank
asa	wing	bandeira	flag
asma	asthma	banheira	bathtub
aspirina	aspirin	banho	bath
assadura das fraldas	diaper rash	banho, calção de	swim trunks
		banho, fato de	swimsuit
assento	seat	banho, casa de	bathroom
assinatura	signature	barata	cockroach
ateu	atheist	barato[a]	cheap
atirar	throw	barba	beard
atleta	athlete	barbeiro	barber
atraente	attractive	barco	boat, ship (n), ferry
atraso	delay (n)	barco de passeio	rowboat
através	through	barco de vela	sailing
atravessar	go through	barulho[a]	noisy
audio guia	audioguide	base	foundation (makeup)
auto serviço	self-service	baseado	joint (marijuana)
autocarro	city bus	basebol	baseball
autoestrada	highway	basquetebol	basketball
automática, caixa	cash machine	batão de cierio	lip salve
		bateria	battery
avião	plane	baton	lipstick
avó	grandmother	bêbado[a]	drunk
avô	grandfather	bebé	baby
azedo[a]	sour	beber	drink (v)
azul	blue	bebida	drink (n)
		beijo	kiss (n)
B		Belgica	Belgium
		beliches	bunk beds
babeiro	bib	bem-vindo	welcome
bagagem	baggage	bexiga	bladder
bagagem	baggage claim	biblioteca	library
bagagem de mão	carry-on luggage	bicicleta	bicycle
		bife	beef
baixo[a]	low	bigode	moustache
balde	bucket	bilhete	ticket
balsa	raft	bloco	block

DICTIONARY

Portuguese / English

blusa	blouse
boca	mouth
bola	ball
boleia, pedir	hitchhike
bolhas	blisters
bolsa	purse
bolso	pocket
bom	good, fine
bomba	bomb; pump (n)
bomba de gasolina	gas station
bom-dia	good day
boné	cap
boneca	doll
bonito[a]	pretty, handsome
borracha	eraser
botão	button
botas	boots
braço	arm
branco[a]	white
brilho de sol	sunshine
brincos	earrings
brinquedo	toy
broche	brooch
broches	clothespins
bronze	bronze
bronzeado	suntan (n)
bronzear	sunbathe
buraco	hole
burro	donkey

C

cabeça	head
cabedal	leather
cabelareiro	beauty salon
cabelo	hair
cada	each
cadeira	chair
cadeira de carro para o bebé	baby car seat
cadeirinha alta	highchair
caderno	notebook
café	coffee; coffee shop
café Internet	Internet café
cãibra	cramps
cair	fall (v)
cais	platform (train)
caixa	cashier; box
caixa automática	cash machine
caixão	crypt
calado[a]	quiet
calção de banho	swim trunks
calças	pants
calções	shorts
calendário	calendar
calor	heat (n)
caloria	calorie
cama	bed
camara	camera
camarote	sleeper (train)
câmbio	exchange (n)
caminho de ferro	railway
camioneta	long-distance bus
camisa	shirt
camisa de dormir	nightgown
campaínha	ring (n)
campeonato	championship
campismo	camping; campsite
campo	countryside; field
Canadá	Canada
canal	canal; channel
canção	song

cancelar	cancel
caneta	pen
canoa	canoe
cansado[a]	tired
cantar	sing
cantor[a]	singer
cão	dog
capela	chapel
capitão	captain
cara	face
carne	meat
caro[a]	expensive
carpete	carpet, rug
carregar	carry
carrinho de bebê	stroller
carro	car
carruagem	train car
carruagem cama	sleeper car (train)
carruagem restaurante	dining car (train)
carta	letter
cartão	card (also business card)
cartão de crédito	credit card
cartão postal	postcard
cartão telefónico	telephone card
cartas	cards (deck)
carteira	wallet
carteirista	pickpocket
casa	house
casa de banho	bathroom
casa de ferragens	hardware store
casa de fotocopias	photocopy shop

casa, á moda de	homemade
casaco	jacket
casaco impermeável	raincoat
casado[a]	married
casamento	wedding
cassete	tape (cassette)
castanho	brown
castelo	castle
catedral	cathedral
Católico[a]	Catholic (adj)
cavaleiro	knight
cavalheiro	gentleman
cavalo	horse
cave	cave
cedo	soon; early
centro	center; downtown
centro comercial	shopping mall
ceramica	ceramic
certo[a]	right (correct)
cerveja	beer
cesto	basket
céu	sky; heaven
chaleira	kettle
chapéu	hat
charcutaria	delicatessen
chateado[a]	angry
chave	key
chave de parafusos	screwdriver
chávena	cup
chegadas	arrivals
chegar	arrive
cheio	no vacancy
cheiro	smell (n)
cheque	check
cheque de viagem	traveler's check
chinélos	slippers

chinês	Chinese
chorar	cry (v)
chupeta	pacifier
chuva	rain (n)
chuveiro	shower
cidade	city; town
ciência	science
cientista	scientist
cigarro	cigarette
cima, em	upstairs
cinto	belt
cintura	waist
cinzeiro	ashtray
cinzento	gray
claro	clear
classe	class
classe, primeira	first class
classe, segunda	second class
clássico[a]	classical
clinica médica	medical clinic
clip	paper clip
cobre	copper
código pessoal	PIN code
código postal	zip code
coelho	rabbit
coisa	thing
colete	vest
colher	spoon
cólicas	menstrual cramps
collants	tights
com	with
com gás	fizzy
combinação	slip
comboio	train
começar	begin
comer	eat
comichão	itch (n)

comida	food
comida para bebés	baby food
como	how
compact disco	compact disc
complicado[a]	complicated
compras	shopping
comprimido	pill
comprimidos para as dores	painkiller (usually non-aspirin)
computador	computer
concerto	concert
concha	shell
condicionador	conditioner (hair)
condutor	conductor; driver
conduzir	drive (v)
conexão	connection (train)
confeitaria	sweets shop
confirmar	confirm
confortável	comfortable; cozy
congestão	congestion (sinus)
constipação	cold (n)
construção na estrada	construction (sign)
conta	bill (payment)
contador	accountant
contagioso	contagious
contracepçaõ	condom
convidado[a]	guest
convite	invitation
copiado	copy
copo	glass
cor de laranja	orange (color)
cor de rosa	pink
coração	heart
coral	choir
corbetor	blanket

corda	rope
cordão de sapatos	shoelaces
cordeiro	lamb
cores	colors
corpo	body
corredor	aisle; corridor
correia de ventoinha	fan belt
correio	mail (n)
correio aéreo	air mail
corrente	stream (n)
correr	run (v)
corrupção	corruption
corta unhas	nail clipper
corte de cabelo	haircut
costa	coast
costas	back
cotovelo	elbow
coxa	thigh
cozinha	kitchen
cozinhar	cook (v)
crédito	credit
crédito, cartão de	credit card
creme	cream; lotion
creme de barbear	shaving cream
creme desinfetante	first-aid cream
creme para as mãos	hand lotion
criado	waiter
criança	child
crianças	children
Cristã[o]	Christian (adj)
cru	raw
cruz	cross
cruzamento	intersection
cruzeta	coat hanger
cuecas	underpants
cuidadoso[a]	careful
culpado[a]	guilty
cúpula	dome
curto[a]	short
custa, quanto	how much ($)

D

dançar	dance (v)
dar	give
de	of; from
de acordo	agree
de repente	suddenly
debaixo	under
declarar	declare (customs)
dedo	finger
dedo do pé	toe
delicioso[a]	delicious
delineador	eyeliner
demasiado	too (much)
democracia	democracy
dente, dor de	toothache
dentes	teeth
dentição	teething (baby)
dentista	dentist
depois	after; afterwards
depois de amanhã	day after tomorrow
depósito	deposit
descanso	relaxation
desconges-tionante	decongestant
desconto	discount
desculpa	apology
desculpe	sorry; excuse me
desejo	wish (v)
desempregado[a]	unemployed

desinfetante	disinfectant
desodorizante	deodorant
despertador	alarm clock
desporto	sport
desventurado[a]	unfortunate
desvio	detour
detergente	laundry detergent
detrás	behind
deus	God
Dezembro	December
dia	day
diabético[a]	diabetic
diafragma	diaphragm (birth control)
diamante	diamond
diarreia	diarrhea
dicionário	dictionary
difícil	difficult
dinheiro	money; cash
direção	direction
directo[a]	direct
direita	right (direction)
disco voador	Frisbee
divertido[a]	funny; fun (adj)
divorciado[a]	divorced
dobrar	double
doce	sweet (adj); candy
doença	disease
doença venéria	venereal disease
doente	sick
domingo	Sunday
donde	where
dono[a]	owner
dor	pain; cramps
dor de cabeça	headache
dor de dente	toothache

dor de estômago	stomachache
dor de garganta	sore throat
dor de ouvido	earache
dor no peito	chest pains
dormir	sleep (v)
dormitorio	dormitory
doutor[a]	doctor
drogado[a]	stoned
dúzia	dozen

E

e	and
ela	she
ele	he
eles	they
elevador	elevator
eliminar	delete
em	in
em cima	upstairs
em frente	straight
em vez de	instead
embaixada	embassy
embalagem	package
embrulhar	wrap (v)
ementa	menu
emergência	emergency
emergência, saída de	emergency exit
emergência, sala de	emergency room
emprestar	borrow; lend
empurrar	push
encantador[a]	charming
encarnado[a]	red
encher	refill (n)
endereço	address

Portuguese / English

DICTIONARY

endereço eletrônico	email address
enfermeiro[a]	nurse
engenheiro	engineer
engolir	swallow (v)
enicologista	gynecologist
entender	understand
entrada	entrance
envenanamento alimentar	food poisoning
enviar	send, ship (v)
enxaqueca	migraine
epilepcia	epilepsy
equipa	team
erro	mistake
erupção	rash
erva	marijuana
escada	ladder
escadas	stairs
Escandinavia	Scandinavia
escanduloso[a]	scandalous
esclarecer	explain
escola	school
escorregadio	slippery
escova	brush
escova de cabelo	hairbrush
escova de dentes	toothbrush
escrever	write
escritório	office
escultor[a]	sculptor
escultura	sculpture
escuro[a]	dark
escutar	listen
esfomeado[a]	hungry
esgotado[a]	exhausted
Espanha	Spain
especialidade	specialty

espectáculo	show (n)
espelho	mirror
espera, sala de	waiting room
esperança	hope
esperar	wait (v)
espirro	sneeze (n)
esposa	wife
esquecer	forget
esquerda	left (direction)
esqui aquático	waterskiing
esquiar	ski (v); skiing
esquina	corner
esta noite	tonight
estação	station
estação de metro	subway station
estacas de tenda	tent pegs
estacionamento, parque de	parking lot
estacionar	park (v)
estado	state
Estados Unidos	United States
estanho	pewter
este	east
estilo	style
estômago	stomach
estômago, dor de	stomachache
estranho[a]	strange
estrangeiro[a]	foreign
estreito[a]	narrow
estrela	star (in sky)
estudante	student
estúpido[a]	stupid
eu	I
Europa	Europe
exactamente	exactly

excelente	excellent
excepto	except
excursão	tour
exemplo	example
explicar	explain

F

fábrica	factory
faca	knife
fácil	easy
fado	mournful Portuguese folk music
falar	talk, speak
falésia	cliff
falso[a]	false
familia	family
famoso[a]	famous
fantástico[a]	fantastic
farmácia	pharmacy
faróis da frente	headlights
fatia	slice
fato de banho	swimsuit
favor, por	please
fazer	make (v)
febre dos fenos	hay fever
fechado	closed
fechadura	lock (n)
fechar	lock (v)
fecho	zipper
feio[a]	ugly
feira	flea market
felicidade	happiness
feliz	happy
feminino[a]	feminine
feriado	holiday
férias	vacation

ferido[a]	injured
fervido	boiled
festa	party
Fevereiro	February
fevre	fever
ficha	token
filha	daughter
filho	son
filme	movie
fio	string; necklace
fio dental	dental floss
fita cola	scotch tape
flor	flower
fogo	fire
fogo de artificio	fireworks
fone	telephone
fonte	fountain
forno	oven
forte	strong
fortificação	wall, fortified
fosforos	matches
fosso	moat
fotocopia	photocopy
fotografia	photo
frágil	fragile
fraldas	diaper
França	France
frente, em	straight
fresco[a]	fresh; cool
frio[a]	cold (adj)
fronteira	border
fruta	fruit
fumador	smoking
fumador, não	non-smoking
fumo	smoke(n)
fundo	bottom
fussil	fuses

futebol	soccer
futebol americano	American football
futuro	future

G

gaivota	paddleboat
galeria	gallery
galeria de arte	art gallery
galinha	chicken
garagem	garage
garantia	guarantee
garfo	fork
garganta	throat
garganta, dor de	sore throat
garrafa	bottle
gás	gas
gás, com	fizzy (water)
gastar	spend
gato	cat
gaze	bandage; gauze
gelado	ice cream
gelo	ice
gêmeos	twins
generouso[a]	generous
genuíno[a]	genuine
gerente	manager
Gilete	razor
ginastica	gymnastics
golfe	golf
gordo[a]	fat (adj)
gordura	fat (n)
gorduroso	greasy
gostar	enjoy, like (v)
gótico[a]	Gothic
Grã-Bretanha	Britain

gramática	grammar
grande	big
grande armazen	department store
granjeiro[a]	farmer
grátis	free (no cost)
grátis, taxa	toll-free
grávida	pregnant
gravidez	pregnancy
Grécia	Greece
gripe	flu
grosso[a]	thick
guarda-chuva	umbrella
guardanapo	napkin
guardar	keep; save (computer)
guerra	war
guia, um (m)	guidebook
guia, uma (f)	guide
guitarra	guitar

H

halito	breath
hashishe	hash (drug)
hemorróidas	hemorrhoids
hidratante	moisturizer
hidroplano	hydrofoil
hífen	hyphen (-)
história	history
hoje	today
Holanda	Netherlands
homem	man
homosexual	gay
honesto[a]	honest
hóquei	hockey
hora	hour

horário	opening hours; timetable
horrível	horrible
humilhante	embarrassing

I

ida e volta	roundtrip
ida, uma	one way (ticket)
idade	age
igreija	church
ilha	island
imediatamente	immediately
imobilizado	stuck
importado[a]	imported
importante	important
impossível	impossible
imposto, sem	duty free
impressionista	Impressionist
imprimir	print (v)
inacreditável	incredible
inchado	swelling (n)
incluido[a]	included
incomudar	disturb
inconciente	unconscious
independente	independent
indigestão	indigestion
industria	industry
infecção	infection
infecção urinaria	urinary infection
inflamação	inflammation
informação	information
Inglaterra	Great Britain
inglês	English
inocente	innocent
insecto	insect

insolação	sunstroke
instante	instant
instrucão	education
inteligente	intelligent
interior	inside
interresante	interesting
intestino	intestines
inverno	winter
iodo	iodine
ir	go
Irlanda	Ireland
irmã	sister
irmão	brother
isqueiro	lighter (n)
Itália	Italy

J

já	already
Janeiro	January
janela	window
jantar	dinner
jardim	garden
jardinagem	gardening
jarro	carafe
jeans	jeans
joalheria	jewelry; jewelry shop
joelho	knee
jogar	play (v)
jogo	game
jornal	newspaper
jovem	young; teenager
jovens	youths
Judeu	Jewish
Julho	July
Junho	June
juntos	together

justo[a]	fair (just)
juventude	youth
juventude, albergue de	youth hostel

K

kitchenete	kitchenette

L

lã	wool
lábio	lip
ladrão	thief
lago	lake
lâmpada	light bulb
lanterna a pilhas	flashlight
lápis	pencil
lápis para os olhos	eyeliner
laranja	orange (fruit)
largo[a]	wide; loose
lata	can (n)
latão	brass
lavandaria	launderette
lavar	wash
lavatório	sink
laxativo	laxative
lembrança	souvenir
lenço	scarf
lençol	sheet
lençol de cama	bedsheet
lenços de papel	facial tissue
lentes de contacto	contact lenses
lento[a]	slow
levar, para	take out (food)
ligadora	bandage, support
limpo[a]	clean (adj)

lindo[a]	beautiful
língua	language
linha	track (train); thread
linha aérea	airline
linha de roupas	clothesline
linho	linen
lista	list
litro	liter
livraria	book shop
livre	vacant
livro	book
local da Web	website
loja	store; shop (n)
loja de brinquedos	toy store
loja de lembranças	souvenir shop
loja de roupa	clothing boutique
loja de telemóveis	cell phone shop
loja de vinhos	wine shop
loja fotográfica	camera shop
longe	far
louro[a]	blond
lua	moon
lua de mel	honeymoon
lugar	seat
lugar sentado	berth (train)
luta	fight (n)
lutar	fight (v)
luvas	gloves
luz	light (n)
luzes traseiras	tail lights

M

madeira	wood
maduro	ripe

mãe	mother	meia de vidro	nylons (panty hose)
magnifico[a]	great		
magro[a]	thin	meia-noite	midnight
Maio	May	meias	socks
mais	more	meio-dia	noon
mais tarde	later	melhor	best
mala	suitcase	Menina	Miss
malenten-dido	misunderstanding	menina	waitress
		menstruação	menstruation; period
mangas	sleeves		
manhã	morning	mentiras	lies
mão	hand	mercado	market
mão, bagagem de	carry-on luggage	mercado de flores	flower market
mapa	map	mercado municipal	open-air market
mapa do metro	subway map		
maquiagem	makeup	mercearia	grocery store
máquina de lavar roupa	washer	mês	month
		mesa	table
mar	sea	mesmo	same
Março	March	mesquita	mosque
marido	husband	metro	subway
marisco	seafood	meu	my
mármore	marble (material)	militares	military
mas	but	minimo	minimum
masculino[a]	masculine	minutos	minutes
masmorra	dungeon	missa	mass
matar	kill	mista	mix (n)
mau	bad	mobilias	furniture
maxila	jaw	mochila	backpack
máximo	maximum	moda	fashion
mecânico[a]	mechanic	moda de casa, á	homemade
mediaval	medieval	moderno[a]	modern
medicina	medicine	moedas	coins
medidor	taxi meter	molhado[a]	wet
médio	medium	momento	moment
medo[a]	afraid	monestério	monastery

Portuguese / English

DICTIONARY

montanha	mountain
montar a cavalo	horse riding
monumento	monument
morrer	die
morto[a]	dead
mosteiro	cloister
mostrar	show (v)
mota	motorcycle
motocicleta	motor scooter
Muçulmano[a]	Muslim (adj)
mudar	change (v); transfer (v)
muito[a]	many; much; very
mulher	woman
mulheres	women
Multibanco	cash machine
multidão	crowd (n)
mundo	world
músculo	muscle
museu	museum
música	music

N

nacionalidade	nationality
nada	nothing
nadar	swim
não	no; not
não fumador	non-smoking
nariz	nose
nascer do sol	sunrise
Natal	Christmas
natureza	nature
náusea	nausea
nebuloso	cloudy
necessário	necessary
necessitar	need

negócio	business
nervoso[a]	nervous
neto[a]	grandchild
nevoeiro	fog
noite	night
noite, esta	tonight
noitecer	evening
nome	name
normal	normal
norte	north
nós	we; us
Novembro	November
novo[a]	new
nunca	never
nuo[a]	naked

O

o quê	what
quê, o	what
O.K.	O.K.
obrigado[a]	thanks
oceano	ocean
oculista	optician
ocúlos	glasses (eye)
óculos de sol	sunglasses
ocupado	occupied
odiar	hate
oeste	west
olá	hello
óleo	oil (n)
óleo de transmissão	transmission fluid
olhar	look; watch (v)
olho	eye
Olímpicos	Olympics
ombros	shoulder

ontem	yesterday
ópera	opera
operador	operator
orelha	ear
orgão	organ
ou	or
ouro	gold
outono	autumn
outra vez	again
outro	other; another
Outubro	October
ouvido, dor de	earache
ouvir	hear

P

padaria	bakery
padre	priest
pagar	pay
página	page
pai	father
Pai-Natal	Santa Claus
pais	parents
país	country
palácio	palace
palavra	word
palito	toothpick
pão	bread
papel	paper
papel higiénico	toilet paper
papelaria	office supplies store
para	for; to
para levar	take out (food)
parabéns	congratulations
para-brisas	windshield wipers
paragem	stop (n, train or bus)
paragem de autocarro	bus stop
paragem do metro	subway stop
parar	stop (v)
parque	park (garden); playpen
parque de diversões	playground
parque de estacionamento	parking lot
partidas	departures
partido[a]	broken
partir	depart
Pascoa	Easter
passado	past
passageiro[a]	passenger
passaporte	passport
pássaro	bird
passatempo	hobby
pasta de dentes	toothpaste
pastelaria	pastry; pastry shop
pastilha elástica	gum
patinagem	skating
patins	roller skates
patrão	boss
paz	peace
pé	foot
pé de atleta	athlete's foot
peão	pedestrian
pedaço	piece
pedir boleia	hitchhike
peito	chest; breast
peito, dor no	chest pains
peixe	fish (n)
pele	skin
pena, que	it's a pity
pénis	penis

Portuguese	English
pensar	think
pensos higiénicos	sanitary napkins
pente	comb (n)
pequeno almoço	breakfast
pequeno[a]	small
percento	percent
perdido[a]	lost
perfeito[a]	perfect (adj)
pergunta	question (n)
perguntar	ask
perigo	danger
perigoso[a]	dangerous
período	period (of time)
perna	leg
perservativo	condom
perto	near
pesado[a]	heavy
pescar	fish (v)
pescoço	neck
peso	weight
pessoa	person
pessoas	people
pessoas de terceira idade	seniors
petisco	snack
piada	joke (n)
pijamas	pajamas
pilula anticoncepcional	birth control pill
pinsa	tweezers
pintura	painting
pior	worst
piquenique	picnic
pisca-pisca	turn signal
piscina	swimming pool
pistola	gun

Portuguese	English
planta	plant
plástico	plastic
pneu	tire (n)
pó	powder
pó de talco	talcum powder
pó para o rosto	face powder
pobre	poor
poder	can (v); power
poderoso[a]	powerful
podre	rotten
polícia	police
poliester	polyester
políticos	politicians
poluição	pollution
ponte	bridge
ponto	dot (computer)
pontual	on time
pôr do sol	sunset
por favor	please
porão	basement
porcelana	porcelain
porco	pig; pork
porquê	why; because
porta	door
portagem	toll
porto	harbor
possível	possible
possuir	own (v)
pouco	few
praça	square (town)
praia	beach
prancha	surfboard
prata	silver
prático[a]	practical
prato	plate
preço	cost, price
prédio	building

preguiçoso[a]	lazy
prenda	gift
Preparação H	Preparation H
presente	present (gift)
preto	black
primavera	spring (n)
primeira classe	first class
primeiro[a]	first
primo[a]	cousin
principal	main
prisão de ventre	constipation
privado[a]	private
problema	problem, trouble
problema no coração	heart condition
produto para a limpeza do rosto	face cleanser
professor	teacher
profissão	occupation
proibido[a]	forbidden
pronto socorro	first aid
pronto[a]	ready
pronúncia	pronunciation
prósperar	prosper
protector solar	sunscreen
Protestante	Protestant (adj)
provar	taste (try)
próximo[a]	next
público	public
pulga	flea
pullover	sweater
pulmões	lungs
púlpito	pulpit
pulsação	pulse
pulseira	bracelet
pulso	wrist
puxador	handle (n)

Q

qualidade	quality
quando	when
quanto	how many
quanto custa	how much ($)
quarta-feira	Wednesday
quarto	room; bedroom; quarter (¼)
quartos	rooms (vacancy sign)
que pena	it's a pity
queda de água	waterfall
queijo	cheese
queimadura	burn (n)
queimadura solar	sunburn
queixar	complain
quem	who
quente	warm; hot (adj)
querer	want
quinta	farm
quinta-feira	Thursday
quiosque	newsstand

R

rabo	tail
rabuçados da tosse	cough drops
racismo	racism
radiador	radiator
rádio	radio
rainha	queen
raio X	X-ray
rapariga	girl
rapaz	boy
reboque	tow truck
recado	message
receber	receive
receita	recipe

receita médica	prescription
recepcionista	receptionist
recibo	receipt
recomendar	recommend
recordar	remember
recto	rectum
rede	cot
reembolso	refund (n)
refigiados	refugees
reformado[a]	retired
rei	king
relaxar	relax
rélica	relic
religião	religion
relógio	clock; watch (n)
remédio	medicine
remédio para a diarréia	diarrhea medicine
remédio para azia	antacid
remédio para constipação	cold medicine
renascimento	Renaissance
renda	lace
reparar	repair
repelente de insectos	insect repellant
repente, de	suddenly
Republica Checa	Czech Republic
reserva	reservation
reservar	reserve
respeito	respect (n)
resposta	answer
ressonar	snore
revista	magazine
rico[a]	rich
rimel	mascara

rio	river
rir	laugh (v)
robe	bathrobe
rock	rock (n)
roda	wheel
rodas-acesso	wheelchair-accessible
rolha	cork
românico	Romanesque
romântico[a]	romantic; Romantic (art)
rotunda	roundabout
roubado[a]	robbed
roulote	R.V. (camper)
roupa	clothes
roxo[a]	purple
rua	street
ruidoso[a]	loud
ruínas	ruins

S

sábado	Saturday
sabão	soap
saber	know
sabor	taste (n); flavor (n)
sacarolhas	corkscrew
saco	bag
saco de dormir	sleeping bag
saco plástico	plastic bag
saco plástico com fecho	zip-lock bag
saia	skirt
saída	exit
saída de emergência	emergency exit
saída do metro	subway exit

sair	leave	sempre	always
sala	hall (big room)	Senhor	Mr.
sala de emergência	emergency room	senhor	sir
		Senhora	Mrs.
sala de espera	waiting room	senhora	waitress
saldos	sale	senhoras	ladies
saltar	jump	sentido único	one-way street
salvagem	wild	separado[a]	separate
sandálias	sandals	ser	is
sandálias de dedo	flip-flops	sério[a]	serious
sande	sandwich	serviço	service
sangrar	bleeding	Setembro	September
sangre	blood	sexo	sex
santo[a]	saint	sexta-feira	Friday
sapatos	shoes	SIDA	AIDS
sapatos de ténis	tennis shoes	silêncio	silence
saudade	homesick	sim	yes
saudavel	healthy	simpático[a]	nice; kind
saúde	health	simples	simple; plain
Saúde!	Cheers!	sinagoga	synagogue
se	if	sinal	sign; moleskin
secador	dryer	sinal de luz	stoplight
secar	dry (v)	sinos	bells
seco	dry (adj)	sinosite	sinus problems
século	century	sintético[a]	synthetic
seda	silk	slide	slide (photo)
sede	thirsty	só	only
segredo	secret	sobre	on
segunda	second	sobremesa	dessert
segunda classe	second class	sobrinha	niece
segunda-feira	Monday	sobrinho	nephew
seguro	insurance	sofrer	suffer
seguro de saúde	health insurance	sol	sun; sunny
seguro[a]	safe; insured	sol, brilho de	sunshine
selo	stamp	sol, nascer do	sunrise
sem	without	sol, óculos de	sunglasses
semana	week	sol, pôr do	sunset

solar, protector	sunscreen
solar, queimadura	sunburn
sólido[a]	sturdy
solteiro[a]	single
sombra	eye shadow
sonhar	dream (v)
sonho	dream (n)
sonolento[a]	sleepy
sorriso	smile (n)
sorte	luck
soutien	bra
sozinho[a]	alone
suar	sweat (v)
subida	up; hill
sublinhar	underscore (_)
suficiente	enough
Suíça	Switzerland
sujo	dirty
sul	south
sumo	juice
supermercado	supermarket
suplemento	supplement
suporte para cadeira	booster seat
surfista	surfer
surpresa	surprise (n)

T

talvez	maybe
tamanho	size
tampa para lava louça	sink stopper
tampões	tampons
tampões de ouvido	earplugs
tantã	crazy
tarde	late; afternoon

tarde, mais	later
taxa	tax
taxa grátis	toll-free
teatro	theater
tecido	cloth
telefone	telephone (n)
telefone publico	phone booth
telefónico, cartão	telephone card
telemóvel	cell phone
televisão	television
telhado	roof
temer	fear (v)
temperatura	temperature
tempestada	storm
tempo	weather
tenda	tent
ténis	tennis; sneakers
tenro[a]	tender
tensão alta	high blood pressure
tépido[a]	lukewarm
ter	have
terça-feira	Tuesday
terceira idade, pessoas de	seniors
terminal das camionetas	bus station
terminar	finish (v)
termómetro	thermometer
terra	earth
terrível	terrible
terroristas	terrorists
tesoraria	treasury
tesouras	scissors
teste de gravidez	pregnancy test
testículos	testicles

tia	aunt
tijela	bowl
tímido[a]	shy
tio	uncle
tirar	pull
toalha	towel
todo	every
tomada	electrical adapter
tomar	take
tonturas	dizziness
torneira	faucet
tornozelo	ankle
torre	tower
tosse	cough (n)
tosser	cough (v)
trabalhar	work (v)
trabalho	job; work (n)
tradicional	traditional
traduzir	translate
tráfico	traffic
transferência	download
traseiro	buttocks
travões	brakes
tripé	tripod
triste	sad
troca	change (n)
tu	you (informal)
tubo para mergulho	snorkel
tudo	everything
tumido[a]	swollen
túnel	tunnel
turista	tourist
Turkia	Turkey

U

último[a]	last
uma ida	one way (ticket)
uma vez	once
úmido	muggy
unha	fingernail
universidade	university
uretra	urethra
urgente	urgent
usar	use (v)
útero	uterus

V

vaca	cow
vale	valley
validade	validate
válido[a]	valid
varanda	balcony
vasilina	Vaseline
vazio[a]	empty
vegetariano[a]	vegetarian
vela	candle
velas	sparkplugs
veleiro	sailboat
velho[a]	old
velocidade	speed
veludo	velvet
vender	sell
vento	wind; windy
ver	see
verão	summer
verde	green
vermelho[a]	red
verniz para as unhas	nail polish
vestido	dress (n)
vez de, em	instead
vez, outra	again
vez, uma	once
via	by (train, car, etc.)

viagem	trip
viagem, cheque de	traveler's check
viajar	travel (v)
vida	life
vijantes	travelers
vinhedo	vineyard
vinho	wine
violação	rape (n)
violência	violence
vir	come
vírus	virus
visita	visit (n)
visita guiada	guided tour
visitar	visit (v)
vista	view
vitaminas	vitamins
viúva	widow
viúvo	widower
viver	live (v)
voar	fly (v)
voçê	you (formal)
volta, ida e	roundtrip
vomitar	vomit
voo	flight
voz	voice

X

xampú	shampoo

ENGLISH/PORTUGUESE

You'll see some adjectives and nouns listed like this: *agresivo[a]*. Use the *a* ending (pronounced "ah") if you're talking about a female (including yourself).

A

abortion	abôrto
above	acima
abstract	abstrato
abuse (v)	abusar
accident	acidente
accountant	contador
adapter, electrical	tomada
address	endereço
address, email	endereço eletrônico
adult	adulto[a]
afraid	medo[a]
Africa	Africa
after	depois
afternoon	tarde
afterwards	depois
again	outra vez
age	idade
aggressive	agressivo[a]
agnostic	agnóstico[a]
agree	de acordo
AIDS	SIDA
air	ar
air mail	correio aéreo
air-conditioned	ar condicionado
airline	linha aérea
airport	aeroporto
aisle	corredor
alarm clock	despertador
alcohol	alcool
allergic	alérgico[a]
allergies	alergias
alone	sozinho[a]
already	já
altar	altar
always	sempre
ambulance	ambulância
ancestor	antepassado[a]
ancient	antigo[a]
and	e
angry	chateado[a]
animal	animal
ankle	tornozelo
another	outro
answer	resposta
antacid	remédio para azia
antibiotic	antibiótico
antiques	antiguidades
antiques shop	antiquário
apartment	apartamento
apology	desculpa
appetizers	aperitivos
appointment	apontamento
approximately	aproximadamente
April	Abril
arm	braço
arrivals	chegadas
arrive	chegar
art	arte
art gallery	galeria de arte

English	Portuguese
Art Nouveau	arte nova
arthritis	artrite
artificial	artificial
artist	artista
ashtray	cinzeiro
ask	perguntar
aspirin	aspirina
aspirin substitute	comprimido para as dores
asthma	asma
at	á
"at" sign (@)	arrôba
atheist	ateu
athlete	atleta
athlete's foot	pé de atleta
attractive	atraente
audioguide	audio guia
August	Agosto
aunt	tia
Austria	Austria
autumn	outono

B

English	Portuguese
baby	bebé
baby booster seat	suporte para cadeira
baby car seat	cadeira de carro para o bebé
baby food	comida para bebés
baby formula	alimento suplementar
babysitter	babysitter
babysitting service	serviços de ajuda com as crianças
back	costas
backpack	mochila

English	Portuguese
bad	mau
bag	saco
bag, plastic	saco plástico
bag, zip-lock	saco plástico com fecho
baggage	bagagem
baggage claim	bagagem
bakery	padaria
balcony	varanda
ball	bola
bandage	gaze
bandage, support	ligadora
Band-Aid	adesivo
bank	banco
barber	barbeiro
baseball	basebol
basement	porão
basket	cesto
basketball	basquetebol
bath	banho
bathrobe	robe
bathroom	casa de banho
bathtub	banheira
battery	bateria
beach	praia
beard	barba
beautiful	lindo[a]
beauty salon	cabelareiro
because	porquê
bed	cama
bedroom	quarto
bedsheet	lençol de cama
beef	bife
beer	cerveja
before	antes
begin	começar
behind	detrás

Belgium	Belgica
bells	sinos
below	abaixo
belt	cinto
berth (train)	lugar sentado
best	melhor
bib	babeiro
bicycle	bicicleta
big	grande
bill (payment)	conta
bird	pássaro
birth	pilula
control pills	anticoncepcional
birthday	aniversário
black	preto
bladder	bexiga
blanket	corbetor
bleeding	sangrar
blisters	bolhas
block	bloco
blond	louro[a]
blood	sangre
blood pressure, high	tensão alta
blouse	blusa
blue	azul
blush (makeup)	blush
boat	barco
body	corpo
boiled	fervido
bomb	bomba
book	livro
book shop	livraria
booster seat	suporte para cadeira
boots	botas
border	fronteira

borrow	emprestar
boss	patrão
bottle	garrafa
bottom	fundo
boutique, clothing	loja de roupa
bowl	tijela
box	caixa
boy	rapaz
bra	soutien
bracelet	pulseira
brakes	travões
brass	latão
bread	pão
breakfast	pequeno almoço
breast	peito
breath	halito
bridge	ponte
Britain	Grã-Bretanha
broken	partido[a]
bronze	bronze
brooch	broche
brother	irmão
brown	castanho
bucket	balde
building	prédio
bulb, light	lâmpada
bunk beds	beliches
burn (n)	queimadura
bus	autocarro
bus station	terminal das camionetas
bus stop	paragem de autocarro
bus, city	autocarro
bus, long-distance	camioneta
business	negócio

but	mas
buttocks	traseiro
button	botão
by (train, car, etc.)	via

C

calendar	calendário
calorie	caloria
camera	camara
camera shop	loja fotográfica
camper (R.V.)	roulote
camping	campismo
campsite	campismo
can (n)	lata
can (v)	poder
can opener	abertor de latas
Canada	Canadá
canal	canal
cancel	cancelar
candle	vela
candy	doce
canoe	canoa
cap	boné
captain	capitão
car	carro
car (train)	carruagem
car seat (baby)	cadeira de carro para o bêbê
car, dining (train)	carruagem restaurante
car, sleeper (train)	carruagem cama
carafe	jarro
card (also business card)	cartão
card, telephone	cartão telefónico

cards (deck)	cartas
careful	cuidadoso[a]
carpet	carpete
carry	carregar
carry-on luggage	bagagem de mão
cash	dinheiro
cash machine	caixa automática, Multibanco
cashier	caixa
cassette	cassete
castle	castelo
cat	gato
catch (v)	apanhar
cathedral	catedral
Catholic (adj)	Católico[a]
cave	cave
cell phone	telemóvel
cell phone shop	loja de telemóveis
cellar	adega
center	centro
century	século
ceramic	ceramica
chair	cadeira
championship	campeonato
change (n)	troca
change (v)	mudar
chapel	capela
charming	encantador[a]
cheap	barato[a]
check	cheque
Cheers!	Saúde!
cheese	queijo
chest	peito
chest pains	dor no peito
chicken	galinha

DICTIONARY

English / Portuguese

child	criança
children	crianças
chills	arrepios
Chinese	chinês
chocolate	chocolate
choir	coral
Christian (adj)	Cristã[o]
Christmas	Natal
church	igreija
church service	serviço
cigarette	cigarro
cinema	cinema
city	cidade
class	classe
class, first	primeira classe
class, second	segunda classe
classical	clássico
clean (adj)	limpo[a]
clear	claro
cliff	falésia
clinic, medical	clinica médica
clock	relógio
clock, alarm	despertador
cloister	mosteiro
closed	fechado[a]
cloth	tecido
clothes	roupa
clothespins	broches
clothesline	linha de roupas
clothing boutique	loja de roupa
cloudy	nebuloso
coast	costa
coat hanger	cruzeta
cockroach	barata
coffee	café
coffee shop	café

coins	moedas
cold (adj)	frio[a]
cold (n)	constipação
cold medicine	remédio para constipação
colors	cores
comb (n)	pente
come	vir
comfortable	confortável
compact disc	compact disco
complain	queixar
complicated	complicado[a]
computer	computador
concert	concerto
conditioner (hair)	condicionador
condom	perservativo
conductor	condutor
confirm	confirmar
congestion (sinus)	congestão
congratulations	parabéns
connection (train)	conexão
constipation	prisão de ventre
construction (sign)	construção na estrada
contact lenses	lentes de contacto
contagious	contagioso
contraceptives	contracepçã
cook (v)	cozinhar
cool	fresco
copper	cobre
copy	copiado
copy shop	casa de fotocopias
cork	rolha
corkscrew	sacarolhas
corner	esquina

corridor	corredor
corruption	corrupção
cost	preço
cot	rede
cotton	algodão
cough (n)	tosse
cough (v)	tosser
cough drops	rabuçados da tosse
country	país
countryside	campo
cousin	primo[a]
cow	vaca
cozy	confortável
crafts	artesanato
cramps	dor, cãibra
cramps, menstrual	cólicas
cream, first-aid	creme desinfetante
credit card	cartão de crédito
cross	cruz
crowd (n)	multidão
cry (v)	chorar
crypt	caixão
cup	chávena
customs	alfândega
Czech Republic	Republica Checa

D

dad	pai
dance (v)	dançar
danger	perigo
dangerous	perigoso[a]
dark	escuro[a]
dash (-)	hífen

daughter	filha
day	dia
day after tomorrow	depois de amanhã
dead	morto[a]
December	Dezembro
declare (customs)	declarar
decongestant	descongestionante
delay (n)	atraso
delete	eliminar
delicatessen	charcutaria
delicious	delicioso[a]
democracy	democracia
dental floss	fio dental
dentist	dentista
deodorant	desodorizante
depart	partir
department store	grande armazen
departures	partidas
deposit	depósito
dessert	sobremesa
detergent	detergente
detour	desvio
diabetes	diabetes
diabetic	diabético[a]
diamond	diamante
diaper	fraldas
diaper rash	assadura das fraldas
diaphragm (birth control)	diafragma
diarrhea	diarreia
diarrhea medicine	remédio para a diarréia
dictionary	dicionário

die	morrer
difficult	difícil
dining car	carruagem
(train)	restaurante
dinner	jantar
direct	directo[a]
direction	direção
dirty	sujo
discount	desconto
disease	doença
disease, venereal	doença venéria
disinfectant	desinfetante
disturb	incomudar
divorced	divorciado[a]
dizziness	tonturas
doctor	doutor[a]
dog	cão
doll	boneca
dome	cúpula
donkey	burro
door	porta
dormitory	dormitorio
dot (computer)	ponto
double	dobrar
down	abaixo
download	transferência
downtown	centro
dozen	dúzia
dream (n)	sonho
dream (v)	sonhar
dress (n)	vestido
drink (n)	bebida
drink (v)	beber
drive (v)	conduzir
driver	condutor
drunk	bêbado[a]
dry (adj)	seco[a]

dry (v)	secar
dryer	secador
dungeon	masmorra
duty free	sem imposto,
	duty free

E

each	cada
ear	orelha
earache	dor de ouvido
early	cedo[a]
earplugs	tampões de ouvido
earrings	brincos
earth	terra
east	este
Easter	Pascoa
easy	fácil
eat	comer
education	instrução
elbow	cotovelo
electrical adapter	tomada
elevator	elevador
email	email
email address	endereço eletrônico
embarrassing	humilhante
embassy	embaixada
emergency	emergência
emergency exit	saída de emergência
emergency room	sala de emergência
empty	vazio[a]
engineer	engenheiro
English	inglês
enjoy	gostar

enough	suficiente
entrance	entrada
entrance (road)	entrada
envelope	envelope
epilepsy	epilepcia
eraser	borracha
Europe	Europa
evening	noitecer
every	todo
everything	tudo
exactly	exactamente
example	exemplo
excellent	excelente
except	excepto
exchange (n)	câmbio
excuse me	desculpe
exhausted	esgotado[a]
exit	saída
exit,	saída de
emergency	emergência
expensive	caro[a]
explain	explicar
eye	olho
eye shadow	sombra
eyeliner	lápis para os olhos,
	delineador

F

face	cara
face	produto para
cleanser	a limpeza do rosto
face powder	pó para o rosto
facial tissue	lenços de papel
factory	fábrica
fair (just)	justo[a]
fall (v)	cair

false	falso[a]
family	familia
famous	famoso[a]
fan belt	correia de ventoinha
fantastic	fantástico[a]
far	longe
farm	quinta
farmer	granjeiro[a]
fashion	moda
fat (adj)	gordo[a]
fat (n)	gordura
father	pai
faucet	torneira
fax	fax
fear (v)	temer
February	Fevereiro
feminine	feminino[a]
ferry	barco
festival	festival
fever	fevre
few	pouco
field	campo
fight (n)	luta
fight (v)	lutar
fine (good)	bom
finger	dedo
fingernail	unha
finish (v)	terminar
fire	fogo
fireworks	fogo de artificio
first	primeiro[a]
first aid	pronto socorro
first class	primeira classe
first-aid	creme desinfetante
cream	
fish (n)	peixe
fish (v)	pescar

fix (v)	arranjar
fizzy	com gás
flag	bandeira
flash (camera)	flash
flashlight	lanterna a pilhas
flavor (n)	sabor
flea	pulga
flea market	feira
flight	voo
flip-flops	sandálias de dedo
floss, dental	fio dental
flower	flor
flower market	mercado de flores
flu	gripe
fly (v)	voar
fog	nevoeiro
food	comida
food poisoning	envenanamento alimentar
foot	pé
football (soccer)	futebol
football, American	futebol americano
for	para
forbidden	proibido[a]
foreign	estrangeiro[a]
forget	esquecer
fork	garfo
formula (for baby)	alimento suplementar
foundation (makeup)	base
fountain	fonte
fragile	frágil
France	França
free (no cost)	grátis
fresh	fresco[a]

Friday	sexta-feira
friend	amigo[a]
friendship	amizade
Frisbee	disco voador
from	de
fruit	fruta
fun (adj)	divertido[a]
funeral	funeral
funny	divertido[a]
furniture	mobilias
fuses	fussil
future	futuro

G

gallery	galeria
game	jogo
garage	garagem
garden	jardim
gardening	jardinagem
gas	gás
gas station	bomba de gasolina
gauze	gaze
gay	gay
generous	generouso[a]
gentleman	cavalheiro
genuine	genuíno[a]
Germany	Alemanha
gift	prenda
girl	rapariga
give	dar
glass	copo
glasses (eye)	óculos
gloves	luvas
go	ir
go through	atravessar
God	deus

gold	ouro
golf	golfe
good	bom
good day	bom-dia
goodbye	adeus
Gothic	gótico[a]
grammar	gramática
grandchild	neto[a]
grandfather	avô
grandmother	avó
gray	cinzento
greasy	gorduroso
great	magnifico[a]
Great Britain	Inglaterra
Greece	Grécia
green	verde
grocery store	mercearia
guarantee	garantia
guest	convidado[a]
guide	uma guia
guidebook	um guia
guided tour	visita guiada
guilty	culpado[a]
guitar	guitarra
gum	pastilha elástica
gun	pistola
gymnastics	ginastica
gynecologist	enicologista

H

hair	cabelo
hairbrush	escova de cabelo
haircut	corte de cabelo
hall (big room)	sala
hand	mão
hand lotion	creme para as mãos

handicapped	aleijado[a]
handicrafts	artesanato
handle (n)	puxador
handsome	bonito[a]
happiness	felicidade
happy	feliz
harbor	porto
hard	difícil
hardware store	casa de ferragens
hash (drug)	hashishe
hat	chapéu
hate	odiar
have	ter
hay fever	febre dos fenos
he	ele
head	cabeça
headache	dor de cabeça
headlights	faróis da frente
health	saúde
health insurance	seguro de saúde
healthy	saudavel
hear	ouvir
heart	coração
heart condition	problema no coração
heat (n)	calor
heaven	céu
heavy	pesado[a]
hello	olá
help (n)	ajuda
help (v)	ajudar
hemorrhoids	hemorróidas
here	aqui
hi	olá
high	alto[a]

DICTIONARY

English / Portuguese

high blood pressure	tensão alta
highchair	cadeirinha alta
highway	autoestrada
hill	subida
history	história
hitchhike	pedir boleia
hobby	passatempo
hockey	hóquei
hole	buraco
holiday	feriado
homemade	á moda de casa
homesick	saudade
honest	honesto[a]
honeymoon	lua de mel
hope	esperança
horrible	horrível
horse	cavalo
horse riding	montar a cavalo
hospital	hospital
hot	quente
hotel	hotel
hour	hora
house	casa
how	como
how many	quanto
how much ($)	quanto custa
hungry	esfomeado[a]
hurry (v)	apressar
husband	marido
hydrofoil	hidroplano
hyphen (-)	hífen

I

I	eu
ice	gelo

ice cream	gelado
if	se
ill	doente
immediately	imediatamente
important	importante
imported	importado[a]
impossible	impossível
Impressionist	impressionista
in	em
included	incluido
incredible	inacreditável
independent	independente
indigestion	indigestão
industry	industria
infection	infecção
infection, urinary	infecção urinaria
inflammation	inflamação
information	informação
injured	ferido[a]
innocent	inocente
insect	insecto
insect repellant	repelente de insectos
inside	interior
instant	instante
instead	em vez de
insurance	seguro
insurance, health	seguro de saúde
insured	seguro[a]
intelligent	inteligente
interesting	interresante
Internet	Internet
Internet access	acesso a Internet
Internet café	café Internet

English / Portuguese

DICTIONARY

intersection	cruzamento
intestines	intestino
invitation	convite
iodine	iodo
Ireland	Irlanda
is	sér
island	ilha
Italy	Itália
itch (n)	comichão

J

jacket	casaco
January	Janeiro
jaw	maxila
jeans	jeans
jewelry	joalheria
jewelry shop	joalheria
Jewish	Judeu
job	trabalho
jogging	jogging
joint (marijuana)	baseado
joke (n)	piada
journey	viagem
juice	sumo
July	Julho
jump	saltar
June	Junho

K

keep	guardar
kettle	chaleira
key	chave
kill	matar
kind	simpático[a]
king	rei
kiss (n)	beijo

kitchen	cozinha
kitchenette	kitchenete
knee	joelho
knife	faca
knight	cavaleiro
know	saber

L

lace	renda
ladder	escada
ladies	senhoras
lake	lago
lamb	cordeiro
language	língua
large	grande
last	último[a]
late	tarde
later	mais tarde
laugh (v)	rir
launderette	lavandaria
laundry soap	detergente
lawyer	advogado[a]
laxative	laxativo
lazy	preguiçoso[a]
learn	aprender
leather	cabedal
leave	sair
left (direction)	esquerda
leg	perna
lend	emprestar
lenses, contact	lentes de contacto
letter	carta
library	biblioteca
lies	mentiras
life	vida

DICTIONARY

English / Portuguese

light (n)	luz
light bulb	lâmpada
lighter (n)	isqueiro
like (v)	gostar
linen	linho
lip	lábio
lip salve	batão de cierio
lipstick	baton
list	lista
listen	escutar
liter	litro
little	pequeno
live (v)	viver
local	local
lock (n)	fechadura
lock (v)	fechar
lockers	armários
look	olhar
lost	perdido[a]
lotion, hand	creme para as mãos
loud	ruidoso[a]
love (n)	amor
love (v)	amar
lover	amante
low	baixo[a]
luck	sorte
luggage	bagagem
luggage, carry-on	bagagem de mão
lukewarm	tépido[a]
lungs	pulmões

M

| macho | macho |
| mad | chateado[a] |

magazine	revista
mail (n)	correio
main	principal
make (v)	fazer
makeup	maquiagem
mall (shopping)	centro comercial
man	homem
manager	gerente
many	muito[a]
map	mapa
marble (material)	mármore
March	Março
marijuana	erva, marijuana
market	mercado
market, flea	feira
market, flower	mercado de flores
market, open-air	mercado municipal
married	casado[a]
mascara	rimel
masculine	masculino[a]
mass	missa
matches	fosforos
maximum	máximo[a]
May	Maio
maybe	talvez
meat	carne
mechanic	mecânico[a]
medicine	medicina
medicine for a cold	remédio para constipação
medicine, non-aspirin substitute	substituto para aspirina
medieval	mediaval
medium	médio[a]

men	homens
menstrual cramps	cólicas
menstruation	menstruação
menu	ementa
message	recado
metal	metal
meter, taxi	medidor
midnight	meia-noite
migraine	enxaqueca
military	militares
mineral water	água mineral
minimum	minimo[a]
minutes	minutos
mirror	espelho
miscarriage	abôrto natural
Miss	Menina
mistake	erro
misunderstanding	malentendido
mix (n)	mista
moat	fosso
modern	moderno
moisturizer	hidratante
moleskin	sinal
mom	mãe
moment	momento
monastery	monestério
Monday	segunda-feira
money	dinheiro
month	mês
monument	monumento
moon	lua
more	mais
morning	manhã
mosque	mesquita
mosquito	mosquito
mother	mãe
motor scooter	motocicleta

motorcycle	mota
mountain	montanha
moustache	bigode
mouth	boca
movie	filme
Mr.	Senhor
Mrs.	Senhora
much	muito
muggy	úmido
muscle	músculo
museum	museu
music	música
Muslim (adj)	Muçulmano[a]
my	meu

N

nail (finger)	unha
nail clippers	corta unhas
nail polish	verniz para as unhas
nail polish remover	acetona
naked	nuo[a]
name	nome
napkin	guardanapo
narrow	estreito[a]
nationality	nacionalidade
natural	natural
nature	natureza
nausea	náusea
near	perto
necessary	necessário
neck	pescoço
necklace	fio
need	necessitar
needle	agulha
nephew	sobrinho
nervous	nervoso[a]

Netherlands	Holanda
never	nunca
new	novo[a]
newspaper	jornal
newsstand	quiosque
next	próximo[a]
nice	simpático[a]
nickname	alcunha
niece	sobrinha
night	noite
nightgown	camisa de dormir
no	não
no vacancy	cheio
noisy	barulho[a]
non-smoking	não fumador
noon	meio-dia
normal	normal
north	norte
nose	nariz
not	não
notebook	caderno
nothing	nada
November	Novembro
now	agora
nurse	enfermeiro[a]
nylon (material)	nylon
nylons (panty hose)	meia de vidro

O

O.K.	O.K.
occupation	profissão
occupied	ocupado
ocean	oceano
October	Outubro
of	de

office	escritório
office supplies store	papelaria
oil (n)	óleo
old	velho[a]
Olympics	Olímpicos
on	sobre
on time	pontual
once	uma vez
one way (street)	sentido único
one way (ticket)	uma ida
one-way street	sentido único
only	só
open (adj)	aberto[a]
open (v)	abrir
open-air market	mercado municipal
opening hours	horário
opera	ópera
operator	operador
optician	oculista
or	ou
orange (color)	cor de laranja
orange (fruit)	laranja
organ	orgão
original	original
other	outro
oven	forno
over (finished)	acabado
own (v)	possuir
owner	dono[a]

P

pacifier	chupeta
package	embalagem
paddleboat	gaivota
page	página

pail	balde	pharmacy	farmácia
pain	dor	phone (n)	telefone
painkiller	comprimidos	phone booth	telefone publico
	para as dores	phone, mobile	telemóvel
pains, chest	dor no peito	photo	fotografia
painting	pintura	photocopy	fotocopia
pajamas	pijamas	photocopy	casa de fotocopias
palace	palácio	shop	
panties	cuecas	pickpocket	carteirista
pants	calças	picnic	piquenique
paper	papel	piece	pedaço
paper clip	clip	pig	porco
parents	pais	pill	comprimido
park (garden)	parque	pill, birth	pilula
park (v)	estacionar	control	anticoncepcional
parking	(parque de)	pillow	almofada
lot	estacionamento	pin	alfinete
party	festa	PIN code	código pessoal
passenger	passageiro[a]	pink	cor de rosa
passport	passaporte	pity, it's a	que pena
past	passado	pizza	pizza
pastry shop	pastelaria	plain	simples
pay	pagar	plane	avião
peace	paz	plant	planta
pedestrian	peão	plastic	plástico
pen	caneta	plastic bag	saco plástico
pencil	lápis	plate	prato
penis	pénis	platform (train)	cais
people	pessoas	play (v)	jogar
percent	percento	playground	parque de
perfect (adj)	perfeito[a]		diversões
perfume	perfume	playpen	parque
period (of time)	período	please	por favor
period (woman's)	menstruação	pliers	alicate
person	pessoa	pneumonia	pneumonia
pet (n)	animal de estimação	pocket	bolso
pewter	estanho	point (v)	apontar

police	polícia	punctual	pontual
politicians	políticos	purple	roxo[a]
pollution	poluição	purse	bolsa
polyester	poliester	push	empurrar
poor	pobre		
porcelain	porcelana	**Q**	
pork	porco	quality	qualidade
Portugal	Portugal	quarter (¼)	quarto
possible	possível	queen	rainha
postcard	cartão postal	question (n)	pergunta
poster	poster	quiet	calado[a]
power	poder		
powerful	poderoso[a]	**R**	
practical	prático[a]	R.V. (camper)	roulote
pregnancy	gravidez	rabbit	coelho
pregnancy test	teste de gravidez	racism	racismo
pregnant	grávida	radiator	radiador
Preparation H	Preparação H	radio	rádio
prescription	receita médica	raft	balsa
present (gift)	presente	railway	caminho de ferro
pretty	bonito[a]	rain (n)	chuva
price	preço	rainbow	arco íris
priest	padre	raincoat	casaco impermeável
print (v)	imprimir	rape (n)	violação
private	privado[a]	rash	erupção
problem	problema	rash, diaper	assadura das fraldas
profession	profissão		
prohibited	proibido[a]	raw	cru
pronunciation	pronúncia	razor	Gilete
prosper	prosperar	ready	pronto[a]
Protestant (adj)	Protestante	receipt	recibo
public	público	receive	receber
pull	tirar	receptionist	recepcionista
pulpit	púlpito	recipe	receita
pulse	pulsação	recommend	recomendar
pump (n)	bomba	rectum	recto

English / Portuguese

DICTIONARY

red	vermelho[a]
refill (n)	encher
refugees	refigiados
refund (n)	reembolso
relax	relaxar
relaxation	descanso
relic	rélica
religion	religião
remember	recordar
Renaissance	renascimento
rent (v)	alugar
repair	reparar
reservation	reserva
reserve	reservar
respect (n)	respeito
retired	reformado[a]
rich	rico[a]
right (correct)	certo[a]
right (direction)	direita
ring (n)	campaínha
ripe	maduro
river	rio
robbed	roubado[a]
rock (n)	rock
roller skates	patins
Romanesque	românico
Romantic (art)	romântico
romantic	romântico[a]
roof	telhado
room	quarto
rope	corda
rotten	podre
roundabout	rotunda
roundtrip	ida e volta
rowboat	barco de passeio
rucksack	mochila
rug	carpete

ruins	ruínas
run (v)	correr
Russia	Russia

S

sad	triste
safe	seguro[a]
safety pin	alfinete de segurança
sailboat	veleiro
sailing	barco de vela
saint	santo[a]
sale	saldos
same	mesmo
sandals	sandálias
sandwich	sande
sanitary napkins	pensos higiénicos
Santa Claus	Pai-Natal
Saturday	sábado
save (computer)	guardar
scandalous	escandulo[a]
Scandinavia	Escandinavia
scarf	lenço
school	escola
science	ciência
scientist	cientista
scissors	tesouras
scotch tape	fita cola
screwdriver	chave de parafusos
sculptor	escultor[a]
sculpture	escultura
sea	mar
seafood	marisco
seat	lugar, assento

second	segunda
second class	segunda classe
secret	segredo
see	ver
self-service	auto serviço
sell	vender
send	enviar
seniors	pessoas de terceira idade
separate	separado[a]
September	Setembro
serious	sério[a]
service	serviço
service (church)	serviço
sex	sexo
sexy	sexy
shampoo	xampú
shaving cream	creme de barbear
she	ela
sheet	lençol
shell	concha
ship (n)	barco
ship (v)	enviar
shirt	camisa
shoelaces	cordão de sapatos
shoes	sapatos
shoes, tennis (sneakers)	ténis
shop (n)	loja
shop, antique	antiquário
shop, barber	barbeiro
shop, camera	loja fotográfica
shop, cell phone	loja de telemóveis
shop, coffee	café
shop, jewelry	joalheria
shop, pastry	pastelaria
shop, photocopy	casa de fotocopias
shop, souvenir	loja de lembranças
shop, sweets	confeitaria
shop, wine	loja de vinhos
shopping	compras
shopping mall	centro comercial
short	curto[a]
shorts	calções
shoulder	ombros
show (n)	espectáculo
show (v)	mostrar
shower	chuveiro
shy	tímido[a]
sick	doente
sign	sinal
signature	assinatura
silence	silêncio
silk	seda
silver	prata
similar	similar
simple	simples
sing	cantar
singer	cantor[a]
single	solteiro[a]
sink	lavatório
sink stopper	tampa para lava louça
sinus problems	sinosite
sir	senhor
sister	irmã
size	tamanho
skating	patinagem
ski (v)	esquiar
skiing	esquiar

skin	pele	sour	azedo[a]
skinny	magro[a]	south	sul
skirt	saia	souvenir shop	loja de lembranças
sky	céu		
sleep (v)	dormir	Spain	Espanha
sleeper (train)	camarote	sparkplugs	velas
sleeper car (train)	carruagem cama	speak	falar
		specialty	especialidade
sleeping bag	saco de dormir	speed	velocidade
sleepy	sonolento[a]	spend	gastar
sleeves	mangas	spider	arranha
slice	fatia	spoon	colher
slide (photo)	slide	sport	desporto
slip	combinação	spring (n)	primavera
slippers	chinélos	square (town)	praça
slippery	escorregadio	stairs	escadas
slow	lento[a]	stamp	selo
small	pequeno[a]	stapler	agrafador
smell (n)	cheiro	star (in sky)	estrela
smile (n)	sorriso	state	estado
smoke	fumo	station	estação
smoking	fumador	stomach	estômago
snack	petisco	stomachache	dor de estômago
sneeze (n)	espirro	stoned	drogado[a]
snore	ressonar	stop (n, train or bus)	paragem
snorkel	tubo para mergulho	stop (v)	parar
soap	sabão	stoplight	sinal de luz
soap, laundry	detergente	stopper, sink	tampa para lava louça
soccer	futebol		
socks	meias	store	loja
some	alguns	store, department	grande armazen
something	alguma coisa		
son	filho	store, hardware	casa de ferragens
song	canção		
soon	cedo	store, office supplies	papelaria
sore throat	dor de garganta		
sorry	desculpe	store, toy	loja de brinquedos

storm	tempestada	sunstroke	insolação
story (floor)	andar	suntan (n)	bronzeado
straight	em frente	supermarket	supermercado
strange	estranho[a]	supplement	suplemento
stream (n)	corrente	surfboard	prancha
street	rua	surfer	surfista
string	fio	surprise (n)	surpresa
stroller	carrinho de bebê	swallow (v)	engolir
strong	forte	sweat (v)	suar
stuck	imobilizado	sweater	pullover
student	estudante	sweet	doce
stupid	estúpido[a]	sweets shop	confeitaria
sturdy	sólido[a]	swelling (n)	inchado
style	estilo	swim	nadar
subway	metro	swimsuit	fato de banho
subway entrance	entrada do metro	swim trunks	calção de banho
		swimming pool	piscina
subway exit	saída do metro	Switzerland	Suíça
subway map	mapa do metro	synagogue	sinagoga
subway station	estação de metro	synthetic	sintético[a]

T

subway stop	paragem do metro	table	mesa
suddenly	de repente	tail	rabo
suffer	sofrer	tail lights	luzes traseiras
suitcase	mala	take	tomar
summer	verão	take out (food)	para levar
sun	sol	talcum powder	pó de talco
sunbathe	bronzear	talk	falar
sunburn	queimadura solar	tall	alto[a]
Sunday	domingo	tampons	tampões
sunglasses	óculos de sol	tape (adhesive)	adesivo
sunny	sol	tape (cassette)	cassete
sunrise	nascer do sol	taste (n)	sabor
sunscreen	protector solar	taste (try)	provar
sunset	pôr do sol	tax	taxa
sunshine	brilho de sol		

taxi meter	medidor
teacher	professor
team	equipa
teenager	jovem
teeth	dentes
teething (baby)	dentição
telephone (n)	telefone
telephone card	cartão telefónico
television	televisão
temperature	temperatura
tender	tenro[a]
tennis	ténis
tennis shoes	sapatos de ténis
tent	tenda
tent pegs	estacas de tenda
terrible	terrível
terrorists	terroristas
testicles	testículos
thanks	obrigado[a]
theater	teatro
thermometer	termómetro
they	eles
thick	grosso
thief	ladrão
thigh	coxa
thin	magro[a]
thing	coisa
think	pensar
thirsty	sede
thread	linha
throat	garganta
through	através
throw	atirar
Thursday	quinta-feira
ticket	bilhete

tight	apretado[a]
tights	collants
time, on	pontual
timetable	horário
tire (n)	pneu
tired	cansado[a]
tires	pneus
tissue, facial	lenços de papel
to	para
today	hoje
toe	dedo do pé
together	juntos
toilet	casa de banho
toilet paper	papel higiénico
token	ficha
toll	portagem
toll-free	taxa grátis
tomorrow	amanhã
tomorrow, day after	depois de amanhã
tonight	esta noite
too (much)	demasiado
tooth	dente
toothache	dor de dente
toothbrush	escova de dentes
toothpaste	pasta de dentes
toothpick	palito
total	total
tour	excursão
tour, guided	visita guiada
tourist	turista
tow truck	reboque
towel	toalha
tower	torre
town	cidade
toy	brinquedo
toy store	loja de brinquedos

track (train)	linha	understand	entender
traditional	tradicional	unemployed	desempregado[a]
traffic	tráfico	unfortunate	desventurado[a]
train	comboio	United States	Estados Unidos
train car	carruagem	university	universidade
transfer (v)	mudar	up	subida
translate	traduzir	upstairs	em cima
transmission fluid	óleo de transmissão	urethra	uretra
		urgent	urgente
travel (v)	viajar	urinary infection	infecção urinaria
travel agency	agência de viagens		
		us	nós
traveler's check	cheque de viagem	use (v)	usar
		uterus	útero
travelers	vijantes		
treasury	tesoraria	**V**	
tree	árvore		
trip	viagem	vacancy sign	quartos
tripod	tripé	vacancy, no	cheio
trouble	problema	vacant	livre
T-shirt	T-shirt	vacation	férias
Tuesday	terça-feira	vagina	vagina
tunnel	túnel	valid	válido[a]
Turkey	Turkia	validate	validade
turn signal	pisca-pisca	valley	vale
tweezers	pinsa	Vaseline	vasilina
twins	gêmeos	vegetarian	vegetariano[a]
		velvet	veludo
U		venereal disease	doença venéria
ugly	feio[a]	very	muito[a]
umbrella	guarda-chuva	vest	colete
uncle	tio	video	vídeo
unconscious	inconciente	video camera	video camera
under	debaixo	view	vista
underpants	cuecas	village	aldeia
underscore (_)	sublinhar	vineyard	vinhedo

English / Portuguese

DICTIONARY

violence	violência
virus	vírus
visit (n)	visita
visit (v)	visitar
vitamins	vitaminas
voice	voz
vomit	vomitar

W

waist	cintura
wait (v)	esperar
waiter	criado
waiting room	sala de espera
waitress	senhora, menina
wake up	acordar
walk (v)	andar
wall, fortified	fortificação
wallet	carteira
want	querer
war	guerra
warm (adj)	quente
wash	lavar
washer	máquina de lavar roupa
watch (n)	relógio
watch (v)	olhar
water	água
water, drinkable	água potável
water, tap	água da torneira
waterfall	queda de água
waterskiing	esqui aquático
we	nós
weather	tempo
website	local da Web
wedding	casamento

Wednesday	quarta-feira
week	semana
weight	peso
welcome	bem-vindo
west	oeste
wet	molhado[a]
what	o quê
wheel	roda
wheelchair-accessible	rodas-acesso
when	quando
where	donde
white	branco[a]
who	quem
why	porquê
widow	viúva
widower	viúvo
wife	esposa
wild	salvagem
wind	vento
window	janela
windshield wipers	para-brisas
windsurfing	windsurfing
windy	vento
wine	vinho
wine shop	loja de vinhos
wing	asa
winter	inverno
wish (v)	desejo
with	com
without	sem
woman	mulher
women	mulheres
wood	madeira
wool	lã
word	palavra

work (n)	trabalho
work (v)	trabalhar
world	mundo
worst	pior
wrap (v)	embrulhar
wrist	pulso
write	escrever

X

| X-ray | raio X |

Y

year	ano
yellow	amarelo[a]
yes	sim
yesterday	ontem

you (formal)	você
you (informal)	tu
young	jovem
youth	juventude
youth hostel	albergue de juventude
youths	jovens

Z

zero	zero
zip code	código postal
zip-lock bag	saco plástico com fecho
zipper	fecho
zoo	zoo

TIPS FOR HURDLING THE LANGUAGE BARRIER

Don't Be Afraid to Communicate

Even the best phrase book won't satisfy your needs in every situation. To really hurdle the language barrier, you need to leap beyond the printed page, and dive into contact with the locals. Never allow your lack of foreign language skills to isolate you from the people and cultures you traveled halfway around the world to experience. Remember that in every country you visit, you're surrounded by expert, native-speaking tutors. Spend bus and train rides letting them teach you.

Start conversations by asking politely in the local language, "Do you speak English?" When you speak English with someone from another country, talk slowly, clearly, and with carefully chosen words. Use what the Voice of America calls "simple English." You're talking to people who are wishing it was written down, hoping to see each letter as it tumbles out of your mouth. Pronounce each letter, avoiding all contractions and slang. For bad examples, listen to other tourists.

Keep things caveman-simple. Make single nouns work as entire sentences ("Photo?"). Use internationally-understood words ("Self-service" works in Lisbon). Butcher the language if you must. The important thing is to make the effort. To get air mail stamps, you can flap your wings and say "tweet, tweet." If you want milk, moo and pull two imaginary udders. Risk looking like a fool.

If you're short on words, make your picnic a potluck. Pull out a map and point out your journey. Draw what you mean. Bring photos from home and introduce your family. Play cards or toss a Frisbee. Fold an origami bird for kids or dazzle 'em with sleight-of-hand magic.

Go ahead and make educated guesses. Many situations are easy-to-fake multiple choice questions. Practice. Read timetables, concert posters, and newspaper headlines. Listen to each language on a multilingual tour. Be melodramatic. Exaggerate the local accent. Self-consciousness is the deadliest communication-killer.

Choose multilingual people to communicate with, such as students, business people, urbanites, young well-dressed people, or anyone in the tourist trade. Use a small note pad to jot down handy phrases and to help you communicate more clearly with the locals by scribbling down numbers, maps, and so on. Some travelers carry important messages written on a small card: allergic to nuts, strict vegetarian, your finest ice cream.

International Words

As our world shrinks, more and more words hop across their linguistic boundaries and become international. Savvy travelers develop a knack for choosing words most likely to be universally understood ("auto" instead of "car," "kaput" instead of "broken," "photo" not "picture"). Internationalize your pronunciation. "University," if you play around with its sound (oo-nee-vehr-see-tay), will be understood anywhere. The average American is a real flunky in this area. Be creative.

Here are a few internationally understood words. Remember, cut out the Yankee accent and give each word a pan-European sound.

Amigo	Bank	Casanova	Coke, Coca-Cola
Attila	Beer	(romantic)	Communist
(mean, crude)	Bill Gates	Central	Computer
Auto	Bon voyage	Chocolate	Disco
Autobus	Bye-bye	Ciao	Disneyland
("booos")	Camping	Coffee	(wonderland)

Elephant
(big clod)
English
("Engleesh")
Europa
Fascist
Hello
Hercules (strong)
Hotel
Information
Internet
Kaput

Mama mia
Mañana
McDonald's
Michelangelo
(artistic)
Moment
No
No problem
Nuclear
OK
Oo la la
Pardon

Passport
Photo
Photocopy
Picnic
Police
Post
Rambo
Restaurant
Rock 'n' roll
Self-service
Sex / Sexy
Sport

Stop
Super
Taxi
Tea
Telephone
Toilet
Tourist
US profanity
University
Vino
Yankee,
Americano

Portuguese Verbs

These conjugated verbs will help you construct a caveman sentence in a pinch.

Portuguese has two different verbs that correspond to the English "to be"—*ser* and *estar.* Generally speaking, *ser* is used to describe a condition that is permanent or longer-lasting, and *estar* is used for something that is temporary. Which verb you use can determine the meaning of the sentence. For example, "*Ricardo é contente*," using *ser,* means that Ricardo is a happy, content person (as a permanent personality trait). "*Ricardo está contente*," using *estar,* means that Ricardo is currently happy (temporarily in a good mood).

TO BE (permanent)	*SER*	sehr
I am	*eu sou*	**eh**-oo soh
you are (formal)	*você é*	voh-**say** eh
you are (informal)	*tú és*	too ehs
he / she is	*ele / ela é*	**eh**-leh / **eh**-lah eh
we are	*nós somos*	nohsh **soh**-moosh
you (plural, formal)	*vocês são*	voh-**saysh** sow
they are	*eles / elas são*	**eh**-lish / **eh**-lahsh sow
(males or coed / females only)		

TO BE (temporary)	*ESTAR*	ish-**tar**
I am	*eu estou*	**eh**-oo ish-**toh**
you are (formal)	*você está*	voh-**say** ish-**tah**
you are (informal)	*tú estás*	too ish-**tahsh**
he / she is	*ele / ela está*	**eh**-leh / **eh**-lah ish-**tah**
we are	*nós estamos*	nohz ish-**tah**-moosh
you (plural, formal)	*vocês estão*	voh-**sayz** ish-**tow**
they are	*eles / elas estão*	**eh**-liz / **eh**-lahz ish-**tow**
(males or coed / females only)		

TO GO	*IR*	eer
I go	*eu vou*	**eh**-oo voh
you go (formal)	*você vai*	voh-**say** vī
you go (informal)	*tú vais*	too vīsh
he / she goes	*ele / ela vai*	**eh**-leh / **eh**-lah vī
we go	*nós vamos*	nohsh **vah**-moosh
you go	*vocês vão*	voh-**saysh** vow
(plural, formal)		
they go	*eles / elas vão*	**eh**-lish / **eh**-lahsh vow
(males or coed / females only)		

TO DO, TO MAKE	*FAZER*	fah-**zehr**
I do	*eu faço*	**eh**-oo fah-**soo**
you do (formal)	*você faz*	voh-**say** fahsh
you do (informal)	*tú fazes*	too **fah**-zish
he / she does	*ele / ela faz*	**eh**-leh / **eh**-lah fahsh
we do	*nós fazemos*	nohsh fah-**zeh**-moosh
you do	*vocês fazem*	voh-**saysh** fah-zay<u>n</u>
(plural, formal)		
they do	*eles / elas fazem*	**eh**-lish / **eh**-lahsh **fah**-zay<u>n</u>
(males or coed / females only)		

TO HAVE	*TER*	tehr
I have	*eu tenho*	**eh**-oo **tayn**-yoo
you have (formal)	*você tem*	voh-**say** tay<u>n</u>
you have (informal)	*tú tens*	too tay<u>n</u>sh
he / she has	*ele / ela tem*	**eh**-leh / **eh**-lah tay<u>n</u>

we have	*nós temos*	nohsh **tay**-moosh
you have	*vocês têm*	voh-**saysh** tay<u>n</u>
(plural, formal)		
they have	*eles / elas têm*	**eh**-lish / **eh**-lahsh tay<u>n</u>
(males or coed / females only)		

TO SEE	*VER*	vehr
I see	*eu vejo*	**eh**-oo **veh**-zhoo
you see (formal)	*você vê*	voh-**say** veh
you see (informal)	*tú vês*	too vehsh
he / she sees	*ele / ela vê*	**eh**-leh / **eh**-lah veh
we see	*nós vemos*	nohsh **veh**-moosh
you see	*vocês vêem*	voh-**saysh veh**-ay<u>n</u>
(plural, formal)		
they see	*eles / elas vêem*	**eh**-lish / **eh**-lahsh **veh**-ay<u>n</u>
(males or coed / females only)		

TO SPEAK	*FALAR*	fah-**lar**
I speak	*eu falo*	**eh**-oo **fah**-loo
you speak (formal)	*você fala*	voh-**say fah**-lah
you speak (informal)	*tú falas*	too **fah**-lahsh
he / she speaks	*ele / ela fala*	**eh**-leh / **eh**-lah **fah**-lah
we speak	*nós falamos*	nohsh fah-**lah**-moosh
you speak	*vocês falam*	voh-**saysh fah**-lahm
(plural, formal)		
they speak	*eles / elas falam*	**eh**-lish / **eh**-lahsh **fah**-lahm
(males or coed / females only)		

TO WALK	*ANDAR*	ahn-**dar**
I walk	*eu ando*	**eh**-oo **ahn**-doo
you walk (formal)	*você anda*	voh-**say ahn**-dah
you walk (informal)	*tú andas*	too **ahn**-dahsh
he / she walks	*ele / ela anda*	**eh**-leh / **eh**-lah **ahn**-dah
we walk	*nós andamos*	nohz ahn-**dah**-moosh
you walk	*vocês andam*	voh-**sayz ahn**-dahm
(plural, formal)		
they walk	*eles / elas andam*	**eh**-lish / **eh**-lahsh **ahn**-dahm
(males or coed / females only)		

LANGUAGE TIPS

TO LIKE	*GOSTAR*	goosh-**tar**
I like	*eu gusto*	**eh**-oo **gohsh**-toh
you like (formal)	*você gosta*	voh-**say gohsh**-tah
you like (informal)	*tú gostas*	too **gohsh**-tahsh
he / she likes	*ele / ela gosta*	**eh**-leh / **eh**-lah **gohsh**-tah
we like	*nós gostamos*	nohsh goosh-**tah**-moosh
you like (plural, formal)	*vocês gostam*	voh-**saysh gohsh**-tahm
they like (males or coed / females only)	*eles / elas gostam*	**eh**-lish / **eh**-lahsh **gohsh**-tahm

TO WANT	*QUERER*	keh-**rehr**
I want	*eu quero*	**eh**-oo **kay**-roo
you want (formal)	*você quer*	voh-**say** kehr
you want (informal)	*tú queres*	too **keh**-rish
he / she wants	*ele / ela quer*	**eh**-leh / **eh**-lah kehr
we want	*nós queremos*	nohsh keh-**ray**-moosh
you want (plural, formal)	*vocês querem*	voh-**saysh keh**-ray<u>n</u>
they want (males or coed / females only)	*eles / elas querem*	**eh**-lish / **eh**-lahsh **keh**-ray<u>n</u>

TO NEED	*PRECISAR*	preh-see-**zar**
I need	*eu preciso*	**eh**-oo preh-**see**-zoo
you need (formal)	*você precisa*	voh-**say** preh-**see**-zah
you need (informal)	*tú precisas*	too preh-**see**-zahsh
he / she needs	*ele / ela precisa*	**eh**-leh / **eh**-lah preh-**see**-zah
we need	*nós precisamos*	nohsh preh-see-**zah**-moosh
you need (plural, formal)	*vocês precisam*	voh-**saysh** preh-**see**-zahm
they need (males or coed / females only)	*eles / elas precisam*	**eh**-lish / **eh**-lahsh preh-**see**-zahm

Portuguese Tongue Twisters

Tongue twisters are a great way to practice a language and break the ice with locals. Here are a few Portuguese tongue twisters that are sure to challenge you and amuse your hosts.

O rato roeu a roupa do rei de Roma.	The mouse nibbled the clothes of the king of Rome.
Um tigre, dois tigres, três tigres.	One tiger, two tigers, three tigers.
Se cá nevasse fazia-se cá ski, mas como cá não neva não se faz cá ski.	If the snow would fall, we'd ski, but since it doesn't, we don't.

English Tongue Twisters

After your Portuguese friends have laughed at you, let them try these tongue twisters in English.

If neither he sells seashells,
  nor she sells seashells,
  who shall sell seashells?
  Shall seashells be sold?

Peter Piper picked a peck
  of pickled peppers.

Rugged rubber baby
  buggy bumpers.

The sixth sick sheik's
  sixth sheep's sick.

Red bug's blood and
  black bug's blood.

Soldiers' shoulders.

Thieves seize skis.

I'm a pleasant mother
pheasant plucker. I pluck
mother pheasants. I'm
the most pleasant mother
pheasant plucker that ever
plucked a mother pheasant.

Portuguese National Anthem

If you ever hear the Portuguese national anthem and you'd like to sing along, here's a little help:

A PORTUGUESA
–Music by Alfredo Keil, lyrics by
Henrique Lopes de Mendonça, 1981

Heróis do mar, nobre Povo,	Heroes of the sea, noble people,
Nação valente, imortal,	Valiant and immortal nation,
Levantai hoje de novo,	Raise up today again
O esplendor de Portugal!	The splendor of Portugal!
Entre as brumas da memória,	From out of the mists of memory,
Ó Pátria sente-se a voz	Oh homeland, we hear the voices
Dos teus egrégios avós	Of your great forefathers
Que há-de guiar-te à vitória!	That shall lead you on to victory!
Às armas! Às armas!	To arms! To arms!
Sobre a terra, sobre o mar!	On land and sea!
Às armas! Às armas!	To arms! To arms!
Pela Pátria lutar!	To fight for our homeland!
Contra os canhões	Against the enemy cannons,
marchar, marchar!	march, march!

Numbers and Stumblers

- Europeans write a few of their numbers differently than we do. 1=1, 4=4 , 7=7 .
- Europeans write the date in this order: day/month/year.
- Commas are decimal points and decimals are commas. A dollar and a half is 1,50 and there are 5.280 feet in a mile.
- The European "first floor" isn't the ground floor, but the first floor up.
- When counting with your fingers, start with your thumb. If you hold up only your first finger, you'll probably get two of something.

APPENDIX

LET'S TALK TELEPHONES

Making Calls within a European Country: About half of all European countries use area codes (like we do); the other half uses a direct-dial system without area codes.

To make calls within a country that uses a direct-dial system (Belgium, Czech Republic, Denmark, France, Greece, Italy, Norway, Poland, Portugal, Spain, and Switzerland), you dial the same number whether you're calling across the country or across the street.

In countries that use area codes (such as Austria, Britain, Croatia, Finland, Germany, Ireland, the Netherlands, Slovakia, Slovenia, and Sweden), you dial the local number when calling within a city, and you add the area code if calling long-distance within the country.

Making International Calls: You always start with the international access code (011 if you're calling from America or Canada, or 00 from Europe), then dial the country code of the country you're calling (see codes on next page).

What you dial next depends on the phone system of the country you're calling. If the country uses area codes, drop the initial zero of the area code, then dial the rest of the number.

Countries that use direct-dial systems (no area codes) vary in how they're accessed internationally by phone. You always start by dialing the international access code, followed by the country code. Then, if you're calling the Czech Republic, Denmark, Italy, Norway, Portugal, or Spain, simply dial the phone number in its entirety. But if you're calling Belgium, France, Poland, or Switzerland, drop the initial zero of the phone number.

Country Codes

After you've dialed the international access code, dial the code of the country you're calling.

Austria—43	France—33	Poland—48
Belgium—32	Germany—49	Portugal—351
Bosnia-	Gibraltar—350	Slovakia—421
Herzegovina—387	Greece—30	Slovenia—386
Britain—44	Hungary—36	Spain—34
Canada—1	Ireland—353	Sweden—46
Croatia—385	Italy—39	Switzerland—41
Czech Rep.—420	Montenegro—382	Turkey—90
Denmark—45	Morocco—212	United States—1
Estonia—372	Netherlands—31	
Finland—358	Norway—47	

Directory Assistance

Dial 118 for local numbers and 177 for international numbers.

Embassies

American Embassy
• Tel. 217-702-122
• Avenida das Forças Armadas, **Lisbon**
• www.american-embassy.pt

Canadian Embassy
• Tel. 213-164-600
• Avenida da Liberdade 198-200, **Lisbon**

NOTES

NOTES

The perfect complement to your phrase book

Travel with Rick Steves' candid, up-to-date advice on the best places to eat and sleep, the must-see sights, getting off the beaten path—and getting the most out of every day and every dollar while you're in Europe.

Start your trip at

Our website enhances this book and turns

Explore Europe

At ricksteves.com you can browse through thousands of articles, videos, photos and radio interviews, plus find a wealth of money-saving travel tips for planning your dream trip. And with our mobile-friendly website, you can easily access all this great travel information anywhere you go.

TV Shows

Preview the places you'll visit by watching entire half-hour episodes of Rick Steves' Europe (choose from all 100 shows) on-demand, for free.

r--ricksteves.com

your travel dreams into affordable reality

Radio Interviews

Enjoy ready access to Rick's vast library of radio interviews covering

travel tips and cultural insights that relate specifically to your Europe travel plans.

Travel Forums

Learn, ask, share! Our online community of savvy travelers is a great resource for first-time travelers to Europe, as well as seasoned pros. You'll find forums on each country, plus travel tips and restaurant/hotel reviews. You can even ask one of our well-traveled staff to chime in with an opinion.

Travel News

Subscribe to our free Travel News e-newsletter, and get monthly updates from Rick on what's happening in Europe.

Audio Europe™

Rick's Free Travel App

Get your FREE **Rick Steves Audio Europe**™ app to enjoy...

- Dozens of self-guided tours of Europe's top museums, sights and historic walks
- Hundreds of tracks filled with cultural insights and sightseeing tips from Rick's radio interviews
- All organized into handy geographic playlists
- For Apple and Android

With Rick whispering in your ear, Europe gets even better.

Find out more at ricksteves.com

Pack Light and Right

*Gear up for your
next adventure at
ricksteves.com*

Light Luggage

Pack light and right with Rick Steves'
affordable, custom-designed rolling
carry-on bags, backpacks, day packs
and shoulder bags.

Accessories

From packing cubes to moneybelts and
beyond, Rick has personally selected the
travel goodies that will help your trip
go smoother.

Shop at ricksteves.com

Experience maximum Europe

Rick Steves Tours

A Rick Steves tour takes you to Europe's most interesting places with great guides and small groups of 28 or less. We follow Rick's favorite itineraries, ride in comfy buses, stay in family-run hotels, and bring you intimately close to the Europe you've traveled so far to see. Most importantly, we take away the logistical headaches so you can focus on the fun.

great tours, too!

with minimum stress

Join the fun

This year we'll take thousands of free-spirited travelers—nearly half of them repeat customers—along with us on four dozen different itineraries, from Ireland to Italy to Istanbul. Is a Rick Steves tour the right fit for your travel dreams? Find out at ricksteves.com, where you can also request Rick's latest tour catalog.

Europe is best experienced with happy travel partners. We hope you can join us.

See our itineraries at ricksteves.com

A Guide for Every Trip

BEST OF GUIDES

*Full color easy-to-scan format,
focusing on Europe's most
popular destinations and sights.*

Best of France
Best of Germany
Best of England
Best of Europe
Best of Ireland
Best of Italy
Best of Spain

COMPREHENSIVE GUIDES

*City, country, and regional guides
with detailed coverage for a
multi-week trip exploring the
most iconic sights and venturing
off the beaten track.*

Amsterdam & the Netherlands
Barcelona
Belgium: Bruges, Brussels,
    Antwerp & Ghent
Berlin
Budapest
Croatia & Slovenia
Eastern Europe
England
Florence & Tuscany
France
Germany
Great Britain
Greece: Athens & the Peloponnese
Iceland
Ireland
Istanbul
Italy
London
Paris
Portugal
Prague & the Czech Republic
Provence & the French Riviera
Rome
Scandinavia
Scotland
Spain
Switzerland
Venice
Vienna, Salzburg & Tirol

THE BEST OF ROME

Rome, Italy's capital, is studded with
Roman remnants and floodlit-fountain
squares. From the Vatican to the Colos-
eum, with crazy traffic in between, Rome
is wonderful, huge, and exhausting. The
crowds, the heat, and the weighty history

of the Eternal City where Caesars walked
can make tourists wilt. Recharge by tak-
ing *siestas*, *gelato* breaks, and after-dark
walks, strolling from one atmospheric
square to another in the refreshing evening air.

umous, gladiators fought
of one another, entertaining
50,000.

e at this Rome ristorante.

of guards at St. Peter's
it work solemnly.

untain, toss in a coin
h to return to Rome. It's
me.

Rick Steves guidebooks are published by Avalon Travel,
an imprint of Perseus Books, a Hachette Book Group company.

POCKET GUIDES

Compact, full color city guides with the essentials for shorter trips.

Amsterdam
Athens
Barcelona
Florence
Italy's Cinque Terre
London
Munich & Salzburg

Paris
Prague
Rome
Venice
Vienna

SNAPSHOT GUIDES

Focused single-destination coverage.

Basque Country: Spain & France
Copenhagen & the Best of Denmark
Dublin
Dubrovnik
Edinburgh
Hill Towns of Central Italy
Krakow, Warsaw & Gdansk
Lisbon
Loire Valley
Madrid & Toledo
Milan & the Italian Lakes District
Naples & the Amalfi Coast
Northern Ireland
Normandy
Norway
Reykjavik
Sevilla, Granada & Southern Spain
St. Petersburg, Helsinki & Tallinn
Stockholm

CRUISE PORTS GUIDES

Reference for cruise ports of call.

Mediterranean Cruise Ports
Northern European Cruise Ports

Complete your library with...

TRAVEL SKILLS & CULTURE

Study up on travel skills and gain insight on history and culture.

Europe 101
European Christmas
European Easter
European Festivals
Europe Through the Back Door
Postcards from Europe
Travel as a Political Act

PHRASE BOOKS & DICTIONARIES

French
French, Italian & German
German
Italian
Portuguese
Spanish

PLANNING MAPS

Britain, Ireland & London
Europe
France & Paris
Germany, Austria & Switzerland
Ireland
Italy
Spain & Portugal

Rick Steves books are available from your favorite bookseller.
Many guides are available as ebooks.

Let's Keep on Travelin'

Your trip doesn't need to end.

Follow Rick on social media!